THE SCOUTS

THE SCOUTS

By the Editors of

TIME-LIFE BOOKS

with text by

Keith Wheeler

TIME-LIFE BOOKS / ALEXANDRIA, VIRGINIA

Time-Life Books Inc.
is a wholly owned subsidiary of

TIME INCORPORATED

Founder: Henry R. Luce 1898-1967

Editor-in-Chief: Henry Anatole Grunwald
Chairman of the Board: Andrew Heiskell
President: James R. Shepley
Editorial Director: Ralph Graves
Vice Chairman: Arthur Temple

TIME-LIFE BOOKS INC.

Managing Editor: Jerry Korn
Executive Editor: David Maness
Assistant Managing Editors: Dale M. Brown (planning),
George Constable, George G. Daniels (acting),
Martin Mann, John Paul Porter
Art Director: Tom Suzuki
Chief of Research: David L. Harrison
Director of Photography: Robert G. Mason
Assistant Art Director: Arnold C. Holeywell
Assistant Chief of Research: Carolyn L. Sackett
Assistant Director of Photography: Dolores A. Littles

Chairman: Joan D. Manley
President: John D. McSweeney
Executive Vice Presidents: Carl G. Jaeger,
John Steven Maxwell, David J. Walsh
Vice Presidents: George Artandi (comptroller);
Stephen L. Bair (legal counsel); Peter G. Barnes;
Nicholas Benton (public relations); John L. Canova;
Beatrice T. Dobie (personnel); Carol Flaumenhaft
(consumer affairs); Nicholas J. C. Ingleton (Asia);
James L. Mercer (Europe/South Pacific); Herbert Sorkin
(production); Paul R. Stewart (marketing)

THE OLD WEST

EDITORIAL STAFF FOR "THE SCOUTS"
Editor: Jim Hicks
Picture Editor: Donna M. Lucey
Text Editors: Russell B. Adams Jr., Bobbie Conlan-Moore,
Lee Hassig, David Johnson
Designer: Edward Frank
Staff Writers: Paul Clancy, Susan Feller, Mark M. Steele,
Lydia Preston
Chief Researcher: Carol Forsyth Mickey
Researchers: Karen M. Bates, Mary G. Burns,
Regina B. Cahill, Mindy A. Daniels, Barbara Fleming,
Sara Mark, Karen Michell, Heather Mason Sandifer,
Nancy Toff, Roger Warner
Art Assistant: Van W. Carney
Editorial Assistant: Barbara Brownell

EDITORIAL PRODUCTION
Production Editor: Douglas B. Graham
Operations Manager: Gennaro C. Esposito,
Gordon E. Buck (assistant)
Assistant Production Editor: Feliciano Madrid
Quality Control: Robert L. Young (director), James J. Cox
(assistant), Daniel J. McSweeney, Michael G. Wight
(associates)
Art Coordinator: Anne B. Landry
Copy Staff: Susan B. Galloway (chief), Patricia Graber,
Barbara Quarmby, Ricki Tarlow, Celia Beattie
Picture Department: Linda Hensel

THE AUTHOR: Keith Wheeler grew up in central North Dakota, a region where both white and Indian scouts once used their special skills to guide settlers, soldiers and explorers. After working as a reporter for newspapers in the West and Middle West, he joined *Life* as a staff writer in 1951. Now a freelancer, he has published five novels and several nonfiction volumes, including *The Railroaders, The Townsmen, The Chroniclers* and *The Alaskans* in the Old West series.

THE COVER: Riding ahead of a small group of cavalrymen, a buckskin-clad scout reins in his pony and readies his just-fired rifle for another shot—presumably at enemy Indians—in this Frederic Remington painting entitled *The Scout.* Aiding troops against hostile tribes was only one aspect of frontier scouting. Craggy mountain man Jim Bridger, in the frontispiece photograph, was also a trapper, professional hunter and explorer's guide who personified the diverse nature of the scouting trade.

CORRESPONDENTS: Elisabeth Kraemer (Bonn); Margot Hapgood, Dorothy Bacon, Lesley Coleman (London); Susan Jonas, Lucy T. Voulgaris (New York); Maria Vincenza Aloisi, Josephine du Brusle (Paris); Ann Natanson (Rome). Valuable assistance was also provided by: Enid Farmer (Boston); Giovanna Brey (Chicago); Karin B. Pearce (London); Carolyn T. Chubet, Miriam Hsia, Christina Lieberman (New York); Mimi Murphy (Rome).

The editors are indebted to Valerie Moolman, text editor.

For information about any Time-Life book, please write:
Reader Information
Time-Life Books
541 North Fairbanks Court
Chicago, Illinois 60611

© 1978 Time-Life Books Inc. All rights reserved.
No part of this book may be reproduced in any form or by any electronic
or mechanical means, including information storage and retrieval devices
or systems, without prior written permission from the publisher, except that
brief passages may be quoted for reviews.
Second printing. Revised 1980.
Published simultaneously in Canada.

Library of Congress Cataloging in Publication Data
Time-Life Books.
  The scouts.
  (The Old West: v. 24)
  Bibliography: p.
  Includes index.
  1. Scouts and scouting—The West—History.
  2. Scouts and scouting—The West—Biography.
  3. The West—History—1848-1950.
  4. Frontier and pioneer life—The West. I. Wheeler, Keith.
II. Title. III. Series: The Old West (New York); v. 24.
F 596.T52   1978   978'.02   78-1364
ISBN 0-8094-2306-5
ISBN 0-8094-2305-7 lib. bdg.

TIME-LIFE is a trademark of Time Incorporated U.S.A.

Other Publications:

THE EPIC OF FLIGHT
THE GOOD COOK
THE SEAFARERS
THE ENCYCLOPEDIA OF COLLECTIBLES
WORLD WAR II
THE GREAT CITIES
HOME REPAIR AND IMPROVEMENT
THE WORLD'S WILD PLACES
THE TIME-LIFE LIBRARY OF BOATING
HUMAN BEHAVIOR
THE ART OF SEWING
THE EMERGENCE OF MAN
THE AMERICAN WILDERNESS
THE TIME-LIFE ENCYCLOPEDIA OF GARDENING
LIFE LIBRARY OF PHOTOGRAPHY
THIS FABULOUS CENTURY
FOODS OF THE WORLD
TIME-LIFE LIBRARY OF AMERICA
TIME-LIFE LIBRARY OF ART
GREAT AGES OF MAN
LIFE SCIENCE LIBRARY
THE LIFE HISTORY OF THE UNITED STATES
TIME READING PROGRAM
LIFE NATURE LIBRARY
LIFE WORLD LIBRARY
FAMILY LIBRARY:
  HOW THINGS WORK IN YOUR HOME
  THE TIME-LIFE BOOK OF THE FAMILY CAR
  THE TIME-LIFE FAMILY LEGAL GUIDE
  THE TIME-LIFE BOOK OF FAMILY FINANCE

CONTENTS

6

1 | Savants of survival in a wild land

Throughout the decades of Western expansion, one group of men served as the eyes, ears and provisioners of those who dared to venture into unsettled territory. Most of these scouts were former fur trappers who had learned how to survive in the wilderness. They knew the country. They knew Indian ways. They could bring down plenty of game to keep their employers fed.

Most important, scouts could "read sign," finding meaning in footprints, bent blades of grass and other subtle clues. A scout could determine from such earthy evidence as a pile of dung whether horses that had crossed the trail were Indian war ponies or a harmless herd of mustangs (wild horses, able to halt at will, left their droppings in piles, while ridden ones left their droppings strung along the ground).

Such perceptiveness could literally mean life or death for those who were dependent on scouts. The well-known explorer John Charles Frémont, who employed these specialists for his expeditions to all parts of the West, put it succinctly: "Scouts are indispensable from the time of leaving the frontiers of Missouri until we return to them."

Sharp-eyed scouts scan the horizon near the Tetons in Wyoming while the Army column they are guiding makes camp to the rear.

In this 1852 painting a dismounted trapper looks for "sign" while companions await his determination. Such skills as reading a trail from broken twigs stood these canny mountain men in good stead when they worked as scouts.

9

Wary trappers employ an Indian trick of walking horses in a stream to conceal their trail. The ability to think like Indians proved a lifesaving talent for trappers who turned to scouting in the 1840s after the beaver trade had declined.

Eyes to the ground, a white scout on foot and a Cheyenne scout on horseback search intently for the faint hoofprints of ponies amid buffalo tracks as they lead a detachment of the U.S. 3rd Cavalry across an arid Southwestern plain.

13

Frederic Remington

Professionals who learned the secrets of the West

Major General Grenville Dodge, who served as chief engineer for the Union Pacific Railroad, once observed the illustrious trapper-turned-scout Jim Bridger and a handful of others in action out West. Dodge was amazed at the scouts' accomplishments, from their ability to track and hunt to the speed with which they were able to build boats of buffalo hides.

"In a few hours they would put together a bull boat and put us across any stream," he wrote many years later in a tribute to Bridger. "Nothing escaped their vision. The dropping of a stick or breaking of a twig, the turning of the growing grass all brought knowledge to them, and they could tell who or what had done it. A single horse or Indian could not cross the trail but that they discovered it, and could tell how long since they had passed. Their methods of hunting game were perfect and we were never out of meat. Herbs, roots, berries, bark of trees and everything that was edible they knew. They could minister to the sick, dress wounds—in fact in all my experience I never saw Bridger or the other voyagers of the plains and mountains meet any obstacle they could not overcome."

It took years to acquire such skills and perfect them. Not surprisingly, thousands of Indians, brought up from childhood to be hunters and warriors, excelled as scouts. But there were also a few dozen white men who came to master the wilderness as thoroughly as their bronze-skinned precursors. The majority of them began as professional trappers or hunters. Their work taught them most of what they needed to survive and prosper in the wilds. The rest of their knowledge they acquired from Indians, by listening to the advice of friendly mentors and by eluding hostile warriors.

These wise men of the wilderness, white and Indian alike, became a national resource of inestimable value to the United States. Without scouts to guide explorers and pioneers, missionaries and surveyors, Indian-fighting armies and railroaders through the perils beyond the frontier, much of the West might well have remained unsettled into the early 20th Century.

A scout's work was both demanding and dangerous. On an expedition, he was chief pathfinder, a man who could rediscover a trail he had followed only once before or blaze a new one where he had never set foot. He was head forager, pinpointing sources of vital food and water for livestock and men. He served as courier when urgent messages had to be carried through hostile territory. His senses and intuition, trained in a dangerous environment to anticipate every threat, made him the nerve center for the safety of his charges. Moreover, a scout had to be something of a diplomat. All his talents and skills were nought if a scout failed to persuade the captain of an expedition—as often as not a headstrong adventurer who was reluctant to take advice—to follow his recommendations. When the scout's advice was ignored, the results were frequently wasted time, unnecessary hardship and, in some instances, outright disaster.

While most scouts shared the common experience of having been trappers, men with the ability to excel in this complex task originated from a great variety of backgrounds. Buffalo Bill Cody, who eventually went into show business, and Christopher Carson, better known by his nickname, Kit, were teen-age runaways from frontier settlements in Kansas and Missouri. Jim Bridger, orphaned in his teens, came West from St. Louis where he had found it difficult to support his younger brothers and sisters. Al Sieber, a scout who

A frontier scout exuberantly signals a clear trail ahead. His ready weapons—rifle, pistol and knife—evidence the dangers encountered in the untracked wilderness.

15

became expert in the ways of Apache Indians, began life in the German Rhineland. Frank Grouard, son of a Mormon missionary and a Polynesian woman, spent his childhood on the South Sea island of Tubuai before becoming one of the best-known scouts in the West.

And from nearly every Plains Indian tribe came scouts who searched out their ancient tribal enemies for the U.S. Army. During the Indian wars, Pawnees scouted for the government against Cheyennes and Cheyennes against Sioux. Apaches in the Southwest extended such treachery to tracking down and fighting other members of their own tribe—or even their own families. Ironically, the excellent work of Indian scouts for the Army not only helped make the West safe for white settlers, but also speeded the day when almost all Indians would be confined on reservations.

The first generation of white scouts grew naturally out of the ranks of mountain men, a few hundred bold souls who, in the first three decades of the 19th Century, pressed up the Missouri River to the northern Rockies and, farther south, fanned across the plains and deserts into California. They went in quest of beaver. The sleek fur of this North American river denizen was highly prized in Europe, where it was made into hats for men of fashion. Entrepreneurs who were seeking the big profits to be had in the fur trade induced hundreds of trappers to go west. One fur company guaranteed a salary of $200 per year, but in a good season a trapper could earn 10 times that amount. By contrast, a skilled carpenter in a city back East could expect to earn no more than $550.

The perilous and uncomfortable fur trapper's life was a toughening experience that was to stand in good stead those who later became scouts. Rheumatism was an occupational hazard for trappers, who waded into icy water to set their traps and retrieve their catch. A man could become lost in a blizzard and freeze. Or he might die of thirst if he chose the wrong direction in looking for water. A broken ankle might mean lonely starvation. Wild animals—grizzly bears in particular—could be an unpredictable peril.

Osborne Russell tells in his trapper's journal of wounding a grizzly bear while hunting buffalo with a companion. Upon approaching the bushes where the bear had retreated, "we heard a sullen growl, which

was instantly followed by a spring of the Bear toward us; his enormous jaws extended and eyes flashing fire," wrote Russell. "Was ever anything so hideous? We could not retain sufficient presence of mind to shoot at him but took to our heels separating as we ran the Bear taking after me. I was obliged to turn about and face him. I pulled the trigger and I knew not what else to do and hardly knew that I did this but it accidentally happened that my Rifle was pointed towards the Bear when I pull and the ball piercing his heart, he uttered a deathly howl and fell dead: but I trembled as if I had an ague fit for half an hour after."

Moreover, there was the ever-present danger of inimical Indians, who plundered traps, stole pelts and killed trappers. Estimates of the damage they did are convincing in their remarkable consistency. One by John Dougherty, an early trapper and Indian agent who first went up the Missouri River in 1809, reckoned that between 1815 and 1831 Indians killed 170 trappers and stole from them more than $100,000 worth of property. William Clark, of Lewis and Clark, put the toll at 150 men and nearly $150,000 in goods. On the other side of the ledger, no one bothered to add up how many Indians the trappers killed in self-defense, retribution or on splenetic rampages.

Many Indians must have been killed by mountain men, however, for the chronicles of trappers and fur traders are filled with stories of bloody confrontations with tribesmen. Experience taught the trappers—and it was a lesson that some of them carried over into later careers as scouts—that most Indians regarded compassion and forbearance as weaknesses and as license to take even greater advantage of whites.

So men in the beaver trade dealt harshly with Indians to establish themselves as a force not to be trifled with. Peter Ogden, with the Hudson's Bay Company, when harassed by Medocs in 1827, recorded a callous but, to his mind, effective approach to newly encountered tribes. "I am of the opinion," he wrote in his journal, "that if on first discovering a strange Tribe a dozen of them were shot, it would be the means of preserving many lives." He meant white lives.

"Old Bill" Williams, a mountain man, trapper and guide for 23 years, made a similar point in a story of an Indian encounter he told to his family on a visit back East. Trapping alone near the source of the Yellow-

stone River, Old Bill was surprised by three Blackfoot Indians. Williams barely escaped to a thicket with his butcher knife as arrows struck his shoulder and thigh. The Indians took his rifle, his mule and his beaver pelts. After recuperating for two days, Williams set out after the thieves and caught up with them four days later.

That night, while the Indians slept soundly after gorging on buffalo, Williams sneaked into their camp. He killed and scalped two of the thieves without waking the third. Then, after stirring up the fire to make a little light, he roused the remaining Blackfoot, who opened his eyes to the bloody scalps of his comrades dangling in front of his face. The terrified Indian took off like an antelope. Asked by his young nephew why he let the last Indian go, Williams replied: "Ef I'd a kilt that Injun, thyar wouldn't a been nobody left ter tell them Blackfeet how them bucks had gone under nor who'd a rubbed 'em out."

But violence was only one side of the ambivalent relationship between trappers and Indians. Offsetting

the tribes that were implacably hostile to white men were tribes into which trappers married, where they became blood brothers of their in-laws and were even installed as chiefs. Close relationships like these meant that a trapper's fame would spread from village to village throughout the tribe's territory. It could mean safe haven in an emergency.

However, most relationships between whites and Indians were more casual. There were Indians with whom the trappers traded, often the very individuals they had fought earlier or might steal from or kill in the future. And there were Indians from whom trappers learned how to survive in the wilderness.

To learn from Indians, trappers had to be able to communicate with them—a skill that later would be even more important to scouts whose duties would include interpreting for their employers. Indian dialects, numerous and for the most part unrelated linguistically, were hard to master. Trapper Osborne Russell noted in his journal that the Crow dialect, spoken along the

17

Yellowstone and Bighorn rivers, "is clear, distinct and not intermingled with guttural sounds, which renders it remarkably easy for a stranger to learn." But most dialects were the opposite, and few trappers learned more than a couple of them.

Indians had the same problem, of course. To solve it they had devised a nearly universal system of signs for communicating across the barrier of spoken languages. Trappers learned to use this sign language with as much facility as the Indians, and such fluency among scouts would later prove invaluable to the leaders of expeditions that journeyed to the West. Interpreters were necessary because sign language could be indecipherable to a novice.

Lieutenant J. Lee Humfreville of the 11th Ohio Volunteer Cavalry noted in his journal that, taken one at a time, individual signs were easy to understand: "The sign language is very figurative. If an Indian desired to say you were not truthful, he would touch his tongue with one finger and hold up two fingers toward you, signifying that you were double tongued. If he desired to speak of being on horseback he did so by putting the first and second fingers over the fingers of the left hand. The signs were innumerable and every one of them illustrated the idea to be conveyed."

But when signs were strung together in a sentence, a translation often called for a knowledge of sign language—and of Indian metaphor—that no novice pos-

Lean Wolf sweeps his brow for "white man." The motion, which represented the brim of a trapper's slouch hat, meant the same whether done with a fist or with fingers extended.

THE ESPERANTO OF THE PLAINS

By the time philologist Garrick Mallery's *Sign Language Among North American Indians* appeared in 1881, trappers, scouts and Indians had long been conversing in prairie pantomine. But Mallery's tome, observing that the silent tongue was universal "from Hudson Bay to the Gulf of Mexico," provided the first comprehensive dictionary of sign language.

The meaning of sign talk lay mostly in the speaker's motions; individual finger positions often were unimportant—akin only to the calligraphic "flourishes of tailed letters," Mallery noted. He illustrated the point with his translation of Hidatsa Chief Lean Wolf's complaint (*right*) that "four years ago the American people agreed to be friends with us, but they lied."

After indicating "four" with fingers held aloft, Lean Wolf most likely made the sign for "winters"—by hugging himself with both arms and shivering—to indicate "years."

Beginning at a point about 15 inches from the right side of his body, Lean Wolf signs "with us" by repeatedly drawing his palm to within a short distance of his breast.

The handshake sign, meaning "friend," stems from the white man's salutation. The more traditional sign, a finger moved up from the lips, depicted smoking a peace pipe.

"Double-tongued" is the literal translation of the chief's two-fingered sign for "lie." A more precise Indian orator would have begun the motion from nearer his mouth.

Lean Wolf makes the sign for "that is all" — "period, end of statement" — by clenching his hands in front of the center of his chest, then sweeping them apart and downward.

sessed. Humfreville continued: "One of the most difficult sign sentences I ever tried to comprehend was in a conversation with some Indians in the South Park. We were expecting to go into battle the next day and the night before one of our Indian allies came to me and talked in the sign language. The first sign given was one of sleep, after which the right hand was passed rapidly under the left, both palms being opened downward which meant 'going in.' The next sign was opening and shutting the fingers of each hand toward each other, rapidly, which meant to fight, then a downward catch of the forefinger which meant good or true.

"And last, the most incomprehensible of all, the making of the figure O with the index finger and thumb of the right hand, turning the hand over as though emptying a bottle. After repeated efforts to interpret the last sign, I gave up in despair, but finally learned the translation of it. The whole sentence translated verbatim was, 'Tomorrow I will go in and fight good, if I pour my life out.' "

Once a trapper could communicate with Indians, he could learn from them how to "read sign," the skill of deducing from the most minute physical evidence a picture of what had recently transpired or what might happen in the near future. Such evaluations were crucial to survival for trappers and scouts alike in a land that probed for a man's weaknesses and destroyed him in a moment of laxity.

Indians, raised from childhood to this heightened awareness of the world around them, were a treasure trove of clues to the wilderness. A white man could learn from an Indian, in a crude example, that lodgepole furrows through the hoofprints of a band of ponies signified Indians on the move with their women and children, rather than a raiding party. But reading sign could be far more subtle. In one instance, an Indian examining a trail that appeared fresh realized that it had been made two days earlier, sometime before 8 a.m. The clue was grains of sand stuck to the grass where horse hoofs had flattened it to the ground. For the sand to have adhered, the grass must have been damp and the most recent dew had occurred two days earlier. The Indian concluded that the horses had passed that day, before the sun had burned off the moisture. In another case, what seemed to be a bear track to a white man was shown by his Indian guide to have been made by blades of grass, bent by the wind to sculpt the loose sand into a shape that resembled a bear-paw print. Such distinctions were critical to a man in the wild. Someone who confused grass marks with bear tracks and vice versa could end up as a meal for a bear—or without a bear for a meal.

Trappers, like their Indian exemplars, subsisted for the most part on a diet of meat alone. Bread was a luxury that trappers learned to live without. Kit Carson said that he managed to eat bread with a meal about once a year. But John Dougherty got along for seven years without once tasting a loaf, and Jim Bridger went 17 years. There were other scarcities. "Vegetables were out of the question in the Rocky Mountains," wrote Osborne Russell, "except a few kinds of roots of spontaneous growth which the Indians dig and prepare for food." Perhaps because they ate almost nothing else, trappers consumed prodigious amounts of meat. The Hudson's Bay Company recommended eight pounds of meat per day for each trapper, and a hungry man could put away more than that.

Even in a game-saturated wilderness, meat on the hoof sometimes vanished for no apparent reason, and then the trappers learned to make do with anything that they could chew. Stray dogs that tagged along with them were early candidates for the pot. In a pinch, mules and horses might be sacrificed to the larder, though men preferred not to eat their transportation. An alternative that kept the transportation was to draw blood from the animal's neck, dilute it with water and drink it as hot soup.

In true "starvin' times," many a moccasin and leather lariat went into the cook pot. There were occasions when a trapper would down a stew of black desert crickets in imitation of the Digger Indians, although the Diggers were widely scorned as the lowest form of human life on the plains for eating insects. Joe Meek, who eventually blazed the last leg of the wagon road to Oregon, could recall plunging his arms into swarming anthills and then licking off the insects with his tongue. Once when a tenderfoot was repelled by watching an Indian sucking down a length of intestine from a freshly killed buffalo, Jim Bridger commented quietly: "I've eaten that kind of stuff myself, when I had to."

What to eat, how to shoot a rifle, how to track men and game, how to find water—the list of skills that a

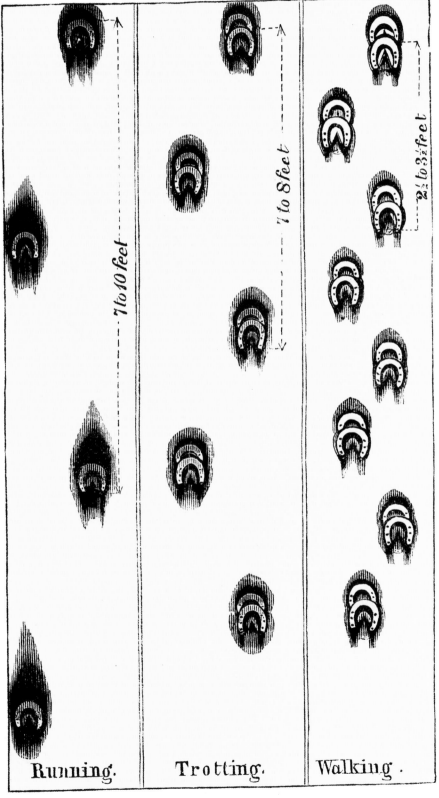

Hoofprints at three common gaits are illustrated in an 1859 trail handbook that sought to explain the techniques of scouting to prairie neophytes. The author, Army Captain Randolph B. Marcy, advised frontier newcomers who found themselves following parties of Indians to determine "the probability of overtaking them and regulate movements accordingly."

A gallery of scouting characters

Contrary to their popular image as gallant, handsome knights-errant of the West, scouts could be unkempt, idiosyncratic and sometimes downright ornery men, a heterogeneous bunch of hardy, self-willed individualists.

Among their number were virtuous men and rascals, teetotalers and drunkards. As a group, they are epitomized, in visage and deed, by the five scouts on these pages.

Mariano Medina bought an Indian bride and was faithful for 30 years. Jim Beckwourth married promiscuously among Indians and frequently had two or more wives at a time. Jim Baker, though kindhearted when sober, was a raging terror when drunk and once had to be physically restrained from slicing off his wife's ear as punishment for suspected unfaithfulness. Tom Tobin loved the life of a scout and resolutely clung to his frontier buckskins long after more civilized garb was widely available, while Stephen Meek tried several times to quit scouting, but was unable to succeed at any other work.

Jim Baker, with 22 fellow trappers in 1841, repulsed some 500 Cheyennes, Arapahos and Sioux at the Little Snake River. He later served as chief scout at Fort Laramie, Wyoming.

In 1857, Mexican mountain man and scout Mariano Medina led a 51-day, midwinter march over the Rocky Mountains. Although 12 soldiers suffered frozen feet, only one perished.

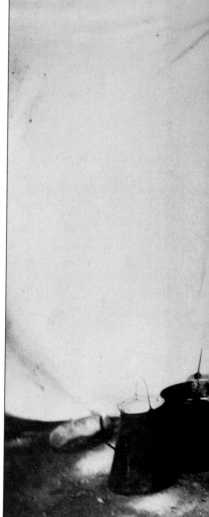

Master tracker Tom Tobin, after stalking a pair of murderers for five days, returned to Fort Garland, Colorado, and dumped their heads out of a sack at the feet of the post commander.

Though best known for enticing an Oregon-bound wagon train to take his shortcut and then getting lost, Stephen Hall Meek successfully made his living as a scout well into his eighties.

Mulatto scout James Beckwourth claimed that he once ran 95 miles in a day to escape a Blackfoot war party. He lived as a Crow Indian and, on his death, was laid to rest in a tree.

trapper absorbed in pursuit of his profession is virtually endless. His talents kept him alive and well and made him a profit besides, at least until around 1840. By then, indiscriminate trapping had all but wiped out the West's beaver population, and quality pelts became rare. At the same time, silk began replacing beaver as the fashionable material for top hats in the cities, and the bottom fell out of the beaver market. The last rendezvous, the annual fur-trading free-for-all where once a year the trappers could relax, was held in the summer of 1840 on the Green River in present-day Wyoming, and soon many trappers were out of jobs they had labored at for as long as 30 years. Most trappers went on to some other business and were never heard of again. But some of the exceptional ones discovered an increasing demand for their skills from another quarter: a swelling stream of greenhorns who wanted to hire them as guides.

Until around 1840 travelers in the domain of the mountain man had been rarities. Lewis and Clark were first in 1803, followed by a couple of Army explorers, Zebulon Pike in 1806 and 1807 and Stephen H. Long in 1818. A pair of British botanists, Thomas Nuttall and John Bradbury, had traveled up the Missouri River in 1811. George Catlin began painting Indians on the Missouri in 1830. He was followed in 1833 by the Swiss painter Karl Bodmer, who traveled with his patron, Maximilian—Prince of the Prussian province of Wied-Neuwied.

There had been a smattering of missionaries. Dr. Marcus Whitman and the Reverend Samuel Parker, Congregational ministers, were first in 1835. Whitman returned the following year leading two more Congregationalists, Henry Spalding and William Gray. Marcus Whitman was a physician as well as a healer of souls, and he more than paid his way. He curbed a cholera epidemic among the fur traders' caravan he accompanied west to the rendezvous.

The mountain men made these neophytes feel welcome, fed them, protected them, guided them and gave freely of their hard-bought expertise in survival. The untutored generally accepted gratefully whatever advice they could get and profited by it. Word spread that trappers could and would look out for tenderfeet, and the demand for such services increased with the frequency of civilization's probes into the wilderness.

In the guiding and scouting business, some men stood out from the others. They attracted the attention and elicited the admiration of influential explorers and adventurers, who chronicled the exploits of their wilderness guardians. The prototypes for these beaver-trappers-turned-scouts were Kit Carson and Jim Bridger, who were by all accounts two of the most trusted and respected men in the West.

Kit Carson, scout extraordinary, and John Charles Frémont, the foremost Western explorer of the mid-19th Century, probably would not be remembered as they are today had they never met. Carson might have remained only a skilled backwoodsman, anonymous to everyone but his comrades in the wilderness, without Frémont as his promoter. And Frémont probably would not have accomplished all that he did without Carson as his scout.

Their historic collaboration began with a chance meeting in June 1842 on the Missouri River steamboat *Rowena*. Carson, who had emerged from the wilderness for the first time in 16 years to enroll his daughter in a St. Louis convent school, was once again headed away from civilization. Frémont, then a lieutenant in the U.S. Army's Corps of Topographical Engineers, was en route "to explore and report upon" a vast tract of territory roughly centered in the Black Hills of Dakota. Learning that Frémont had failed to connect with one Captain Drips, a seasoned mountaineer whom the engineer had hoped to employ as a guide, Carson offered himself as an alternative.

Frémont was impressed with the slightly built Carson from the start. "I was pleased with him and his manner of address at this first meeting," wrote Frémont in his memoirs. "He was a man of frank speech and address; quiet and unassuming." After making inquiries into Carson's background and capabilities, Frémont hired him at a salary of $100 per month.

Frémont no doubt discovered through his investigation of Carson that the trapper had a reputation among his fellows for courage, trustworthiness and honesty. Carson was brave by anyone's standards. At the rendezvous on the Green River in 1835, there was a bully of a French trapper—many mountain men were French Canadians—named Chouinard. It was not uncommon for men of surpassing strength like Chouinard

An 1826 newspaper notice offers an insultingly small reward — one cent — for the return of a runaway apprentice named Carson. The future scout joined a wagon train headed for Santa Fe and escaped capture.

Notice is hereby given to all persons,

THAT CHRISTOPHER CARSON, a boy about 16 years old, small of his age, but thick set; light hair, ran away from the subscriber, living in Franklin, Howard county, Missouri, to whom he had been bound to learn the saddler's trade, on or about the first of September last. He is supposed to have made his way towards the upper part of the state. All persons are notified not to harbor, support or assist said boy under the penalty of the law. One cent reward will be given to a by person who will bring back the said boy.

DAVID WORKMAN.

Franklin, Oct. 6, 1826   16-3w

allowed him to draw his gun. We both fired at the same time; all present said but one report was heard. I shot him through the arm and his ball passed my head, cutting my hair and the powder burning my eye, the muzzle of his gun being near my head when he fired. During our stay in camp we had no more bother with this bully Frenchman." Carson's version of the story ends here. Another account, however, has it that the scout went for a second pistol to finish off his adversary but relented when the man begged for his life.

Brave as he was, Carson was not quite fearless. Hunting dinner for a camp of trappers, he had just shot an elk when two outraged grizzly bears charged him from behind. "My gun was unloaded and I could not possibly reload it in time to fire," reminisced Carson. "There were some trees at a short distance. I made for them, the bears after me. As I got to one of the trees, I had to drop my gun — the bears rushing for me, I had to make all haste to ascend the tree. I got up some ten or fifteen feet and then had to remain till the bears would find it convenient to leave." One of the bears lost interest quickly, but the other kept Carson clinging to the tree for hours. By the time he returned to camp, "never having been so scared in my life," it was too dark to fetch the elk, so Carson and his comrades went supperless after all.

Other incidents during his formative years as a trapper betray in Carson a youthful impulse toward rash action that sometimes propelled him into potentially disastrous situations. Once in 1833, Carson and a few men rode out of their base camp to check for signs of beaver in a promising stream. The trappers had been plagued by horse-stealing Indians for days, so when Carson sighted four Indians in the distance as his party returned from a fruitless examination of the stream, he and his companions charged.

It was a mistake in judgment that nearly led to catastrophe; the four Indians turned out to be only a part of a band of some 60 Indians hidden by a hill. "They had surrounded us," Carson recalled, "and our only chance to save our lives was a good run. We done so, the Indians firing on us from all directions. We run the gauntlet for about two hundred yards, the Indians were often as near as twenty yards of us. We durst not fire, not knowing what moment our horses might be shot from under us and the idea of being left afoot, your

to load up on whiskey and challenge all comers to a brawl. After beating two or three men one day, he began boasting that he could take a switch to any of the Americans as if they were little children. This was too much for Carson, who happened to be the puniest American in camp. "I did not like such talk from any man," related Carson to his biographer, who no doubt translated Carson's words into agreeable English, "so I told him that if he made use of any more such expressions, I would rip his guts."

Without a word Chouinard went for his horse and his rifle. Carson mounted his own horse, grabbed a pistol, then "galloped up to him and demanded if I was the one which he intended to shoot. Our horses were touching. He said no, but at the same time drawing his gun so he could have a fair shot. I was prepared and

A letter for John Charles Frémont, carried by Kit Carson in 1847, bears a vague address. But the sender, Senator Thomas Hart Benton, Frémont's father-in-law, trusted Carson to find the Pathfinder somewhere in the West, and Carson did.

gun unloaded, was enough for to make any man retain the shot which his gun contained." Carson's party escaped with only one man wounded.

By the time Frémont met Carson, however, the woodsman's more impetuous days were behind him; he had acquired the careful, levelheaded demeanor that Lieutenant Douglas Brewerton would observe in him on the trail from California to New Mexico in 1848. "Carson, while traveling, scarcely spoke; his keen eye was continually examining the country," Brewerton wrote for *Harper's Magazine* in 1853. "I often watched with great curiosity Carson's preparations for the night. A braver man than Kit perhaps never lived, in fact I doubt if he knew what fear was, but with all this he exercised great caution.

"While arranging his bed, his saddle, which he always used as a pillow, was disposed in such a manner as to form a barricade for his head; his pistols, half cocked, were laid above it, and his trusty rifle reposed beneath the blanket by his side, where it was not only ready for instant use but perfectly protected from the damp. Except now and then to light his pipe, you never caught Kit exposing himself in the full glare of the campfire." It was this approach to his work that made Carson a premier scout and allowed him to keep his scalp in situations where others lost theirs.

Carson also embodied a spirit of brotherhood rare among mountain men, who commonly looked out for themselves first. Once when he was in a fight with 30

Blackfoot Indians over some stolen horses, concern for a companion nearly cost Carson his life. He and a man named Mark Head were stalking two of the Indian warriors in the snow. Distracted by a faulty rifle mechanism, Head failed to notice that the Indian he was tracking had turned and was about to shoot him. Carson saw what was developing, swung his aim from his own target to Head's and dispatched the Indian. Now Carson, his single-shot rifle discharged, was defenseless against his own adversary, who had drawn a bead on his chest. Only by frantically dodging about did Carson escape with no more than a temporarily disabling bullet wound in the shoulder.

The personal qualities that Carson displayed made him the perfect choice for Frémont as a scout and guide. Moreover, the 29-year-old Frémont got along with Carson, who was only three years older than he, better than he did with older scouts he employed. Carson, never having been a leader of trappers, was more flexible and willing to take orders than men who had commanded large trapping parties. Frémont, in the reports of his expeditions, showed little favoritism toward Carson and recounted noteworthy exploits of other scouts as well. Once Frémont waxed hyperbolic about all his scouts, expressing the opinion that under Napoleon, any of them would have risen to the rank of marshal of the armies. But when Frémont's reports were published, the adventures of Kit Carson were the ones that stimulated the American public and excited the imagi-

Despite his ramrod-straight, totally masculine appearance in this rare formal portrait, Kit Carson disappointed most people who met him by his stooped shoulders, short stature, gentle voice and weak gaze.

nations of more than one author of the sensational (if groundless) dime novels.

Charles Averill's *Kit Carson, Prince of the Gold Hunters* portrayed the scout as a killer of Indian "critters" and "varmints" as well as the discoverer of gold in California. When Carson is asked in *The Prairie Flower, or Adventures in the Far West* how he intends to respond to the appearance of overwhelming numbers of hostile Indians, author Emerson Bennet attributes the following absurd plan to the illiterate scout: "Why, sir, to arm and mount on good horses a dozen or fifteen of us, dash into them and fight our way out." On one occasion, shown the cover of a similar work that depicted him knocking off Indians with his right hand while rescuing a distressed maiden with his left, Carson mildly remarked: "That thar may be true but I hain't got no recollection of it."

Most of Frémont's characterizations of Carson, on the other hand, ring as true and unexaggerated as his description of Carson riding out to verify a report of Indians in the distance: "Mounted on a fine horse, without a saddle, and scouring bareheaded over the prairies, Kit was one of the finest pictures of a horseman I have ever seen."

As Frémont's scout on three exploratory expeditions between 1842 and 1845 and during the Mexican War, which commenced the following year, Carson was responsible for keeping his employer out of trouble. Most of the time this assignment presented no extraordinary problems to Carson and the other scouts whom Frémont had hired. But the wilderness was as unpredictable as ever, and from time to time Carson found himself in situations that continued to spice his life with danger and adventure.

In 1844 an incident occurred that at first blush appears to be an act of sheer bravado on Carson's part, but in fact probably contributed significantly to the safety of Frémont's party. As Carson and Alexis Godey, another scout, guided Frémont across the Mojave Desert in 1844, they chanced upon two distraught Mexicans, an old man and a boy, who told of Paiutes who had driven off their stock and murdered the boy's parents. Carson and Godey volunteered to apprehend the killers, anticipating that other members of their party would offer to help. None did, so Carson and Godey set out alone. All one day and night they fol-

lowed the trail and at dawn came upon a camp of some 30 Indians who were butchering some of the stolen horses for a feast.

Carson and Godey sneaked close to the camp on foot but were given away by whinnies of alarm from the Indians' war ponies. As the Paiutes rushed for their weapons, Carson and Godey attacked. Their first shots brought down two Indians while the others fled, presumably judging that two would not dare attack so many without a larger force waiting in ambush.

Carson and Godey then set to the business of scalping the fallen. One Indian, not yet dead despite two rifle balls in him, felt the sear of the knife and leaped to his feet with a howl of agony. "The frightful spectacle appalled the stout hearts of our men," Frémont later wrote of Carson and Godey, "but they did what humanity required," and killed the wretched Indian.

The exploit greatly impressed Frémont, who considered it an act of singular gallantry. "The time, place, object and numbers considered, this expedition may be considered among the boldest and most disinterested which the annals of western adventure can present. Two men in a savage desert pursue day and night an unknown body of Indians into the defiles of an unknown mountain—attack them on sight, without counting numbers—and defeat them in an instant—and for what? To punish the robbers of the desert and avenge the wrongs of Mexicans."

Charles Preuss, Frémont's acidulous German cartographer, saw the episode as a grisly display of the scouts' cowardice. "Godey rode into camp with a yelling war cry," Preuss told his journal. "Are these whites not much worse than the Indians? The more noble Indian takes from the killed enemy only a piece of the scalp as large as a dollar, somewhat like the tonsure of a priest. These two heroes, who shot the Indians creeping up on them from behind, brought along the entire scalp." Neither Preuss nor Frémont seemed to have understood that Carson's actual motivation was to punish the Indians in order to dissuade them from future attacks on his own party.

Frémont was an explorer to the core: his aim was to go where others had not, even across a trackless desert if necessary. He did just that in 1845. Finding himself on the shores of the Great Salt Lake for the second time in two years, Frémont proposed to strike westward from the lake, straight across a parched section of real estate that even Indians avoided. Frémont ordered Carson and Lucien Maxwell, a fellow scout, and a couple of others to reconnoiter for water, without which the trek would be impossible for man or beast. Carson set out in the cool of the evening with his three companions and a mule loaded with water. Frémont was aware that others had ventured far into this wasteland without being able to find water, but rising above the horizon—some 60 miles distant—were mountain peaks that appeared to be less parched. Perhaps water could be found there.

Carson's party made the distance in a grueling forced march over country with "no water or grass, not a particle of vegetation, as level and bare as a barn door," as Carson told it. The mountains did indeed offer an abundance of water, grass and firewood. As arranged beforehand, Carson relayed news of the scouting party's good fortune to Frémont with smoke from a signal fire, and Frémont started across the desert with the main party. This route proved a shortcut compared to earlier trails leading westward from the Great Salt Lake. Emigrant wagon trains used it frequently, and it became the route for the Pony Express, daily Overland Mail and a telegraph line.

By early 1846, during Frémont's third expedition, war with Mexico appeared to be imminent. As the only American military presence in the Far West, Frémont and his band of 60 armed explorers would play an important role in the conquest of California for the United States.

Frémont, along with the members of his party, recently had been chased out of California by the Mexican authorities and was moving north through Oregon toward the Columbia River. On May 8 a messenger reached Frémont with word that Archibald Gillespie, a Marine lieutenant who had set out from Washington six months earlier on a covert mission that took him to Mexico and Hawaii, was trying to catch Frémont to deliver official dispatches and personal letters from home and the capital. Upon hearing of Gillespie, Frémont turned back with a party of 10 to intercept him. After a hard day's march, Frémont found Gillespie near the southern end of Lake Klamath.

The documents Gillespie carried pulled Frémont irreversibly into the mounting conflict with Mexico, but not before they nearly cost him his life. That night Frémont sat up late by the campfire, eagerly poring over the news. Perhaps because he was so absorbed in the dispatches, he neglected to post sentries. More unaccountably, so did the woods-wise Carson.

Late that night, not long after Frémont had at last rolled up in his blankets, Carson awoke to a thud in the dark, the sound of an Indian tomahawk splitting a human skull. In an instant Carson was on his feet shouting the alarm, but it was already too late for scout Basil LaJeunesse and one of the four Delaware Indian scouts who had accompanied Frémont. In the skirmish that followed, another Delaware scout was killed, shot with five arrows. The chief of the attacking Klamaths died inside Frémont's camp, swinging his hatchet. During the rest of the night, the Klamaths continued to snipe at the camp with arrows, which Carson and his comrades intercepted with thick wool blankets hung in trees and spread over bushes. Before dawn, the Indians slipped away.

Of the Klamath leader, Carson later said: "He was the bravest Indian I ever saw. If his men had been as brave as himself we would surely all have been killed." At the sight of the bloody scene that greeted the party in the gray light of dawn, Carson was less generous toward this fallen hero of the enemy. Distraught at the loss of LaJeunesse, Carson grabbed the dead chief's hatchet and, in a rare outburst of temper, smashed the Indian's skull to pulp. Nor was that the end of the carnage. The following day, the two surviving Delaware scouts killed an additional two Klamaths to avenge their tribesmen. And the day after that, Carson led a punitive raid against a large Klamath village on the Williamson River, putting it to the torch and killing at least 20 Indians.

During the hostilities, Frémont came to Carson's rescue twice, saving his life on both occasions. Pressing the initial attack on the Indian village, Carson and the nine other men with him crossed the river at a point where it appeared fordable, but where the water was actually almost 15 feet deep. In the resulting plunge, Carson and his men wet their powder; they would have been defenseless against Klamath arrows had Frémont and the rest of the party not arrived with dry powder at that moment. A little later, Frémont rode down an Indian aiming at Carson, causing the arrow to fly wide

Kit Carson and John Charles Frémont's forces battle Klamath warriors in Oregon, having torched the Indians' village to retaliate for a raid on Frémont's camp. Carson called the flames "a beautiful sight."

of its mark; one of the Delaware scouts then clubbed the Indian to death. In his memoirs, Carson recognized his debt to his boss: "I considered that Frémont saved my life for, in all probability, if he had not run over the Indian as he did, I would have been shot."

While Carson and Frémont fought Indians on the Williamson River, General Zachary Taylor and the American Army had already clashed with Mexican forces along the Rio Grande in Texas, beginning a war that would last nearly two years and send Carson the width of the continent and back carrying dispatches.

After the Mexican War, Carson, considering himself old at 40, made an attempt to settle down and establish a ranch in New Mexico with his Mexican wife of five years and his children, whom he had rarely seen. But the frontier was not yet ready to let him lead a quiet life. The Army called on him frequently to lead one detachment or another in pursuit of hostile Indians.

One such foray was an effort to rescue Mrs. James White from Jicarilla Apaches, who had carried her off after killing her husband and four other men on the Santa Fe Trail. Mrs. White was in the hands of the Apaches for two weeks before word of her plight reached the Army in Taos. A rescue party under Major William Grier started out immediately, and Carson joined the column when it passed near his ranch. "It was the most difficult trail that I ever followed," said Carson of the meager sign left by the Apaches. "As they would leave the camps, they, in numbers from one to two, went in different directions, to meet at some appointed place. In nearly every camp we would find some of Mrs. White's clothing, which was the cause of renewed energy on our part to continue the pursuit."

When Carson found the Indians after 12 days, he counseled an immediate attack, hoping to snatch Mrs. White while the Apaches were occupied defending

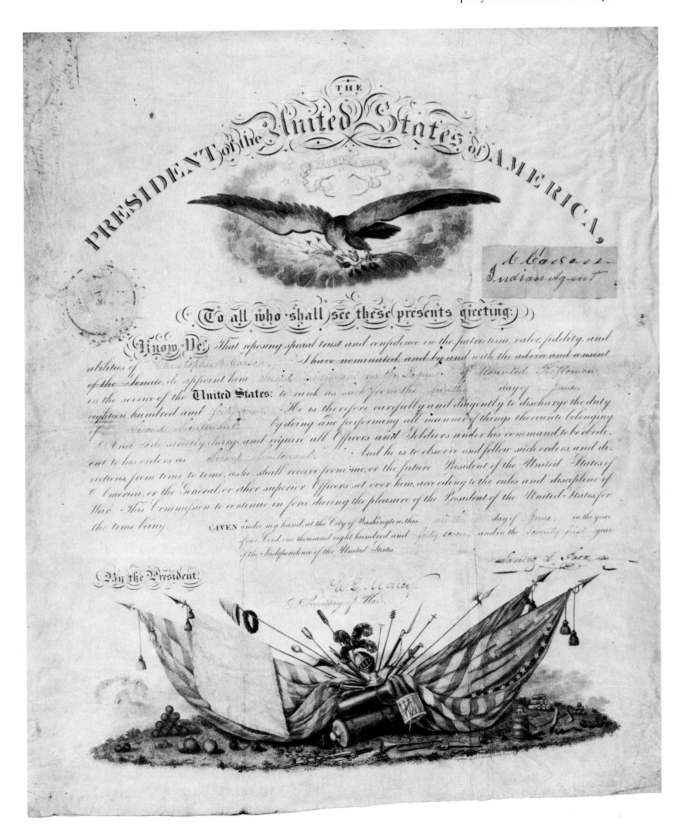

themselves. But the cavalry charge was delayed—at least in part because of the confusion that arose when Major Grier was struck by a ball from an Apache rifle—and Mrs. White's body was found still warm, an arrow through the heart.

For Carson it was an occasion of special distress, for among the dead woman's effects lay one of those lurid dime novels that celebrated Carson as the premier Indian slayer of the age. "I have often thought as Mrs. White would read the same, and knowing that I lived near, she would pray for my appearance," he reminisced through his biographer. "I did come but had not the power to convince those in command to pursue my plan for her rescue."

In 1853, Carson was appointed Indian agent for the Utes of New Mexico. It was a job for which he was superbly qualified. No one knew the Indians better than he and, when not fighting them, he was sympathetic to their needs. Since Carson had no reading, writing or arithmetic, he was hopeless at keeping accounts. Fortunately, as an Indian agent he was allowed $500 a year for an interpreter for which he had no need. Instead the money went to hire a bookkeeper.

When the Civil War broke out, Carson left the agency and signed on with the New Mexico Volunteers as a lieutenant colonel. For the remainder of his public career he employed scouts and guides—mostly Utes and knowledgeable Mexicans—instead of serving as one himself. In recognition of his outstanding Civil War record, Carson was brevetted brigadier general, as the citation read, "for gallantry and for distinguished services in New Mexico."

Kit Carson and Jim Bridger were two of a kind, the one as skilled as the other at scouting. They knew each other, having trapped for beaver together in 1831 and again in 1834. They both attended the fur traders' rendezvous of 1835, where Carson fought the French troublemaker Chouinard, as well as a similar convocation in 1837. To be sure, there were differences between them. By far the biggest one was Carson's good fortune in finding a chronicler in Frémont. Bridger had no such luck; consequently, and unjustly, he won a lesser share of glory in the annals of scouting exploits.

Bridger was five years older than Carson and had already been tramping through the woods for seven years before Carson started work as a trapper in 1829. Bridger had an affinity for nicknames that Carson apparently did not have. "Old Gabe" was one of Bridger's handles; he was given it by Jedediah Smith, a Bible-reading mountain man, because the self-assured Bridger reminded Smith of the Angel Gabriel spreading the word of God. Indians gave Bridger the name of "Blanket Chief" for a red-and-blue robe, sewn and decorated by his Indian wife, that he wore on special occasions. Carson preferred the life of an independent trapper. Bridger spent much of his career leading contingents of trappers numbering 60 or more for large fur-trading enterprises such as the Rocky Mountain Fur Company, of which he was a founder, and the American Fur Company.

In the summer of 1842, confronted with the virtual disappearance of the beaver trade and anticipating the coming tide of westward emigration, Bridger and Louis Vasquez—"Old Vaskiss," as he was known to his fellow trappers—founded a settlement in what is now Wyoming. It consisted of a ramshackle trading post and smithy on Black's Fork of the Green River. Here the overland trail west would, the next year, fork southwestward for California and northwestward for Oregon. Fort Bridger, as the assemblage of cabins and Indian lodges became known, soon evolved into an important stop for repairing broken wagons, feasting on a rare hot meal—from Mrs. Bridger's oven—and swapping trail-worn livestock for fresh animals.

Weary emigrants found Bridger a helpful host. "He was excessively kind and patient with me in laying down the route to Salt Lake," reported William Kelly, who passed that way, "taking the trouble of drawing a chart with charcoal on the door, pointing out a new line that had never yet been attempted, which would be a short cut of thirty miles."

Bridger was a walking atlas of the West. The vast expanse of wilderness from the headwaters of the Missouri to the Rio Grande, down the Colorado River and across the Sierra Nevada to California, lay in his memory like a panoramic mural. And his knowledge helped other travelers besides Kelly. "With a buffalo skin and a piece of charcoal he will map out any portion of this vast region with wonderful accuracy," Captain John W. Gunnison reported in 1834. Or he might use handfuls of sand on a blanket to build peaks and ranges

An old scout at war

At the outset of the Civil War in 1861, the federal government ordered all Army units stationed in the Southwest to return east to fight for the Union. In the absence of troops to keep them subjugated, the Navajos, Comanches, Kiowas and Apaches went on the warpath. Observed one contemporary chronicler: "The savages indulged in a saturnalia of slaughter. The horribly mutilated bodies of men, women and children marked nearly every mile of the road to the Rio Grande."

Unable to spare any regular soldiers for Western duty, the U.S. Army called on Kit Carson to recruit a corps of volunteers to reestablish the peace.

Commissioned a lieutenant colonel in the New Mexico Volunteers and quickly promoted to colonel, Carson began training his raw recruits. The former scout became an employer of scouts, hiring scores of Utes and Jicarillas eager to strike

In this locket miniature, Carson wears the shoulder straps and eagles of a full colonel.

back at their longtime tribal enemies.

After many small-scale skirmishes Carson, in September 1863, began an eight-month scorched-earth campaign that starved the marauding Navajos out of northern New Mexico. His militia laid waste to hundreds of lodges and burned tons of grain and fruit that the tribes had gathered for winter provisions.

In 1864 Carson proved his ability as a commander in a bloody battle at

Adobe Walls, an abandoned trading post in the Texas Panhandle. There Carson's 335 volunteers and 75 scouts beat back about 3,000 massed Indians and escaped with only 25 fatalities. The only other American officer who ever faced as many Indians was George Armstrong Custer, some 12 years later, and he, with nearly twice as many soldiers, suffered one of the most ignominious defeats in military history.

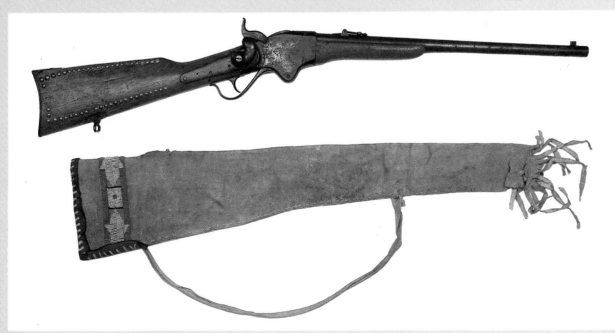

Carson decorated his deadly Spencer carbine Indian style. The sheath was crafted for him by a Taos, New Mexico, Indian friend.

with intervening valleys and then trace rivers and streams with a finger tip. In 1851 when the Plains tribes gathered at Fort Laramie in Wyoming Territory to sign a peace treaty among themselves and with the United States, Jim Bridger was at the elbow of Father De Smet, a Jesuit missionary assigned by the government to draw the official maps that established the domain of each tribe.

Bridger was a physical specimen worth noticing. "Tall — six feet at least — muscular, without an ounce of superfluous flesh to impede its force or exhaust its elasticity," wrote David Brown, a newspaper reporter who ventured out to the 1837 fur rendezvous for the Cincinnati *Atlas*. "His cheek bones were high, his nose hooked or acquiline, the expression of his eyes mild and thoughtful, that of his face grave almost to solemnity."

But Old Gabe enjoyed the rendezvous as much as any other mountain man. He was a crafty campfire raconteur, many of whose tales, tall and true alike, became woven into the fabric of the West's folklore. At least two of the wonders he swore to have seen, a river that ran so fast it got hot at the bottom and one stream that ran toward two seas, had some basis in fact. The first was the Fire Hole River in the Yellowstone region, heated by a subterranean hot spring. The other was Two Ocean Creek, which rose at the crest of the continental divide in the Grand Tetons and split into two branches, one flowing east and eventually into the Atlantic, the other west to the Pacific.

Other stories were pure fantasy — such as the one about Crystal Mountain, so transparent as to be invisible; the only evidence of its existence was scores of

by passing travelers as a "shabby concern" that consisted of "two or three log cabins bearing faint resemblance to human habitation."

lifeless birds at its base, the victims of fatal collisions. Bridger had a wry sense of humor. Pressed once by a British journalist to relate how he escaped from a box canyon blocked by a horde of ravening Indians, the Blanket Chief replied, "Oh, that time I never did. They killed us right there."

As a fireside entertainer, Bridger could get a rise out of Indians too, even if he had to use sign language; so attested Captain Howard Stansbury of the Topographical Engineers after watching Bridger perform before a party of Sioux and Cheyenne in 1850. "He held the whole circle for more than an hour perfectly enchained and evidently most deeply interested in a conversation and narrative, the whole of which was carried on without the utterance of a single word. Exclamations of surprise or interest, and occasional laughter,

showed that the whole party perfectly understood."

However, anyone, white man or Indian, who wanted to hear Old Gabe spin a yarn or describe how to get from here to there stood little chance of finding him at Fort Bridger. Between 1842 when he gave up trapping, and 1867 when failing eyesight relegated him to a Missouri farm, he was too busy guiding and scouting to sit at home. Bridger played diplomat, persuading a pair of recalcitrant Indian tribes to attend an important peace conference near Laramie. He laid out a stage route west from Denver for the Central Overland & Pike's Peak Express Company. He guided 300 prospectors to Montana gold fields. He shepherded explorers and, with the Army, took out after Indians.

One Army expedition in pursuit of Indians in 1865 provided Bridger with an opportunity to demonstrate

At the trappers' rendezvous of 1837, Jim Bridger sports the steel breastplate and plumed helmet given him by Captain William Drummond Stewart, a wealthy Scots sportsman who hired Bridger as a scout.

his acute eyesight. Scouting ahead of the column one day near the Tongue River in Wyoming Territory, Bridger drew the attention of his companion, a Captain Palmer, to smoke "over there by that there saddle." The scout was pointing to a saddle-shaped depression in the hills nearly 50 miles distant. Palmer could not see the smoke, even when he used field glasses. Neither could General P. Edward Connor, the expedition commander. This led the scout to mutter about "these damn paper-collar soldiers" who were not able to see smoke where there was smoke. Soon other scouts rode in and reported an Indian village with campfires where Bridger had seen the smoke.

During his years of scouting and trapping, Bridger must have killed his share of Indians—especially Blackfeet, who were responsible for an arrowhead that Bridger carried embedded in his shoulder for three years. Heading a large group of trappers with Tom Fitzpatrick in 1832, Bridger encountered a band of hostile Blackfeet. The Indians, seeing that they had no clear advantage in numbers, resorted to a ruse. One warrior rode forward on his pony with a peace pipe and Bridger went to meet him halfway. Something about the other Indians aroused Bridger's suspicion, and he cocked his rifle just as the Indian emissary extended his hand in apparent friendship.

But the Blackfoot seized the gun, turning away the trapper's shot, then cracked Bridger on the head. A heated battle erupted. The fighting ended at dusk with nine Blackfeet and three trappers killed. Bridger took two arrows in the shoulder. His companions were able to remove one of them; the other was embedded so securely that the untutored surgeons could only cut

off the arrowshaft at the skin and leave the arrowhead in Bridger's body.

Not until the rendezvous of 1835 did Bridger find a physician who could remove the three-inch piece of barbed iron. It was Dr. Whitman, the Congregational minister who had saved a caravan of fur traders from cholera. Marveling that the wound had not putrified, Whitman cut out the arrow before a fascinated audience of fur trappers and Indians. Bridger attributed his healthy shoulder to the cool mountain air. "In the mountains, Doctor," observed the Blanket Chief, "meat don't spoil."

Strangely, there are few such stories of bloodletting among Bridger's recorded adventures. Perhaps Captain Eugene F. Ware, who met Old Gabe at Fort Laramie, explained the anomaly with this observation about Bridger in *The Indian War of 1864:* "He never in my presence vaunted himself, about his own personal actions. He never told about how brave he was, nor how many Indians he had killed."

One witness, however, did describe an incident that, while enigmatically recounted, indicates that Bridger could be murderous in his dealings with Indians. The observer was Lieutenant J. Lee Humfreville, the same soldier who described the difficulty of interpreting the Indians' sign language. While scouting with Bridger, a few Ohio Volunteer Cavalry and some Arapahos, Humfreville and his companions were attacked by a group of Indians.

Humfreville later recounted Bridger's part in the event: "After a sharp engagement with a war party of much greater numbers than ours, we withdrew to a hillside. Some of the enemy warriors dismounted; and hiding in the grass and bushes, began firing upon us. Bridger challenged an Arapaho to join him in a close-up reconnaissance. The Arapaho refused, and Bridger abused him soundly by means of the sign language. At last the Arapaho took Bridger's hand and they proceeded. I heard a shot; and in a few minutes Bridger returned with a warm, bloody scalp."

Humfreville did not say whether the scalp came from one of the attackers—nor did he say what became of the reluctant Arapaho. The incident—and what it implies about Jim Bridger's moral character—was left clouded in mystery.

Even if tales of Bridger as an Indian fighter had abounded, they could hardly have been more intriguing than his experiences with two noblemen from the British Isles, Sir George Gore and Captain William Drummond Stewart.

Old Gabe met and entered the service of Sir George, Eighth Baronet and Lord of the Manor Gore in Ireland, in 1854. Sir George was a hunter who not only wanted to see the West but also, by the evidence, to kill as much of it as he could.

For the next two years, at $30 a day, Bridger shepherded Sir George and his safari through game country between Fort Laramie in Wyoming and Fort Union in Dakota. It was a sizable responsibility, for the Irish knight's entourage, paid for out of Sir George's $200,000 annual income, included 40 men—among whom were gunbearers, chefs, drovers, wine stewards, secretaries and one specialist whose only duty was to tie trout flies—14 imported hunting hounds, 112 horses, 12 yoke of oxen, 21 carts and six wagons.

On this marathon hunt, Bridger pointed out and Sir George contrived to slaughter 105 grizzlies, 1,600 elk and deer, 2,500 buffalo and countless trout. He left such a trail of havoc that the Indians began muttering about taking to the warpath to protect their food supply. Sir George, unmindful of his limited prerogatives as a foreigner in America, responded by building a personal fort 100 feet square. In so doing, complained Indian agent A. J. Vaughan, Sir George had "most palpably" violated his passport.

Unabashed, the knight errant, with Old Gabe for company, dined on buffalo steaks and rare wines. After supper he would read aloud to Bridger from Shakespeare, Sir Walter Scott and others. Of Longfellow's *Hiawatha,* the Blanket Chief was of the scornful opinion that "no such Injun" had ever lived. Shakespeare's Falstaff, Bridger said, would have been leaner had he taken his alcohol in Taos Lightning rotgut instead of lager. On occasion, to the delight of Sir George, Bridger would turn the tables and recite long passages of Shakespeare that he had heard only once, a feat of recall that rivaled his formidable memory for geographic detail. Late at night after the readings Bridger would retire to his blanket under the stars and Sir George to his canopied brass bedstead.

Bridger could hardly have helped comparing Sir George Gore's remarkable behavior with that of the other nobleman, Captain Stewart, whom the scout had guided through the wilderness back in 1833. Except for noble blood, Stewart bore no resemblance whatsoever to Sir George. For starters he was a Scotsman. Moreover, as a second son in a social system that gave rank and riches to the firstborn, Stewart was comparatively impecunious. And as it turned out, Stewart needed little nursemaiding even on an illegal and dangerous trapping expedition to the Mexican southwest. By the time Stewart had spent his second season in the mountains, trappers were treating him as a talented amateur who, in an emergency, could be called upon to handle a pack train on his own. Eventually they came to look on him as one of their number scarcely different from them except that his firearms were costly handmade masterpieces from London.

Or perhaps there was one other, trifling difference. It would have been an eccentric mountain man indeed who imported from England, as Stewart did for his friend Bridger, nothing less than the steel armor of a British guardsman. For a trapper accustomed to buckskins, such a costume might have seemed an inappropriate gift, heavy and cumbersome, an oven in the summer sun. The gift may well have been an expensive joke; certainly there was a great deal of laughter when Bridger received and donned the armor at the 1837 fur rendezvous. But, joke or not, perhaps Stewart intended the helmet and breastplate as a symbolic protection against all the hazards that the backwoods presented. If so, it worked. Because Jim Bridger died on his farm near Kansas City, Missouri, in 1881 with his boots off, virtually unscathed after nearly six decades of trapping and scouting in the American wilderness.

Scout Jim Bridger mounts guard over his employer, Captain William Stewart, as the Scots adventurer scans the prairie with a telescope.

2 | The men who knew the way

"Our ignorance of the route was complete," said a member of the first emigrant wagon train to the West Coast. "We knew that California lay west, and that was the extent of our knowledge." It was 1841, and few white Americans knew anything about paths to the Pacific—or the stark, punishing land along the way. For the most part, maps of the mountains, plains and deserts existed only in the minds of scouts like Thomas "Broken Hand" Fitzpatrick, whose services that first emigrant train was fortunate enough to secure.

In the years that followed, scouts were much in demand, both for their knowledge of established trails and for their ability to blaze new ones. They led not only parties of settlers but expeditions of soldiers, mapmakers and scientists. An act of Congress in 1853 spurred this scout-led exploration of the West to new, feverish heights: the Army's Corps of Topographical Engineers was charged with determining "the most practicable and economical route for a railroad from the Mississippi to the Pacific Ocean."

Corps expeditions like that of Lieutenant Robert S. Williamson (*below*) pushed across deserts and studied the curves and grades of mountain passes. These parties included botanists, geologists and artists, who inventoried and described the land and the life it supported. In the process they opened new routes and filled in many of the blank spaces on the map of the West.

Only a distant mountain breaks the vast horizon facing the members of a railroad survey team as they cross a California desert in 1853. The domelike shape imposed on this lithograph by the artist enhances the sense of limitless space.

A railroad survey team in the Northwest receives word from a white scout that the trail ahead is too rough for the wagons that carry the party's scientific instruments. An Indian scout, on horseback, later helped to reroute the course of the expedition.

A group of Army explorers surveys the timberless foothills of California's Coast Ranges, seeking a suitable railroad route. The party, which started from San Francisco and worked its way east, was guided by scout Alexis Godey through the treacherous peaks of the Sierra Nevadas.

Finding new trails across the wilderness

The most vital work of scouts in the two decades before the Civil War was discovering new and better pathways to the Pacific Coast and, in the process, opening the whole West to settlement. They guided the wagon trains and the exploratory expeditions that changed a region of uncharted mystery into a land whose rivers, mountains, valleys and deserts were mapped, described and traversed by proven routes (map, page 59).

When a scout known as "Broken Hand" Fitzpatrick led the first emigrant wagon train across the Rockies in 1841, the vast expanse between that mighty mountain chain and the Sierra Nevada to the west was so little known that it was not generally suspected of being a great basin with its own landlocked system of rivers and lakes. Explorer John Charles Frémont himself thought that the Great Salt Lake in Utah ran directly, by means of a presumed river, into the Pacific Ocean. Twelve years later, thanks to men like Fitzpatrick, the lay of the land was sufficiently known for Congress to begin planning a transcontinental railroad.

Most of the scouts who took part in this process of finding new routes and dispelling the enigmas of Western geography won little recognition for their work. For instance, fame never visited Caleb Greenwood, Elisha Stevens or Isaac Hitchcock, and yet this trio of mountain men opened a new wagon road to California that became a major emigrant thoroughfare: the California Trail (map, page 59).

Before 1844, wagon trains bound for northern California followed the Oregon Trail all the way to its end at present-day Portland and then made a long trek

south down the coast. But in that year the three scouts, working together, turned the train they were guiding off the Oregon Trail and led the wagons down the Humboldt River and over Donner Pass into California. Before long the new route was being traveled by hundreds of California-bound emigrants, many of whom had never heard of the men who blazed the trail.

Another little-celebrated routefinder was Moses Harris, whom a contemporary described as "a mountaineer without special education, but with five sound senses." Besides being an accomplished scout, Harris was a fascinating character. An air of mystery surrounded him. People were not certain where he came from or what his racial origin was. His complexion was so dark that he was known as "Black" Harris, and one man who met him said his skin was "apparently composed of tan leather and whip cord, finished off with a peculiar blue-black tint, as if gun powder had been burnt into his face."

In 1846, Black Harris and another scout named Jesse Applegate were the mainstays of a scouting party that discovered, after several unsuccessful tries, a new route running from the California Trail through the Cascade mountains to Oregon. This new road greatly facilitated travel to southern Oregon, and soon was being heavily used by emigrants. But Harris enjoyed no particular fame for his part in finding it. His partner was luckier; the road became known as Applegate's Cutoff.

Two of the West's greatest pathfinders, however, were also renowned in their own day, with names that were familiar to both generals and Congressmen. They were Thomas "Broken Hand" Fitzpatrick and a trapper-turned-scout named Antoine Leroux. Both were described as being among the "oldest backwoodsmen in existence" by the German artist-naturalist Balduin Möllhausen, a member of a trailblazing expedition guided by Leroux in 1853. They were "grey-headed

Moses "Black" Harris was reported to know every hill and hollow from St. Louis to Oregon. The scout could hold his companions spellbound with hair-raising tales.

old fellows," Möllhausen noted in his diary, "whom one cannot avoid looking at with a certain respect and admiration, when one remembers how often during their long wanderings death in many forms has threatened them." It was their mode of life, he thought, that kept them "vigorous, and one may say young in mind and body, though they have reached an advanced age." At the time Möllhausen was writing, Fitzpatrick was 55 and Leroux 53.

Yet the German—who later achieved fame in his own country with a stream of novels set in the American West—was not alone in assuming the scouts to be not only grizzled but ancient as well; many other acquaintances spoke of Fitzpatrick and Leroux that way. It may well have been reassuring to believe that the men on whom one's own survival depended had themselves survived to the age of Methuselah. But these scouts probably did look old before their time: a life lived in constant battle with nature and Indians could do that to a man.

Thomas Fitzpatrick, born in 1799 of County Cavan gentlefolk, left Ireland for America when he was 17. In 1822 he answered a memorable help-wanted notice in a St. Louis newspaper. General William Ashley was seeking "enterprising young men" to trap beaver for him on the upper Missouri. The list of youthful adventure-seekers who signed on reads like a roll call of great mountain men: besides Fitzpatrick they included Jedediah Smith, Antoine Leroux, Jim Bridger, Hugh Glass, Jim Clyman and Bill Sublette.

For the next 20 years, Fitzpatrick earned his living as a trapper, eventually becoming a major partner in the Rocky Mountain Fur Company. During that time he built a reputation as a canny mountaineer who knew most of the uncharted West like the back of his hand.

To the Indians, Fitzpatrick was something of a legend. They not only dubbed him Broken Hand after his wrist was shattered in a rifle accident, but they called him White Hair as well. That last nickname was bestowed after an incident that helps explain how Fitzpatrick acquired his acumen in the wilderness and why he looked 10 to 20 years older than he was.

In 1832, while riding in advance of a pack train he was guiding, Fitzpatrick ran into a migrating group of dangerous Gros Ventre Indians near South Pass in the Rockies. He lit out for the nearby mountains with the

Based on contemporary likenesses, this portrait of Thomas Fitzpatrick late in life reveals the gentlemanly demeanor of the former scout. After guiding his last expedition in 1846, he was an Indian agent on the Plains until he died at age 55 in 1854.

Indians in yelling pursuit. His horse, spurred through brush and across jagged rocks, soon gave out and Fitzpatrick had to streak up the mountainside on foot. He found a crevice in the rock and crawled in, heaping up stones and leaves around the opening. The Gros Ventres found his horse but, though they came within inches, they missed his hiding place. Enraged that somehow he had given them the slip, they camped nearby and for several excruciating days Fitzpatrick remained hidden. Finally he slipped out by night, making a wide circle around their camp.

Although his immediate surroundings were strange to him, he was able to orient himself by familiar mountain peaks in the distance and headed toward his intended rendezvous at Pierre's Hole, a valley in what is now southeastern Idaho. In order to get across the Snake River, he built a small raft, but it was dashed against rocks in midstream and Fitzpatrick reached the

48

opposite bank without his rifle, powder or shot-pouch.

For five days he struggled onward, subsisting mainly on roots and berries. He escaped a wolf pack by climbing a tree, and later made a meal of the raw meat of a buffalo carcass left by the wolves. When his moccasins became shredded, he cut his leather hat into strips and bound his bloodied feet. When at last he was found by two trappers sent out to search for him, he was near death and unable to walk. But his course had been as true as an arrow's and he was only a few miles from his destination. With rest he recovered, but the ordeal had turned his hair white. He was 33.

In 1841, Broken Hand Fitzpatrick secured for himself a special position not only in the lore of scouts, but in the history of America, when he led the first emigrant wagon train to cross the wilderness to the West Coast. The job fell to him almost by accident.

In May 1841, sixty-nine emigrants, eager to reach California, the reputed land of milk and honey, had paused at the frontier jumping-off point of Westport, Missouri. They had been particularly enchanted by the accounts of the veteran trapper Antoine Robidoux, who not only spoke of oranges, grapes and olive trees, but also insisted that sickness was virtually unknown to Californians. According to John Bidwell, one of the leaders, the emigrants had been preparing to start without a guide and with only the vaguest notion of how to get to California when they heard that a group of missionaries was on the way from St. Louis "with an old Rocky Mountaineer for a guide." The guide was Broken Hand Fitzpatrick, who had been hired by a Belgian priest, Pierre-Jean De Smet, to lead his party to the Flathead Indians in Oregon Territory.

"At first we were independent, and thought we could not afford to wait for a slow missionary party," wrote Bidwell. "But when we found that no one knew which way to go, we sobered down and waited for them to come up; and it is well we did, for otherwise not one of us would ever have reached California, because of our inexperience." The genial, roly-poly Father De Smet, whom Bidwell called "one of the saintliest men I have ever known," was glad to have the greenhorns along and Fitzpatrick raised no objections. On May 10 the caravan, its members apparently unaware of its historic significance, rolled out from the westernmost edge of civilized America for the Pacific Coast. It was the prototype of countless wagon trains that were to follow. The emigrants had 13 wagons, drawn by mules, horses and oxen; the missionaries were mounted on mules and hauled their belongings in five Red River carts — awkward two-wheeled vehicles drawn by mules hitched in tandem.

Father Nicolas Point, one of De Smet's two assistants, kept a journal of the daily routine; it bears evidence that Fitzpatrick, though nominally only the guide, was in effect the leader of the train. Point and others in the party called the scout "Captain." "Each day the captain gave the signal to rise and depart, ordered the march and the stops, chose the spot in which to camp, and maintained discipline. Whenever possible, camp was pitched on the wooded bank of some river that there would be no lack of drinking water or of wood for cooking. First, the captain would mark a spot for our tents; then the vehicles would be arranged one beside the other in a circle or in a square in such a manner to provide the pack animals a secure enclosure for the night."

Everyone in the train, including the priests, took turns standing watch at night, but they had only one real Indian scare. A party of 40 Cheyenne warriors set upon one of the party, a young schoolteacher named Nicholas Dawson who was hunting antelope. When Dawson returned without his mule, gun and most of his clothes, a panic ensued, and the train broke into a full gallop — oxen and all. Fitzpatrick managed to calm the party; then, after forming the wagons into a protective square, he went out with a force to find the Cheyennes.

Dawson later recalled following with a borrowed gun and horse, bent on vengeance. "I came on at full speed and was aiming at the first Indian within range, when I was stopped by some forcible language from Fitzpatrick." Broken Hand managed to barter back most of Dawson's articles, but the scout's "patience gave out before all was got back, and declaring that I ought to be satisfied to have got off with my life, he refused to intercede further." From then on, the company dubbed the teacher "Cheyenne" Dawson.

One night, while they were encamped on the south fork of the Platte River, the expedition's members found themselves in the path of a buffalo stampede. "We had to sit up and fire guns and make what fires we could to keep them from trampling us into the dust," said Bidwell. "We were obliged to go out some distance from camp to turn them: Captain Fitzpatrick told us that if we did not do this the buffaloes in front could not turn aside for the pressure of those behind. We could hear them thundering all night long; the ground fairly trembled with vast approaching bands; and if they had not been diverted, wagons, animals and emigrants would have been trodden under their feet."

The group crossed the Continental Divide at South Pass, and after reaching Soda Springs on the Bear River, the train split up. Half of Bidwell's emigrants decided to play it safe and remain with Fitzpatrick and the missionaries as far as Oregon country; they reached it safely and expeditiously, and thus established the Oregon Trail as the prime route to the West.

The remainder struck off without a guide to California. "We knew nothing positive of the route, except that it went west," recalled Cheyenne Dawson. Fitzpatrick gave them what advice he could, but since he had not traveled that route himself he could not prevent, nor could they foresee, the harrowing events that awaited them. Eventually they did push through to the San Joaquin Valley, but only after abandoning their wagons, devouring their oxen and most of their horses and mules, and being reduced to eating crows, coyote and anything else they could shoot, including a wildcat. When they staggered over the Sierra Nevada about November 1 and found themselves in a valley full of deer, antelope and wild grapes, they had no idea that they had actually reached their promised land. "We were really almost down to tidewater, but did not know it," wrote Bidwell. "Some thought it was 500 miles yet to California."

Tom Fitzpatrick piloted a second wagon train over part of the Oregon Trail in the following year. This time the group was much larger, with 112 emigrants strung out in a long procession of prairie schooners, horses, pack mules and cattle. They had been traveling without a scout and trouble was brewing when Fitzpatrick ran into them and took over as guide after the wagon train was past Fort Laramie, in what is now eastern Wyoming. "All appeared to be determined to govern, but not to be governed," wrote Lansford W. Hastings, a member of the company who was later to turn his experiences to practical use by publishing the

first guidebook for emigrants to Oregon and California.

If the emigrants had had the benefit of Fitzpatrick's leadership from the first, they would have undoubtedly avoided bickering. And if he had been with them when they arrived at Fort Laramie—which was still a private post—he could have saved them from being bilked by unscrupulous traders, who induced some of the group to swap their wagons and oxen for pack horses at a great disadvantage, alleging falsely that they would never get wheels over the passes to Oregon.

But when Broken Hand did join them, a mile or so out of Laramie, and contracted, at a fee of $250, to take them across the divide to Fort Hall, he managed to bring a semblance of order—and even to save the lives of a couple of recalcitrants. One of his cardinal rules was no straggling. Anyone who lingered behind or wandered off the trail was vulnerable to Indian attack. Unfortunately this rule was disregarded by Hastings and A. L. Lovejoy (one of the future founders of Portland), who dallied to carve their names on Independence Rock, a landmark in present-day Wyoming. Suddenly they were surrounded by several hundred Sioux, who seized and stripped them. They were held prisoner for several hours, during which they were beaten with bows and rifle ramrods. Then the Indians took the prisoners along as they pursued the wagon train.

Fitzpatrick had already surmised the situation and had drawn his camp into battle formation. The Indians stopped short, parleyed, and eventually traded Hastings and Lovejoy for a supply of ammunition. The two truants ran to their friends with tears of joy streaming down their cheeks. Once again Fitzpatrick had shown the combination of tact, firmness and knowledge of Indian custom that won for scouts like him the respect of Indians and white men alike.

The next year, 1843, came to be known as the year of the Great Emigration. What had started as a trickle of 69 hardy spirits two short years before was now turning into a flood. Westport and nearby towns were thronged with emigrants laying in supplies for Oregon. The trail, so new to wagons in 1841 that John Bidwell could still make out the tracks of a trading caravan that had passed over it several years earlier, was now deep-rutted by the wheels of hundreds of vehicles. Two years later, in 1845, Colonel Stephen Watts Kearny, on his way to South Pass with a force of dragoons, counted one wagon train after another; he estimated that he had passed half that year's emigration of nearly 5,000 men, women and children, with their vehicles and their thousands of horses, mules and cattle. The route through South Pass, the great northern gateway through the Rockies, had been a mere pathway for trappers since March 1824, when it was discovered by a trapping party that included Tom Fitzpatrick. Twenty years later the incessant trampling of emigrant feet and turning of wagon wheels had transformed it into a broad avenue.

The famous Captain Fitzpatrick—his honorary rank was later elevated to "Major"—accompanied the Kearny expedition as guide and interpreter. This flashy assemblage of five companies of the 1st Dragoons, totaling 250 men, was sent out by the government to impress the Plains Indians between Fort Leavenworth and South Pass with the military strength of the white man and to admonish them not to molest the wagon trains that passed through their hunting grounds. To heighten the Indians' awe, Kearny took along two howitzers and he arranged his dragoons in parade-ground splendor. Lieutenant J. H. Carleton, one of Kearny's subordinates, described the order of march:

"First the guide"—Fitzpatrick—"is seen by himself, some quarter of a mile ahead of all: then the commanding officer, followed by his orderly and the chief bugler: then the staff officers: then a division, mounted on black horses, marching by twos: then another on greys—another on bays—another on sorrels, and a fifth on blacks again, with an interval of one hundred paces between each division to avoid one another's dust: then the howitzers, followed by a party of dragoons: then the train of wagons, with a detail to assist in getting them over bad places, under the immediate command of the quartermaster-sergeant: then the drove of cattle and sheep, followed by their guard of nine men under the command of a corporal—and lastly, the main guard, under an officer to bring up the extreme rear."

Not surprisingly, Kearny did not meet as many Indians as he hoped he would on his march; they judiciously kept well outside the range of his gorgeous dragoons and their howitzers. "Yet"—he wrote in his official report—"the fact of our having been through their country is, no doubt, at this time known to every man, woman and child in it. And as these were the first soldiers ever seen by those upper Indians it is most probable, in their accounts to those who did not see us, they have rather exaggerated than lessened our numbers, power, and force."

Kearny was wrong on one score. The Plains Indians were not lastingly cowed by a parade of American soldiery, as the Army was to discover in the following decades. But in the two powwows he managed to convoke, his mission seemed most effective. The first took place near Fort Laramie, where tribes of several Indian nations gathered and spread their buffalo robes, sitting in a great semicircle, with their women and children behind them. The peace pipe was passed around and Kearny addressed the assembled throng. Tom Fitzpatrick, who had a thorough, even scholarly knowledge of Indian languages, was probably the interpreter as Kearny declared that the road opened by the dragoons must not be closed and that the white men who traveled it must not be molested. The officer also warned the Indians of the evils of drinking whiskey. One of the chiefs, Bull Tail, made a dignified response, after which the soldiers passed out trinkets.

To cap the ceremony a sky rocket and the howitzers were fired. At this, according to historian Francis Parkman, who was at Fort Laramie a year later, "many of the Arapahos fell prostrate on the ground, while others ran away screaming with amazement and terror. The following day they withdrew to their mountains, confounded with awe at the appearance of the Dragoons, at their big guns that went off twice at one shot"—the howitzers threw explosive shells—"and the fiery messenger they had sent up to the Great Spirit."

The troopers covered 1,700 miles in only 72 days, with their horses subsisting solely on grass—a significant indication of how efficiently, thanks to the help of scouts, Americans could operate in country that recently had been terra incognita. In his report, Kearny had only praise for his famous scout. In urging that the Army explore shorter routes to the Pacific than the circuitous Oregon Trail, he recommended, as the man to lead such expeditions, "Mr. Thomas Fitzpatrick, who was our guide during the late expedition, an excellent woodsman—one who has been much west of the mountains, and who has as good, if not a better knowledge of the country than any other man in existence." ◉

A traveler's sketches of history in the making

To the Jesuit missionaries and California-bound laymen led westward by Thomas "Broken Hand" Fitzpatrick in 1841, Indians, grizzly bears and black clouds of buffalo were new and awesome sights. Deeply impressed, Father Nicolas Point, a Belgian priest and artist, made primitive, often whimsical, sketches of what he saw. "What a beautiful perspective for a Missionary!" Point wrote in his journal when at the edge of the boundless prairie. "But especially for me, who for twenty years have seen nothing but the walls of a college."

From the time the wagon train left Westport, Missouri, the artist sketched prolifically. One "good effect" of the pictures, said the modest Point, was that they at least "contributed in some small measure to the innocent amusement of the company." But they were much more: an eyewitness record of that historic enterprise, the first wagon train to the West Coast.

Fitzpatrick talks with Indians who display an American flag and a human scalp. One traveler said these trophies, presumably from white victims, "made us tremble."

Les deux Pawnies conversant par signes avec le capitaine. le premier a pour manteau un drapeau americain. le second a une chevelure humaine pandue au mors de son cheval. Une douzaine sont venus nous visiter — distribution de tabac.

With three priests on horseback, the missionary party's two-wheeled supply carts roll out of Westport, passing the small chapel in which Father Point had served.

Thomas Fitzpatrick, called "Thom" in Point's caption, is pictured here twice: first killing elk as food for the emigrants, and then carrying the game back to the camp.

53

In Point's opinion, "the most remarkable landmark in this beautiful solitude" was Independence Rock in what is now Wyoming. His sketch (*bottom left*) includes the members of his party who etched their signatures on "The Great Register of the Wilderness." Point was also evidently impressed by a half-Iroquois scout (*below*), Ignace Hatchiorauquasha, who became known as John Gray. One missionary said that Gray, who was with Fitzpatrick for much of the trip, often showed "extraordinary courage and dexterity, especially when on one occasion he dared to attack five bears at once."

Point gave the half-Indian scout John Gray a French first name and a European aspect.

Wielding his gun, Gray holds

Even the seasoned Broken Hand Fitzpatrick and Gray succumbed to tradition by signing their names on Independence Rock.

John aux prises avec cinq ours. Gray.
b. 183.

five grizzlies at bay. Hearing shots, his companions rushed to the scene and found the scout "in a circle of bears finishing off the last."

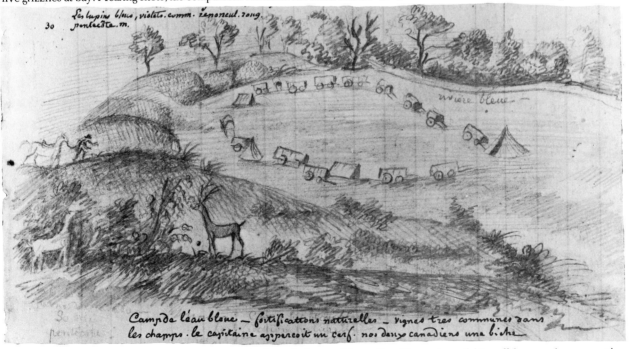

30 Les lupins bleus, violets. comm. ęenoncul. roug.
pentecôte. m.

rivière bleue

Camp de l'eau bleue — fortifications naturelles — vignes tres communes dans les champs. le capitaine apperçoit un cerf. nos deux canadiens une biche.

Father Point's sketch of wagons pulled into a circle for the night is one of the earliest illustrations of this well-known pioneer practice.

Dwarfed in a panorama of the northern Rockies, surveyors *(left)* push westward toward Little Blackfoot Pass while their Indian scout detours to shoot deer. Beyond the scout lies Cadotte's Pass, which the survey leader would later recommend as the best rail route across the Great Divide.

A man whose knowledge of the country was probably as good as Fitzpatrick's was Antoine Leroux. Leroux proved extremely valuable to the Army as a finder of new routes. He led four important path-breaking expeditions in the Southwest and was consulted by Congress as an expert on routes for the planned transcontinental railroad. As a free trapper, Leroux came to know every mountain pass and stream of the upper Rio Grande region; the whole of the San Luis Valley and southern Colorado was his backyard. Because he so frequently got there first, maps of the region are sprinkled with his name: Leroux Springs in present-day Arizona, Leroux Fork on the Little Colorado, Leroux Peak near the Green River in Utah.

Born in St. Louis in 1801 of mixed French and Spanish ancestry, with a touch of Indian on the mother's side, Leroux was a French subject until the Louisiana Purchase of 1803 made him a citizen of the United States. He spoke French-accented English and grew up listening to the lore of French-Canadian trappers who were his neighbors in St. Louis. Like Fitzpat-

rick he was one of the young woodsmen who trapped for General Ashley at the headwaters of the Missouri in 1822, but after visiting his mother's kinfolk in Taos, New Mexico, in 1824, he made the Southwest the center of his trapping activity. Leroux became a naturalized Mexican citizen in 1830 to avoid the stiff taxes leveled on foreigners who trapped in Mexican-owned territory, which then included most of the Southwest as well as California.

In 1833 he married Juana Catarina Valdez de Vigil, heiress to a Spanish land grant of nearly half a million acres in the vicinity of Taos. Much of this huge domain was desert, suited at best for grazing, but Leroux was now a man of some wealth. He chose to continue the life of a trapper, however, working the vast territory of the Gila and Colorado rivers and their tributaries. He relished this outdoor life and he took an amateur scientist's interest in the largely unknown terrain he ranged over—its flora and fauna, its geology, even its archeology (it was Leroux who discovered the prehistoric Indian ruins in the Verde Valley now

called Montezuma's Castle and Montezuma's Well).

With his skills and knowledge, Antoine Leroux was just the man for the U.S. Army to call on when it undertook a massive stocktaking of the West and all it contained that might be of advantage to the white man. The dimensions of the project were staggering. Few accurate large-scale maps of the trans-Mississippi regions existed, much less detailed topographical surveys of specific areas. Passable trails and navigable rivers had to be charted. Passes through the forbidding mountain ranges needed to be investigated for wagons and rails. Grades and elevations had to be determined with mathematical accuracy.

Of nearly equal importance was an accounting of the vast resources that the region contained. Where were water, grass and timber? How much fertile land was there? What areas were rich in minerals? What plants and animals were native to the region? What of value could be learned about the history, culture and economy of the native tribes and their attitude toward white intruders? These were questions for geologists, botanists, ethnologists, archeologists and artists, as well as surveyors, geographers, cartographers and topographical draftsmen.

All this work proceeded under the auspices and protection of the Army, and most of it was carried forward by a remarkable, minuscule Army unit known as the Corps of Topographical Engineers. The Corps was created in 1838 and in all its existence—it was disbanded during the Civil War—never had a roster exceeding 36 officers. But no other group, of any size, contributed more to the exploration and development of the American West than the Topographical Engineers and the scouts who guided them.

The Corps attracted the cream of West Point's engineering graduates, and on its various expeditions it employed independent scientists and artists of sundry nationalities as co-workers. Some of its work had an immediate military purpose—it was, in fact, a fighting unit when necessary. More often it served the practical purpose of encouraging settlement by finding mountain passes, rivers and harbors and establishing roads. Simultaneously it functioned as a body of scientists, producing reports on the natural phenomena it found on its expeditions. These reports were accompanied by maps, drawings, paintings and narrative journals that give a day-by-day account of the adventures and misadventures that befell the expeditions.

Nothing was irrelevant to the scientific, cataloguing minds of these Corpsmen. John C. Frémont — who was the most famous of the Topographical Engineers, as well as one of the few non-West Pointers — carried this passion for observation to the extreme when he commented at length on the peculiarities of a bumblebee that he found buzzing around at the summit of a peak in the Wind River Mountains.

The Topographical Engineers were a new breed. At West Point they did not waste their time on Latin and Greek; their only foreign language was French, the universally acknowledged tongue of scientific discourse in their day. In addition, most of them studied drawing and could set down — sometimes elegantly — the main details of a landscape or sketch the appearance of an Indian. They took classes with John Torrey, one of the leading botanists of the era, and studied techniques of microscopy with Jacob Bailey, a specialist in algae. Some of them corresponded with the era's great scientists like Alexander von Humboldt and Louis Agassiz. On the whole, these Army engineers came close to the ideal of the Renaissance man.

At the base of their adventurous spirit and thirst for knowledge was a romantic awe of the land they were engaged in discovering — of its vast canyons, breathtaking rivers and lakes, parched deserts, primitive tribes. Impelled by this awe, as well as by the widely held faith in their country's Manifest Destiny to possess the continent from ocean to ocean, they produced in a mere 25 years one of the swiftest and most comprehensive inventories ever made of any part of the earth. They could not have done it without the aid of scouts such as Antoine Leroux.

Leroux's first assignment for the U.S. Army came at what must have been a traumatic moment in his life. When the Army of the West under Stephen Watts Kearny invaded New Mexico soon after the outbreak of the Mexican War, the governor of that Mexican province issued an order drafting all able-bodied males

to its defense. Although he was a naturalized citizen of Mexico, Leroux had strong loyalties to the United States, the country in which he had been reared and educated. He was now faced with the dilemma of either taking up arms against the Americans or joining them and being branded a traitor by Mexico, the native land of his wife and children.

Fortunately, before a choice was forced on him, Governor Armijo fled Santa Fe. Kearny captured the town without firing a shot, declaring all of New Mexico to be American territory. Leroux soon gave evidence of his renewed allegiance to the United States by agreeing to act as guide for Captain Philip St. George Cooke, under orders from General Kearny to find a wagon road from Santa Fe to San Diego. Besides the engineering staff, Cooke's expedition included the so-called Mormon Battalion, 399 volunteers furnished by Brigham Young, whose purpose was to conduct a contingent of the Saints westward at government expense.

Consulting his new chief guide, the red-bearded Cooke learned that some 1,200 grueling miles lay ahead of him and that his pack mules and oxen could carry only 60 days' worth of rations; they were in poor condition and there were no more to be had. "Very discouraging," Cooke told his journal, adding that he doubted his guides knew the country.

Leroux knew it well enough to realize that Cooke could not go the way he wanted, which was more or less directly west. The best course, Leroux advised,

---

A LACEWORK OF WESTWARD ROUTES

The trails that the scouts added to the map in the 1840s and 1850s became pathways along which civilization moved westward. Within two years after Thomas Fitzpatrick led the first emigrant wagon train over the Oregon Trail in 1841, some 1,500 settlers had followed that road to the Northwest. The new trails across Utah marked out by Captain James Hervey Simpson and his scout John Reese were among routes that, by 1860, more than 300,000 pioneers had taken to California. Other new paths — such as the one blazed by Captain Lorenzo Sitgreaves and scout Antoine Leroux in 1851 — eventually became routes for railroads that stretched across the continent.

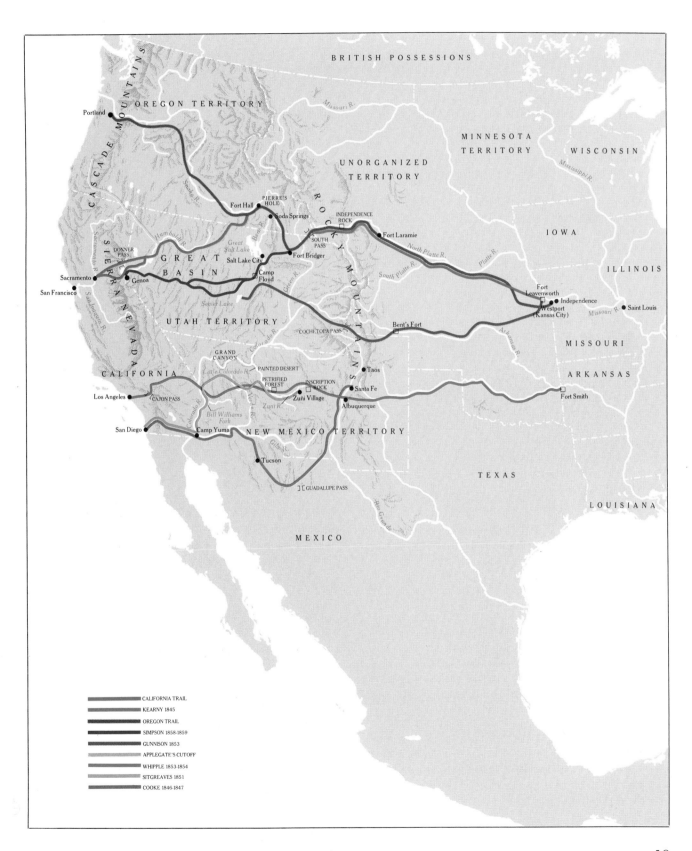

BRITISH POSSESSIONS

OREGON TERRITORY

MINNESOTA TERRITORY

WISCONSIN

CASCADE MOUNTAINS

Portland

Missouri R.

UNORGANIZED TERRITORY

Mississippi R.

Snake R.

PIERRE'S HOLE

Fort Hall

INDEPENDENCE ROCK

IOWA

Soda Springs

Bear R.

SOUTH PASS

Fort Laramie

North Platte R.

Humboldt R.

Great Salt Lake

Fort Bridger

ILLINOIS

ROCKY MOUNTAINS

Salt Lake City

South Platte R.

Green R.

GREAT BASIN

DONNER PASS

Camp Floyd

Platte R.

SIERRA NEVADA

Sacramento

Genoa

Fort Leavenworth

Sevier Lake

UTAH TERRITORY

Independence

San Francisco

San Joaquin R.

Westport (Kansas City)

Saint Louis

Bent's Fort

Missouri R.

Arkansas R.

MISSOURI

COCHETOPA PASS

GRAND CANYON

Colorado R.

ARKANSAS

PAINTED DESERT

Taos

CALIFORNIA

Little Colorado R.

PETRIFIED FOREST

INSCRIPTION ROCK

Los Angeles

CAJON PASS

Zuñi Village

Santa Fe

Fort Smith

Virgin R.

Bill Williams Fork

Zuñi R.

Albuquerque

San Diego

Colorado R.

Camp Yuma

Gila R.

NEW MEXICO TERRITORY

TEXAS

Tucson

Rio Grande

LOUISIANA

GUADALUPE PASS

MEXICO

CALIFORNIA TRAIL
KEARNY 1845
OREGON TRAIL
SIMPSON 1858-1859
GUNNISON 1853
APPLEGATE'S CUTOFF
WHIPPLE 1853-1854
SITGREAVES 1851
COOKE 1846-1847

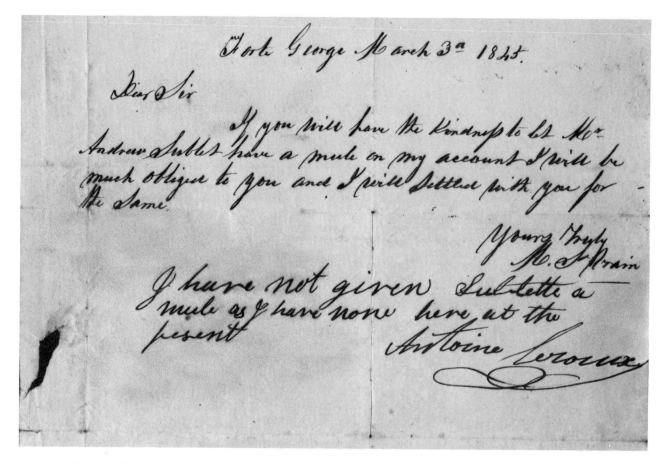

was to follow the Rio Grande for some 230 miles to the south *(map, page 59),* and then swing to the southwest for another 160 miles to reach an easy wagon road over Guadalupe Pass to Tucson. With reluctance, Cooke agreed to the roundabout route, at least for a while.

As the expedition pressed south from Santa Fe, Leroux scouted as far as 60 miles ahead of the party, looking for water, forage and terrain fit for wheels to turn on. He had set up with Cooke a communication system of smoke signals and messages attached to poles or trees. He also took along a number of assistant scouts, sending one of them back each day with directions for camping places or the following day's march. Frequently, Cooke would not see Leroux himself for a week at a time.

When they left the Rio Grande and struck out for Guadalupe Pass the going became slow and mean, mostly through desert. Cooke began to grow weary of their eternal southwestering; California, after all, lay to

the west. One day, he abruptly decided to countermand his scout. A member of the battalion wrote in his diary that Cooke "was riding at the head of his command with his pilots when he made a sudden halt and ordered his men to turn square to the right and swore he would be damned if he was going all around the world to reach California."

Now, having picked his own course, Cooke had to find a wagon pass through the mountains ahead or confess failure. He thought he had his problem solved when Leroux, hunting for someone from whom Cooke might buy fresh livestock, brought in a drunken Apache chief who pointed out what he said was a pass. But even in his cups, the chief admitted that getting through the pass would be difficult. He understated the problem. To cross craggy declivities, far too steep and boulder-studded to be negotiated on wheels, Cooke's exhausted men lowered the ungainly wagons by ropes and then hauled them up the other side. Sheer, groaning manpower finally got the vehicles over the pass, but some of the wagons came through in such sorry shape that they were cannibalized to patch up others.

And then Cooke learned that he had battered his way over the divide less than half a dozen miles north of the easily crossed Guadalupe Pass toward which Leroux had been attempting to lead him. Unwilling to admit the fact that he himself had chosen the road after a consultation with an inebriated Indian, Cooke complained, "My guides are ignorant of the country." As though he had found it out for himself, he declared his belief that Guadalupe Pass, the one he had bullheadedly missed, was "the only pass to the Pacific for a thousand miles south."

Sixty-four days out, having limped and stumbled over 780 miles of sere desert and rugged mountain, Cooke's force reached the Colorado River at the point where it is joined by the Gila. On the other side of the Colorado lay California and well-known trails all the way to San Diego. In spite of the difficulties, Leroux had helped blaze the first wagon road through the Southwest, a road soon to be trodden by thousands heading for the California gold fields.

Antoine Leroux returned to Taos, built up his ranch, took out a license to trade with the Comanches and, in 1849, was elected one of 19 delegates to organize the Territory of New Mexico. Then, five years after the Cooke expedition, the Corps of Topographical Engineers knocked on the door of his hacienda.

By 1851 many settlers and gold rushers were using Cooke's 1846 route to California—except that now they went the few extra miles to cross easy Guadalupe Pass. But it was still a hard road. Furthermore, much of it ran through territory that was and would remain Mexican until the Gadsden Purchase of 1853 fixed the international boundary where it is today. More and better ways of reaching California, now American territory, were needed.

The commander of the Topographical Engineers, Colonel John James Abert, put the problem in its grim political context: "Unless some easy, cheap and rapid means of communicating with these distant provinces be accomplished, there is danger, great danger, that they will not constitute parts of our union. We shall sink into two second rate governments if we are even able to maintain as good a position as second rate."

In 1851, Colonel Abert dispatched Captain Lorenzo Sitgreaves to look for another road well to the north of Cooke's track and entirely within American territory. The plan was to start at the Zuñi villages in present-day northwestern New Mexico, then descend the Zuni River to the Little Colorado and thence to the Colorado itself. In Santa Fe, Sitgreaves hired Antoine Leroux as the expedition's scout.

The small party—two topographical engineers, a physician-naturalist, a draftsman, 15 packers and muleteers and an escort of 30 soldiers—left the flourishing cornfields and orchards of the placid Zuñi Indian village in September 1851. They followed the Little Colorado to the arid plain now known as the Painted Desert in Eastern Arizona, where they stumbled on a phenomenon of nature that was later to be known as the Petrified Forest.

Pushing on, the party was deep in the valley of the Little Colorado by mid-October. Leroux warned Sitgreaves that unless they left the river and turned westward they would find themselves in the practically bottomless pit through which the Colorado River flowed, the Grand Canyon—which, like most of the geography of the region, had not yet received its official name (Sitgreaves referred to it as "the great cañon"). As yet, no white man was known to have set foot on the floor of that stupefying chasm. The first to do so was probably Joseph Christmas Ives of the Topographical Engineers, who snaked his way down with the aid of two Indian guides in 1858.

On the high Coconino Plateau, they passed the ruins of a long-abandoned pueblo—great stone houses three stories high, perched in the cliffs. In his report, Sitgreaves speculated that the ancient populace departed when their springs and watercourses dried up.

And now his own expedition began to feel the effects of long desert marches without water. "No indications of water in any direction . . . no appearance of water," Sitgreaves noted. Leroux found a small spring, but it soon gave out. Taking half the party with him, Leroux scouted ahead for water and came upon an encampment of primitive Indians, possibly Yampai. The women fled but the men held their ground, hostile and aloof. Unfortunately, Leroux allowed his men to pilfer articles and food from these impoverished people—watertight baskets, piñones and grass seed, and

bread made of mesquite beans. Sitgreaves regretted this breach of civilized behavior and Leroux made amends at a second Indian camp (whose timid occupants fled at the sight of the white men) by leaving small gifts of tobacco, handkerchiefs and knives.

The explorers badly needed a native guide to take them to water but the Indians were so shy that the expedition finally had to capture one. He was an old man, unable to bolt with his tribesmen, whom Sitgreaves described as "ten or twelve of the most wretched looking Indians I have ever seen, naked, and apparently almost starved." Pressed into unwilling service, the ancient native did show the party to several spring-fed water holes but slipped away at the first opportunity. The mules, in their eagerness to drink, trampled the springs to a mass of mud and Sitgreaves' exhausted men had to clear them out again. Then they led the animals, two or three at a time, to a trickle of water that provided "enough to keep them alive, but not enough to allay their thirst, as their refusal to eat and plaintive cries too clearly proved."

Leroux's scouting party at last discovered a rivulet that had abundant grass growing on its banks. Sit-greaves named it the Yampai River, and everyone enjoyed a bath—a luxury not fully appreciable by those who have not gone a week without water to wash even their faces and hands."

Next morning, the first ominous sign of Indian trouble occurred. A warrior slipped into the camp and attempted to make off with some of the mules. He was caught but soon escaped under a protective shower of arrows from his companions, who had been lurking in the nearby hills. The arrows killed three of the mules but the explorers were unharmed.

They were not so lucky several days later. The mules gave out on a steep, rough climb and Sitgreaves called a halt to rest them. Taking advantage of this pause, Leroux set out alone to climb an adjoining escarpment for a better look at the countryside. When he was part of the way up, a barrage of arrows rained on him from behind a rock buttress, and three of them struck home. The soldiers immediately rushed to the defense of their guide. "The Indians were driven from rock to rock," Sitgreaves wrote, "but always contrived to keep out of rifle range; and, after the pursuit was abandoned as fruitless, they returned as near as their

safety would permit, watching our movements and making gestures of rage."

Leroux had been struck behind an ear and in both a forearm and a wrist. Doctor S. W. Woodhouse, who was the physician for the party, had no trouble doctoring two out of three of the wounds, but a stone arrowhead had embedded itself in one of the bones in Leroux's wrist and Woodhouse had to cut away the flesh to expose it. One of Woodhouse's own arms had been put out of commission by a rattlesnake bite early in the expedition; he was forced to perform the difficult surgery with one hand. The physician blistered his thumb and bent his forceps before he finally managed to pull the arrowhead out. Leroux was unable to use his arm for the rest of the journey.

For a seasoned woodsman like Leroux, the humiliation of having rashly exposed himself to Indian arrows must have been more painful than the actual wounds. Two years later, crossing the same region with another exploring party, he met some of the Indians from the tribe that had attacked him. They were now disposed to be friendly and showed signs of recognizing him, but he pulled the brim of his hat low over the head wound

they had given him and firmly denied that he had ever seen them before.

After the Indian attack, the members of the company began to wonder if they would ever catch sight of the Colorado; behind every mountain loomed another. Finally Sitgreaves saw the river "winding far below through a broad valley. The smoke of numerous fires in the valley gave evidence of a large Indian population, and the sight brought a spontaneous cheer from the men, who believed that this was to be the end of their privations and the labors and anxieties of the journey." They cheered too soon. The Mojaves they found in the valley were friendly enough, joining the whites' cavalcade, laughing, talking, crowding into camp that evening to barter pumpkins, beans and corn. Both Sitgreaves and Leroux thought the presence of Indians in the camp was dangerous, and ejected them.

But it was another tribe on the Colorado, the Yumas, that proved truly dangerous. About a week later, as the expedition moved toward the river, Leroux gave a warning to stay clear of a thicket of willows, a perfect place of concealment for marauders. Most of the party was well past the thicket when 50 or 60 Yumas erupted from it, yelling and swinging war clubs shaped like potato mashers. A laggard soldier named Jones was caught and beaten to death. The Yumas seized his rifle but had no idea how to fire it. Sitgreaves and the small force managed to rally and fight off their attackers, leaving four Indians dead.

From then on they were free of Indian attacks. But the food they had obtained from the Indians gave out and the mules began to drop of starvation. To keep going, the men discarded everything that could be dispensed with—spare saddles, blankets, tents, ammunition, books—and finally began slaughtering the remaining mules for food. Dr. Woodhouse later reported that nearly everyone in the party became ill, at one time or another, from the diet of mule meat "without condiments of any kind." Other illnesses recorded by the physician were influenza, diarrhea and cholera.

Ill and exhausted, the men of Sitgreaves' expedition finally straggled into Camp Yuma at the confluence of the Colorado and Gila rivers in November 1851. At first it seemed they had accomplished little more than a feat of endurance. Leroux had led his charges across 657 miles of some of the most forbidding land in America, but it was not likely that a road soon would pass through that arid terrain of mesa and jagged mountains. Congress duly received and filed away the expedition's report and maps of the area. Thirty-four years later there was a payoff: when the Santa Fe Railroad was built, much of its route followed the trail that Leroux and Sitgreaves had blazed.

But that dividend was in the future. At the time of the Sitgreaves expedition, the routes of long-dreamed-of cross-country railroads were hotly debated issues. For years the United States Congress and every city along the Mississippi had simmered with contention over where the jumping-off point should be for the nation's first transcontinental railroad. The debate came to a preliminary boil on March 2, 1853, when Congress passed the Pacific Railroad Survey Bill, ordering the Secretary of War, within 10 months, to reconnoiter all feasible rail routes to the Pacific to decide which was the best, most practicable and cheapest to build.

Four primary lines of exploration were laid out: between the 47th and 49th parallels in the north; between the 38th and 39th parallels across the middle of American territory; along the 35th parallel through New Mexico to Southern California; and in the extreme south, where explorers would search for mountain passes connecting the 35th and 32nd parallels. The entire project was handed over to the Army's Corps of Topographical Engineers, to be dealt with by separate teams.

Before the year was out Antoine Leroux became chief scout for two of these expeditions. He was in Taos in August when two Army officers came 100 miles from Fort Massachusetts to see if he would help Captain John W. Gunnison explore the 38th parallel. Leroux agreed to guide the topographers part of the way, but said that he would have to leave by October in order to honor a contract to lead another expedition along the 35th parallel.

With no particular difficulty, Leroux brought Gunnison through Cochetopa Pass in southwestern Colorado, a crucial segment of any 38th parallel route. In the process, Dr. Jacob H. W. Schiel, a German geologist with the party, caused Leroux some professional concern by wandering off alone on side excursions. "He recommended very definitely that I stop all further explorations of that kind if I wanted to keep my scalp a few days longer," Schiel wrote. Soon thereafter, Schiel had reason to take the warning to heart.

"We were climbing down from a mesa and camping at Cebolla, or Onion, Creek when we found ourselves surrounded by a crowd of Tabawatshi Utahs, who seemed to grow literally out of the floor in that country. At first their talk was haughty, almost threatening, and they let us know openly that if we would not make presents they would take them."

It was the sort of situation Leroux had faced before and he knew how to handle it. He made a short speech, pointing out that Gunnison's men carried good rifles and had plenty of powder and lead; if the Utes, or Utahs, wanted to fight, he said, let them come ahead. If not, they should come and smoke the pipe of peace. The chiefs chose to do the latter.

But later the Utes staged an intimidating dance, complete with war whoops. They had recognized Leroux as the trapper who, many years earlier, had killed one of their chiefs when he tried to steal Leroux's horses. Leroux showed no fear but privately voiced regrets that a skirmish of long ago might put Gunni-

Dr. Samuel Woodhouse traded his city clothes for buckskins to serve as surgeon and naturalist with the Topographical Engineers. This daguerreotype and the one below were taken in 1850 during surveys of Creek and Cherokee Indian territories.

Woodhouse *(below, nearest the pony's head)* and fellow explorers relax at their camp on the Red Fork of the Arkansas River. A year later, the doctor joined the arduous Sitgreaves expedition in the Southwest, led by scout Antoine Leroux.

Dressed in buckskins and smoking a pipe, the Delaware Indian Black Beaver, shown above as he was portrayed by John Woodhouse

Black Beaver: a cosmopolitan Indian pathfinder

Some of the most valued scouts who helped explore the West in the mid-1800s were Delaware Indians, members of a fabled tribe that had gradually migrated from their Eastern homeland. They had, as one Army diarist wrote, "exact knowledge of all parts of the West, having traded, hunted and trapped among nearly every tribe." The most sought-after Delaware scout was Black Beaver *(left)*, who became a trusted friend and guide of famed pathfinder Captain Randolph Marcy.

Black Beaver helped Marcy lead a train of 500 emigrants to New Mexico in 1849, and on his way back blazed a new trail between the Brazos River in Texas and Fort Smith, Arkansas. Marcy said his Delaware scout was "a veritable cosmopolite," who "converses fluently with the Comanche and most other prairie tribes." The Army officer also was impressed by his scout's ability to read sign. When a member of the 1849 expedition was found dead in a ravine, Black Beaver quickly deduced, from only the lay of trampled grass and the hoofprints of horses and mules, that the man had been overpowered by a pair of Indians who had come upon him at full gallop, stolen his rifle and shot him without a fight.

The Delawares were comfortable with white men and even accepted white men's ideas that outraged some other Indians. A Cheyenne chief once said disparagingly that he regarded the "Delawares and whites as one people."

But even Black Beaver's trust of his white friends had a limit: after Marcy described the wonders of the telegraph to the Indian and asked him to translate the story for a Comanche, the scout replied: "I don't think I tell him that, Captain; for the truth is, I don't believe it myself."

Audubon, resembles the white men who were eager to employ his services as a scout.

Two members of Lieutenant Amiel Whipple's railroad survey team take a rest break on top of a petrified log in the Arizona desert.

Men with the Whipple expedition pull their instrument carriage across the Colorado River on an inflated pontoon. The clumsy craft

68

son's party in jeopardy. He knew, moreover, that he personally was in danger and when he left Captain Gunnison to return to Taos on September 25, he and his two Mexican employees traveled by night and kept hidden by day. Later Dr. Schiel was to write: "All the experience, courage and cold-bloodedness of a man who had spent almost 50 years in the mountains was necessary to deceive these deadly enemies."

After Leroux departed, Gunnison was killed when he and several members of his party were ambushed by Ute Indians near Sevier Lake in western Utah. Although Gunnison did not complete his journey to the Pacific, his unfinished journal demonstrated conclusively that a railroad along the 38th parallel could be constructed only by a gigantic and costly engineering feat—tunneling for miles through mountains, bridging many rivers and spanning countless gullies.

Leroux joined topographical engineer Amiel Weeks Whipple early in November at Albuquerque. The Whipple expedition was to explore the feasibility of a

railroad along the 35th parallel, a route extending from Fort Smith, Arkansas, to Los Angeles. Leroux had traveled much of this terrain earlier with Sitgreaves. Sitgreaves' report and maps were insufficiently detailed to indicate the feasibility of a railroad route, but they were invaluable to Whipple's survey. So was Leroux. The experienced and now-famous scout was well worth his considerable fee of $2,400.

Lieutenant Whipple's outfit was twice the size of Sitgreaves': 114 men, including surveyors, topographers, geologists and naturalists, 16 heavy wagons and a light carriage suspended on springs to protect the delicate surveying instruments it carried. Among the nonmilitary scientists was Balduin Möllhausen, the German artist and naturalist, who viewed Leroux's presence thankfully.

After leaving Fort Smith and moving about 800 miles westward through known country, the group was joined by an escort of two dozen soldiers from Fort Defiance, in what is now northeastern Arizona. They continued their journey, and soon came upon a famous gray giant of a monolith known as Inscription Rock. There they saw messages scratched into the sandstone by Spanish conquistadors who had passed that way as much as 200 years earlier. One legend read, in Spanish: "In the year 1716, on the 26th of August, came past this place Don Felix Martinez, Governor and Captain-General of this kingdom." The earliest inscription, barely legible, bore the date 1606.

When it reached the Zuñi village in northwestern New Mexico, the company found the Indians in the throes of a terrible smallpox epidemic. Out of 1,000 villagers, 100 were already dead. "The survivors," wrote one of Whipple's officers, "in all stages of convalescence, shedding their scabs and spotted like leopards, were lounging around or running into our camp everywhere." Nine of the exploration party contracted the disease but Whipple pushed on and the invalids all recovered in due time.

Since they were heading into desert country where Leroux had had harrowing difficulties finding water and forage for the Sitgreaves expedition, Whipple wanted to obtain the temporary services of Indian guides. After some hesitation, a Zuñi Indian named José Hacha agreed to show them the easiest way to the Little Colorado, where they would be able to find Moqui

capsized a number of times in the river's three-mile-an-hour current.

A welcoming oasis for the trail-weary

When brothers Charles and William Bent opened their mammoth fortified trading post on the Arkansas River in southeastern Colorado in 1833, they launched what would become a near-monopoly of trade and commercial hospitality in that region for the next 16 years. Bent's Fort was almost impregnable. Its adobe walls, which enclosed more than half an acre, were three feet thick and 14 feet high, and defenses were buttressed at two corners by towers equipped to accommodate musketry and small field pieces.

From the fort, rugged scouts like Kit Carson and Jim Beckwourth led the Bents' freight caravans laden with everything from farm tools to fish hooks, which were traded to the Plains Indians for buffalo hides. Local Cheyennes gathered at the fort to trade, mingling with mountain men, explorers and Army troops.

Besides storerooms, the fort included a main dining hall, carpenter's,

Charles Bent, proprietor of Bent's Fort.

tailor's and blacksmith's shops, and lodging for up to 200 men built around a courtyard. The Bents treated their guests in style. In 1844, John C. Frémont was welcomed with a cannon salute and cheers. Lieutenant James W. Abert of the Topo-

graphical Engineers, en route to survey Kiowa and Comanche country, was "invited by the gentlemen of the Fort" to witness Cheyennes performing their celebrated scalp dance.

The Bents' cook, Charlotte Green, was renowned for her sumptuous feasts: roast buffalo meat, beef and turkey, vegetables and freshly baked cakes and pies—a far cry from wilderness rations of hardtack and jerky. For a thirst, a man could order a "hailstorm," a brew contrived by the St. Louis-bred Bents of shaved ice, wild mint and local whiskey. (The ice was preserved in an ice house for summer use.)

Charles Bent died in 1847. The fort operated until 1849, when a cholera epidemic, borne westward by gold seekers, decimated the Cheyennes who supported most of the Bents' trade. Unwilling to let the fort be overrun by drifters, William Bent removed its contents and blew up the desert landmark that bore his name.

A huge American flag became a sought-for signal of comfort to travelers approaching the fort, near present-day Pueblo, Colorado.

guides to accompany them on the next leg of the journey, to the San Francisco mountains.

Several days later, they passed through the Petrified Forest, which made Möllhausen gasp with wonder even though he almost certainly had heard Leroux's description of it. "Trees of all sizes lay irregularly scattered about; some of them were more than 60 feet long and of corresponding girth, and looking as if they had been cut into regular blocks," the naturalist noted. "On closer examination we found they were fossil trees that had been gradually washed bare by the torrents and had broken off by their own weight."

The party celebrated Christmas Eve while camped near the site of the present-day city of Flagstaff, Arizona. All the rum and wine in the train were brought forth, in addition to a case of eggs, and a gigantic eggnog was concocted. In the absence of fireworks, the Mexican packers were given some superfluous gunpowder. "The Mexicans sang their *Soli,* with choruses emphasized by continual firing of pistols," wrote Möllhausen. "Favorite Negro melodies were volunteered by the American part of the company, and every fresh beaker was greeted with a fresh song." To make a bonfire, they set an entire thicket of cedar trees aflame. "The pointed leaves or needles, rich in resin, caught fire immediately, the flames blazed over the tops of the trees and sent millions of sparks up to the sky. It was a most beautiful spectacle!"

The only man who seemed to keep his head through all this was Antoine Leroux. He observed calmly, as he took a puff of his pipe: "What a splendid opportunity it would be for the Indians to surprise us tonight!" But hostile Indians, knowing of the smallpox outbreak, were giving the explorers a wide berth. "Two years ago these hills were covered with Indians," Leroux remarked to Whipple. "Now there is none."

They were getting close to the Colorado River in the middle of February but as they entered the rough gorge of Bill Williams Fork, Whipple came more and more to agree with Leroux that this was not promising railroad country, or even wagon country for that matter. He sent Leroux backtracking to see if he could discover more negotiable terrain. There was little of that sort to be found and within a few days Whipple abandoned all the wagons except the light spring carriage that was used to carry the surveying instruments.

After being close-herded in scanty forage, the mules were fast playing out and the men were down to half rations. Still, the party was of good heart. As early as February 9 they had caught a distant glimpse of their immediate goal. "From the top of a high hill, a great valley filled with smoke, supposed to be that of Rio Colorado, seemed to proceed from the northwest and unite with Bill Williams Fork," Whipple wrote. But getting there was another matter. "Having travelled four miles, we entered a narrow chasm, the precipitous walls of which grew higher as we proceeded. We therefore despaired of being able to make an exit from its head; and turning, ascended the mountain ridges." That maneuver brought them back at sunset to their campsite of two days before.

Ten days later they pushed into what at first seemed another futile cul-de-sac. But, although nobody would have believed it at the moment, that canyon was the last one. The cliffs began to fall away and the valley to widen. A tangled thicket of willow and vines blocked the explorer's path, but when they hacked a road through this last obstacle, they found themselves on an open field of grass. Four miles more and they were on the banks of the Colorado.

Before them the valley lay broad and fertile and here they met a welcome surprise. This was the land of the Chemehuevis Paiutes and the stately Mojaves, and both were friendly and hospitable. The Mojaves were superior farmers, and soon the expedition was dining well again. A brisk trade in white porcelain beads and calico fetched an abundance of beans, pumpkins, melons, corn and flour.

Leroux guided Whipple and his group some 60 miles up the Colorado River from Bill Williams Fork. There Whipple decided to cross the Colorado and head into California. But getting his outfit across the river proved tricky and was attended by minor calamity. The river was rapid, from six to 12 feet deep and about 500 yards wide. Several times a leaky India-rubber pontoon turned turtle in midstream, once while carrying the unwheeled body of the instrument carriage. By the time Whipple's chief survey officer, Lieutenant J. C. Ives, had righted the craft with the help of a fleet of enthusiastic Mojave swimmers, some of his precious instruments and some of the expedition's scientific records were hopelessly waterlogged or lost.

Not knowing whether the Indians on the far side of the river would be as friendly as those they left behind, Leroux repeated earlier warnings about staying alert and keeping closed up. The disappearance of a Mexican teamster gave point to the admonition. The man was never found, but in a Paiute camp a search party discovered his mule being roasted and other evidence of what had befallen him. "The clothes of the murdered Mexican were also found, literally riddled by arrows and stiff with hardened blood," Whipple wrote. Leroux did not waste sympathy with the man. "He was too lazy to carry his gun, but left it on his mule," the scout remarked. "So he was murdered."

As the expedition moved westward into California it found easier going. Just east of Cajon Pass, the explorers met a party of Mormons who gave them their first news of the outbreak of the Crimean War. It was March 14, 1854; they had been out of touch with civilization since November 10, 1853.

Whipple felt that their time had not been wasted. Now that they had mapped the terrain, future engineers could avoid their mistakes and backtrackings. "We have discovered passes that render the route practicable," he reported, "if not easy." More exploration was needed to shorten the route and diminish the grades involved, he admitted. But, he concluded, "there is no serious obstacle to the construction of a railway."

At San Pedro, Antoine Leroux bade farewell to the Topographical Engineers for the last time. Whipple wrote that Leroux "shook hands with us all, with hearty good wishes, but like a man accustomed to find acquaintances on every steppe, to remain with them for awhile, sharing all hardships and privations like brothers, and then say good-bye forever."

Leroux returned to his Taos ranch and, except for brief excursions, did no further scouting. His many narrow escapes and his advancing age perhaps persuaded him to end his years of adventure. He died in 1861, at 60, of "asthma complicated by spear wounds" according to the official Taos records. The arrows that struck him on the Sitgreaves journey may have been more deadly than he or Dr. Woodhouse had supposed.

In addition to searching for the ideal transcontinental railroad route, the Topographical Engineers and the scouts who worked with the Corps put a great deal of effort into the improvement and shortening of the existing wagon routes in the 1850s. The officer who achieved the most brilliant success in this endeavor was Captain James Hervey Simpson. A conservative man, who was precise in everything he undertook, Simpson was convinced that before constructing a railroad to the Pacific, the United States should build up its wagon roads, improve its postal routes, populate the West and develop its natural resources. In the summer of 1858 he set an example by establishing a new road from Camp Floyd, south of Salt Lake City, to Fort Bridger, some 155 miles to the northeast.

In the winter of 1858-1859 Simpson submitted to the Secretary of War a proposal that he take a reconnaissance group from Camp Floyd across the forbidding deserts and mountains of the Great Basin to Genoa, at the foot of the Sierra Nevada. From Genoa, in Utah Territory near the California border, there was already an established, easygoing road to San Francisco. This new wagon route, he claimed, would be less than 800 miles long, 260 miles shorter than the usual emigrant road by way of the Humboldt River and 390 miles shorter than circling to the south by way of the Los Angeles route.

This would be progress indeed. The War Department quickly approved the expedition and the Simpson party started from Camp Floyd on May 2, 1859; it consisted of 44 officers and men, including scientists and an artist. Simpson did not have a Carson, Fitzpatrick or Leroux, but he did obtain the services of a scout named John Reese, who had been over some of the route they would travel, though he was far from intimately acquainted with it.

They struck directly through the Great Salt Lake Desert, which Simpson described in his report as "a somber, dreary waste, where neither man nor beast can live." He soon discovered that human life did subsist here, however, for the party met numbers of Goshoot and Digger Indians on their journey. The diet of these half-starved people consisted largely of grass seed, roots and whatever small desert creatures they were able to catch—principally rats.

Reese, the guide, followed the classic pattern of a scout: he ranged a few days in advance and sent back one assistant each day to advise the party of watering places, easy passes through the various isolated moun-

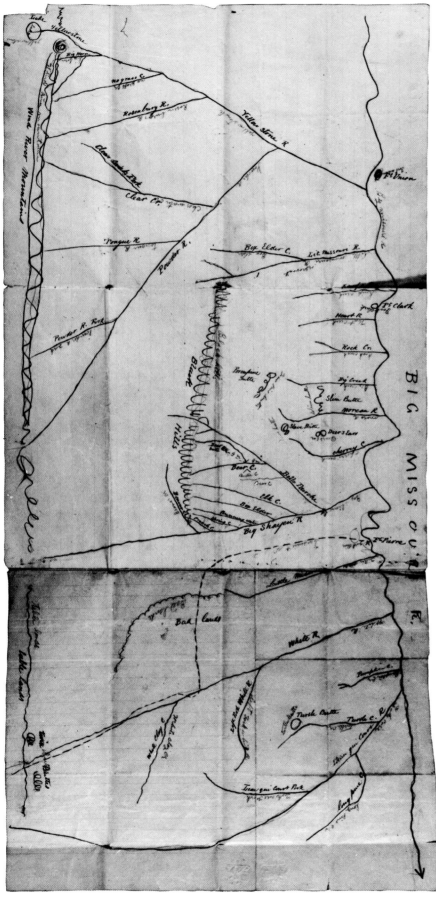

Crudely sketched on scrap paper, this map of Sioux country was made in 1857 for the Army by mountain man Joseph Jewitt. Such firsthand information was indispensable to Army exploratory expeditions.

Captain James H. Simpson's exploring party threads its way through the Timpanogos Canyon in Utah. This 1858 expedition considerably shortened the supply route from Camp Floyd to Fort Bridger.

Scout John Reese *(left)* and Captain
James H. Simpson teamed up to explore
western Utah Territory in 1859. The
roads they blazed cut nearly 300 miles off
the trip from Salt Lake City to California.

tain ranges, and possible camping sites. Simpson
thought highly enough of Reese to name a river and a
valley after him, but occasionally the scout irritated
the captain by a tendency to ignore instructions. On
the 30th of May, Reese failed to rendezvous with the
expedition at an agreed-upon campsite. "As he is
alone, contrary to my orders, which require him always
to come in with the last man of his party, I am not
gratified, though doubtless his zeal had led him to this
unauthorized venture." Simpson noted in his journal.
"I feel anxious about him."

Simpson delayed departure for two days, but still
Reese did not appear. The explorer sent out several
parties to search for the missing scout and finally decided the expedition could wait no longer. Simpson had
just ordered his soldiers to resume their march when a
man hobbled into camp, supporting himself with two
makeshift crutches. "At first I took him for a Digger
Indian," wrote Simpson. "On more close scrutiny,
however, I found it to be Mr. Reese, our guide, who,
as soon as we reached him, sank down exhausted into
a sage-bush. His clothes were nearly torn off him,

and altogether he presented a most pitiable aspect."

Reese's mule had given out, but he had made it back
to camp on foot, without provisions or even matches to
make a fire to warm himself during the cold nights.
Fortunately, the Indians he had met were friendly, but
in their bitter poverty could be of little help to him.
Some Diggers had offered Reese three fat rats, Simpson noted, "but as they had been roasted with entrails
and offal unremoved, he said he did not feel hungry
enough to accept their generous hospitality." After a
good meal and a long sleep in one of the wagons, Reese
was ready to go out scouting again.

Through the parched and rugged country, the party
made its slow way, carefully cataloguing everything of
scientific interest in its path, and especially making note
of whatever would aid the emigrant wagons that might
soon be traveling along this route. Distances between
watering places were critical factors, and Reese not
only explored the direct route for creeks and springs,
but also surveyed a parallel course to the south. "If
water is found there," Simpson said, "I shall change the
road accordingly on my return from Carson Valley."

Three days after completing his round-trip exploration of the new shortcuts to California, Simpson announced his findings and, in the Mormon weekly, *The Deseret News,* recommended Reese as a guide.

On June 12, 1859, the soldiers reached the end of their newly blazed trail at Genoa in the foothills of the Sierra. Here they were greeted by a 13-gun salute and the raising of the American flag. The townspeople, who numbered fewer than 200 souls, were overjoyed that Simpson had opened up a direct mail and emigrant route to their front door; it promised to turn Genoa into a boom town. As soon as the expedition arrived, the news of its success was flashed to San Francisco newspapers: the telegraph had already come to Genoa, its wires strung over the mountains through the branches of living trees.

Simpson returned to Camp Floyd, Utah, along the parallel route 40 miles to the south that Reese had explored. Reese again served as scout. As before, his work did not always please the expedition's commander. Simpson wanted to stay in close touch with his guide while Reese preferred the old school of scouting, staying far out in front and communicating by proxy. Simpson grew angry when he discovered a note from Reese "stuck in a cleft-stick near a rush pond, informing me that the Indian with him says there are water and grass ten miles beyond this locality. This mode of guiding me by notes stuck up, depending upon the contingency of my reaching or getting them, is a new feature introduced by the guide since I have approached the desert, and is entirely unauthorized." Apparently Simpson was unaware that this was a traditional method of communication, used by such famous scouts as Fitzpatrick and Leroux.

Water was even more scarce on the homebound trek than it had been on the outgoing one. "O, the value of water, and how little it is prized when it is to be had in abundance!" exclaimed the captain, "These trips across our desert plains make it very plain why such value, in the days of Abraham, Isaac, and Jacob, was placed on wells." Just at the point when all the mules were in danger of perishing from thirst, Reese encountered a crippled Indian who temporarily took over the duties of scout and guided them to a plenteous spring. One of the mules drank 14 bucketfuls of water before it was satisfied.

Simpson dubbed the watering place Good Indian Spring and the grateful soldiers showered the surprised Indian guide with presents as a sign of their gratitude. "He is treated so much like a king," Simpson re-

[For the Deseret News.

To California Emigrants and the Citizens of Utah Territory.

The undersigned is informed that there are many persons at Salt Lake City destined for California, who are in doubt as to the route they should take. He would inform all such, that by direction of General Johnston, he has within the past three months, explored and surveyed two new routes to California, either of which is about 300 miles shorter than the old Humboldt or St. Mary's river route; and, from all he can hear and has read, incomparably better in respect to wood, water and grass.— Indeed, by this route, the Great Salt Lake desert is entirely avoided, except at few points.

The best route is that from Camp Floyd, through General Johnston's pass, and thence along the rim between the Great Salt Lake desert and the Sevier Lake desert, keeping generally from 25 to 40 miles south of the General Johnston and Hasting's Pass road.

Mr. John Reese, of Genoa, and his son have just come over the route with me and will be enabled and are ready to conduct any parties of emigrants or herds of animals which may be tending towards California. The young man will doubtless be in the city at the time this notice appears, and Mr. John Reese in the course of about twelve days; as soon as he returns from an expedition under the direction of Lieut. J. L. K. Smith, Top'l Engineers, who has been charged by Gen'l Johnston with the duty of improving the direction of the road within the last one hundred miles and establishing troughs at a particular spring.

The undersigned is confident that this route will be found from 25 to 50 per cent. better than the old Humboldt River route and particularly fine for stock driving. It has also the advantage of being a later fall and earlier spring route.

He will, as soon as Lieut. Smith returns, have an itinerary of the route prepared, setting forth the distances between the camping places, and where wood, grass and water can be found and will send it to the papers of the Territory for publication. This itinerary, it would be well for emigrants and others interested in the route, to procure and keep.

J. H. SIMPSON,
Capt. Corps Top'l Eng'rs.
Camp Floyd, U. T., Aug. 7, 1859.

marked, "that he looks upon us occasionally with a look of wonder and then breaks out into a laugh, in which is intermingled as much of astonishment as joy. At his request, I have permitted him to sleep in camp, the only strange Indian to whom this privilege has been granted on the trip."

Along the trail, Simpson had signs erected bearing such legends as, "To good camp and road, 8 miles (a short cut)." No sooner was he back at Camp Floyd than he was directing eager emigrants along the southerly route, and John Reese was offering his services as guide. The Chorpenning Mail Company soon set up posts along this new road for its pack-mule mail service;

the firm of Russell, Majors & Waddell was driving its stagecoaches over the same path, and the telegraph followed close behind.

By the end of the 1850s, personal scouts like Tom Fitzpatrick and John Reese were being replaced by guidebooks carried by westward-streaming emigrants. "We crossed the Rocky Mountains at South Pass, according to the instructions given in *Horn's Guide for Emigrants,* which we had carefully observed during our trip," one oldtimer later wrote in his memoirs. Because his family "had grown somewhat careless about consulting our handbook," they made their camp

by a stream whose poisoned waters almost did away with their livestock. "Had we consulted our guidebook before camping at that pretty spot, we would have been spared all this trouble, as it warned travelers of the poison existing there."

The West seemingly was tamed, charted and published in book form. In reality, there still was great need for scouts, as the ensuing years of Indian warfare were to prove. But for John Bidwell, who had gone west with the first emigrant wagon train in 1841 and who had found wealth and power in California as an agriculturalist and politician, it was an astonishing experience to return eastward by rail several decades later.

Instead of riding a slow-moving oxcart he was "swiftly borne along on an observation car amid cliffs and over rushing streams." He recalled that in that first emigrant wagon train was an old codger named Bill Overton who, over the evening campfire, used to proclaim that nothing could surprise him. "I should not be surprised," Overton had said, "if I were to see a steamboat come plowing over these mountains this minute."

"In rattling down the canyon of Weber River," Bidwell went on to say, "it occurred to me that the reality was almost equal to Bill Overton's extravaganza, and I could but wonder what he would have said had he suddenly come upon this modern scene."

As the number of emigrant parties outstripped the supply of scouts, guidebooks like these led travelers to "those wild regions upon the great Pacific which had become the topic of conversation in every circle," as Lansford Hastings put it in his 1848 edition (left). More than 100 such manuals were published in the years that preceded the Civil War.

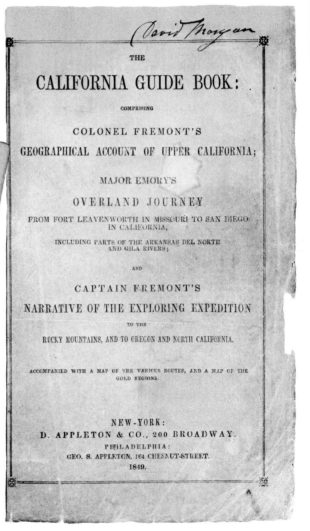

3 | The eyes and ears of the Army

A beleaguered detachment attempts to hold off a band of swift-riding Sioux while its commander consults with his buckskin-clad scout.

After the Civil War, white settlement in the West provoked a great eruption of hostility from Indians who knew their lands and way of life were in peril. Soldiers sent to fight the Indians must have felt at times that they were battling with ghosts. The elusive warriors, able to travel light, seemed to appear and disappear at will. When they outnumbered an enemy, they swooped down with impunity, stealing livestock and taking scalps. But when a numerically superior force took the field, the Indians maddeningly vanished.

For help, the Army turned to civilian scouts who understood both the land and the inhabitants. Scouts instinctively knew, as Jim Bridger once put it, that "where you don't see no Injuns, there they're certain to be thickest." For decades scouts had labored to steer explorers, missionaries and settlers clear of the Indians. Now their mission was to lead an Army burdened with hulking gun carriages and clumsy supply wagons to the Indians. An Army scout's job was never easy. And—as scouts involved in battles like that portrayed below understood only too well—it was often dangerous.

81

Frederic Remington

"Congenial employment, leading to a terrible death"

Riding at the head of an Army wagon train bound for Fort Wallace, Kansas, in June of 1867, scout Will Comstock peered across miles of unrelenting prairie. "If the Indians strike us at all," he said, "it will be just about the time we are coming back over this very spot."

Two Army officers riding alongside him were puzzled by his words. Schooled in combat during the Civil War, they saw nothing in the featureless terrain to enhance the chance of a successful ambush by a skulking enemy. But Will Comstock's schooling had been far different from theirs, and he knew better. "Now mind what I tell you," he said.

At Fort Wallace the wagons were freighted with supplies for George Armstrong Custer's 7th Cavalry, out hunting for hostile Indians that season on the Kansas and Nebraska plains between the Smoky Hill and Platte rivers. With an escort of 48 cavalrymen, the caravan then moved back over the same course, lumbering northward to rejoin Custer.

Comstock, as always, spearheaded the column, his practiced eyes ceaselessly scanning the ground and horizon. As he came closer to the place that he had earlier marked for danger, he saw what he was expecting: far off in the distance to the right, a line of small silhouettes appeared on the crest of a gently rising hill. Comstock raised his field glasses to scrutinize the hill. Indians, their heads barely visible above the rise, were watching as the heavily laden wagons rolled across the prairie.

John Y. Nelson, photographed at the age of 64 in 1890, was typical of the scouts who occupied the twilight world between white and Indian civilizations. He had taken at least nine Indian wives, but often scouted for the Army against their people.

Realizing that they had been seen, the mounted Cheyennes and Sioux rode brazenly into full view. At first they seemed to be only 20 to 30 warriors strong, but before long hundreds of warriors materialized from the prairie—which was not, as Comstock well knew, quite so flat as it appeared to be to the untutored observer. Instead, it was slashed by gullies that were deep enough to conceal horsemen, ideal staging areas for surprise attack.

Thanks to Comstock, this attack would be no surprise. As the full band of some 600 to 700 well-armed warriors began bearing down on the train, the teamsters maneuvered their vehicles into two parallel columns. The cavalry commander ordered his men to dismount and move out to form a marching shield on either side to protect the horses, the wagons and their own lives. The column then resumed its steady advance, while Comstock—"a host in himself," he would later be called by George Armstrong Custer—"galloped from point to point wherever his presence was most valuable." A hail of well-placed carbine fire broke the Indians' first assault, and as they withdrew Comstock taunted them loudly in their own tongue.

The warriors then regrouped and attacked again. For the next three hours, they circled the thin line of skirmishers, whose expert marksmanship continued to beat them back. With their supply of ammunition running lower with each volley, however, the soldiers' only hope was that reinforcements would arrive in enough time to drive the Indians from the field.

Suddenly, as the beleaguered troopers looked on in disbelief, the attackers disappeared from sight, carrying their casualties with them. The soldiers, whose losses amounted to only two wounded, learned why the Indians had fled so precipitously when an advancing column of blue-coated horsemen appeared on the horizon. Custer, fearing for the safety of his supply train, had dis-

patched two squadrons of cavalry to meet the wagons.

Although Will Comstock had guided the Army wagon train and fought side-by-side with its defenders, he was not a soldier. He was a civilian contract scout, one of the many hired by Army quartermasters to perform duties that could range from guide, hunter and courier to interpreter, intelligence officer and diplomat. It was difficult and hazardous work that Custer once described as "congenial employment, most often leading to a terrible death."

Custer had an abiding respect for the counsel of his scouts. He also respected the privacy that they so frequently demanded, and wrote: "Who they are,

whence they come or whither they go, their names even, except such as they choose to adopt or which may be given them, are all questions which none but themselves can answer."

Some, possibly for good reason, preferred not to answer, or to be asked, many questions. But as their stories unfold, the Army scouts emerge as one of the most fascinating groups of men in the history of the American West. Half a dozen in particular became famous on the frontier. Comstock was one of these. Frank Grouard was another; he was known to have lived for a number of years in the camps of Sitting Bull, and there were those on the Plains who said that

Grouard had gone willingly on the warpath with the Sioux chief's braves. Johnnie "Big Leggins" Bruguier, son of a white trader and his Santee Sioux wife, was another scout whose special relationship with Sitting Bull sometimes raised white suspicions, though both Bruguier and Grouard would more than once prove their fidelity to the Army and its cause.

Other scouts, like Charles A. "Lonesome Charley" Reynolds and Luther "Yellowstone" Kelly, came from more conventional backgrounds and were men of mystery out of choice or modesty. (Such a man was Will Comstock, whose carefully guarded secret was that he was a grandnephew of James Fenimore Cooper,

whose romantic portrayals of the "noble savage" were frequently hooted at on the Plains.)

Civilian scouts were needed because the United States Army, firmly wedded to the textbook tactics of conventional battle, was unprepared to deal with as unconventional a foe as the American Indian. There was little in an old-school soldier's training—whether in the classrooms of West Point or on the fields of Manassas, Antietam or Gettysburg—that would serve him well on the Plains against such an enemy. The Indian declined to fight at all unless the odds were clearly in his favor, and whether in combat or in flight, he was swift, elusive and wary as a wolf. An Army unit on its own, burdened with heavy equipment and slowed to the pace of mule-drawn wagons or slogging infantry, was no match for him.

Military commanders on the Plains conceded at least some of their deficiencies and turned to civilian scouts for help. Chosen for their knowledge of the country and of Indian ways, these bold frontiersmen quickly became all but indispensable to the Indian-fighting Army, and it has been said that one good scout was worth a regiment of soldiers.

Scouts could do little to move the Army much faster than was its cumbersome habit, but they smoothed its progress and bolstered its effectiveness in many ways. On the march, they chose the route, an exacting business when thousands of men and horses and hundreds of clumsy vehicles had to move through a roadless wilderness. Scouts selected river-crossing points; when unaided by scouts, the Army's heavy wagons, wheeled artillery and burdened cavalrymen often foundered in streams that even Indian women and children could traverse with ease. The scouts picked campsites, always with a canny eye for animal forage, drinking water and fuel for cookfires. And when rations began to run low, they frequently bagged fresh game to feed their famished charges.

Essential as such workaday duties were, the responsibilities of a scout went far beyond logistics and basic housekeeping chores. The Army's mission, after all, was to pacify belligerent Indian tribes—by show of force if possible, in battle if all else failed. Skilled in plainscraft, able to converse with the Indians in their tribal tongues or in sign language, the scouts tracked the enemy on his native ground and made knowledgeable estimates of his strength and aims. In a conflict with no clearly drawn front lines, scouts often ventured into hostile villages to parley with chiefs and to attempt to divine their intentions. And on occasion they even managed to shepherd bugle-blowing, saber-rattling military units into position to spring a surprise attack on an unsuspecting cluster of tipis.

But it was as couriers that the scouts showed in fullest measure their skills, their bravery and their devotion to duty—and even, sometimes, their foolhardy love of adventure. Operating in a vast region served only sparsely by telegraph, the scouts were frequently called upon to bear military dispatches across hundreds of miles of dangerous territory. Traveling alone at night, hiding by day as best they could, they were the vital communications link between far-flung Army commands. Scouts were often praised for such deeds, but perhaps the most heartfelt tribute of all came from Elizabeth Custer some years after her husband fell at the Little Bighorn. "I would far rather go into battle with the inspiration of the trumpet call and the clash of arms," she wrote, "than go off alone and take my life in my hands as did the scouts."

In spite of their loyalty, the scouts did not align themselves with the U.S. Army out of any love for military ways and discipline. Fiercely independent, they were sometimes careless—if not downright slovenly—in their dress and manner. Many of them, moreover, were not altogether comfortable living in white civilization. John Young Nelson, as an example, had more in common with the nomadic tribesman of the Plains than with the Army that he often served as a scout, and he became as adept as any Indian at the fine art of scalping. He could speak derisively of cunning "redskins," yet he spent much of his life living among them, marrying at least nine Indian women. And in the end, Nelson lamented the passing of the Sioux nation, noting almost with regret the part he had played in humbling a race that had been "masters of the continent before a white man ever set foot on it."

It is doubtful that scouts faced the dangers of their profession simply for money; certainly they did not do it for job security. Though paid more than a common soldier, and sometimes more than a junior officer, a scout was expected to assume far greater risks and responsibilities, and his employment was likely to cease without ceremony at the end of a mission. Performing one of his first major duties as a scout in January of 1866, Will Comstock guided several starving Army garrisons on a two-week march through blinding prairie blizzards. He was removed from the payroll on the same day he found a safe haven for them.

Because his roughhewn frontier colleagues generally distrusted anyone who came from genteel surroundings, William Averill Comstock tried to maintain the amiable fiction that he was a true son of the wilderness who had never traveled east of the Missouri River and never seen a railroad train. As a matter of fact, Com-

'HO! FOR THE PLAINS!'

RECRUITS WANTED!

50 MEN ARE WANTED

To complete the organization of the body of "Scouts" that are now operating upon the Kansas Frontier.

EVERY MAN TO FURNISH HIS OWN HORSE!

For further particulars enquire for five days at the

ADJUTANT GENERAL'S OFFICE, Topeka, Kan.

Topeka, Kan., June 23d, 1869.

COMMONWEALTH TOWER PRESS PRINT, TOPEKA, KANSAS

stock was born in Michigan in 1842, the son of a lawyer and state legislator who was also a prosperous Indian trader and dealer in military supplies. His mother died in 1846; three years later, when he was 7 years old, Will was farmed out to uncles in New York state. Sometime in his teens, he joined a sister in Wisconsin, and later moved with her to Nebraska. There he became, like his father, an Indian trader.

Like many people in his line of work, Comstock lived among his customers, sleeping in their smoky lodges and learning their ways. His teachers were the Cheyennes, Arapahos and Southern Sioux, and while he never said so, it is likely that he was tutored in the native languages by compliant Indian women. Comstock also earned a nickname, Medicine Bill, from his Indian hosts. Later he would explain that he received this sobriquet after he saved a man's life by cutting off a

finger that had been bitten by a rattlesnake. Another version of the story had it that the victim was a young Sioux woman and that Comstock performed the amputation with his teeth.

Although he relished his carefree life among the Indians, Comstock drifted into civilian service with the U.S. Army, which highly prized his peculiar talents. Captain Richard Musgrove wrote glowingly of the scout's knowledge of the ways of Indians: "He could easily read all the 'signs' they left for the information of other Indians, could interpret their smoke columns used in telegraphing, and after a party had passed, could tell with remarkable accuracy from its trail how many were in the party." Comstock's reputation was spreading, and when Custer, recently posted to Fort Riley, first sent for him in January of 1867, Comstock came armed with a letter of recommendation from Captain

George Custer inspects the mutilated corpses of Lieutenant Lyman Kidder and his men. Custer's scout, William Comstock, believed Kidder might have escaped had he heeded the advice of his own scout.

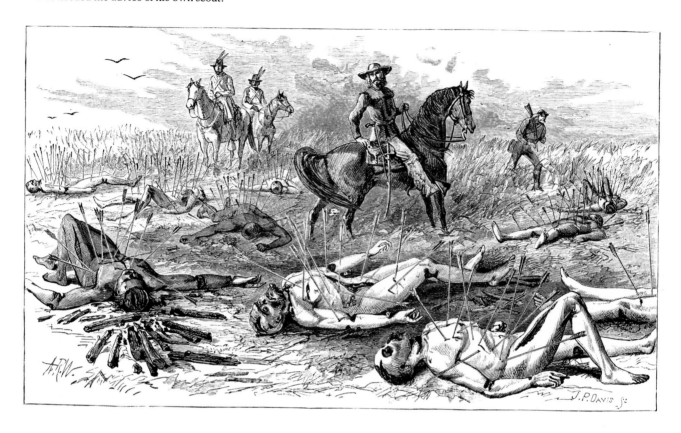

Myles W. Keogh describing the scout as being "an eccentric genius and an ardent admirer of everything reckless and daring."

Comstock's initial stint with Custer was brief and apparently unremarkable, but in April he was summoned again. "He is a worthy man," Custer wrote to his wife, "and I am constantly learning valuable information from him regarding the Indians, their habits, etc." And soon enough, Comstock would lead Custer to grisly evidence of what could happen if an Army officer declined to heed the advice of a civilian guide.

Not long after Comstock's timely warning of attack had helped save Custer's supply train from almost certain annihilation, Custer learned at a nearby telegraph station that still another military unit was in peril. Lieutenant Lyman Kidder, with 10 troopers and a Sioux guide named Red Bead, had left Fort Sedgwick to find Custer and deliver important dispatches from General William T. Sherman, commander of the Army's Division of the Missouri. Traveling through hostile territory, Kidder and his men were alarmingly overdue. Custer consulted Comstock, who said that

Kidder's safety would depend on how willing he was to do what Red Bead told him. But Comstock added: "My experience with you army folks has always been that the youngsters among you think they know the most, and this is particularly true if they have just come from West Point." The 25-year-old Kidder was no West Pointer, but he had won his Regular Army commission just six months before.

With Comstock scouting in the lead, Custer's column set out in search of Kidder. His trail was found to lead toward Fort Wallace, Kansas, over the same ground where the wagon train had been attacked just days before. If Kidder's detachment had reached the fort without a skirmish, said Comstock, "I'll lose my confidence in Indians."

The first sign of trouble was a dead cavalry horse sprawled at the side of the trail. Two miles farther along Comstock spotted another dead horse, and now he saw that the hoofprints of Kidder's heavily shod mounts were trampled over by the tracks of pursuing Indian ponies. Then a wheeling flight of buzzards led Comstock to the missing detachment.

Kidder and his men were lying in a tight circle, their bodies bristled with arrows and had been mutilated beyond recognition. Only Red Bead, the Sioux guide, could be distinguished, by the color of his skin. All of the men had been scalped, but Red Bead's bloodied tonsure still lay in the dust at his side. Comstock explained that Indians were barred by custom from carrying off scalps belonging to their own tribesmen; the massacre was Sioux handiwork.

Soon after this, hostilities waned and the government pursued a policy of negotiating with the Indians rather than fighting them. In October of 1867, chiefs of the Kiowas, Kiowa-Apaches, Comanches, Cheyennes and Arapahos signed a treaty at the site of what is today Medicine Lodge, Kansas. Under terms of this pact, the tribes agreed to stop killing whites and withdraw to reservations.

While Comstock's activities during this period are unclear, it is known that he agreed to provide an Army firewood contractor, H. P. Wyatt, with information about stands of timber in the area. It is also certain that on the 14th of January, 1868, Comstock displayed an uncharacteristic streak of brutality. When Wyatt refused to pay him as promised, Comstock whipped out his pistol and shot the contractor on the spot. "It is a most strange thing," the fort's quartermaster wrote to a friend in Denver.

Comstock's preliminary hearing before a justice of the peace was most strange, too. According to one account, the post sutler, Val Todd, described how Comstock had gunned Wyatt down and was then asked, "Did he shoot with felonious intent?"

"I do not know what his intentions were," Todd replied, "but I did see him shoot and Wyatt ran out of the store and fell dead."

Then the justice, perhaps mindful of Comstock's importance as a scout and unwilling to see him jailed, announced his ruling: "If the shooting was not done with felonious intent, and there is no evidence that it was, the prisoner is discharged for want of said proof."

Comstock, possibly fearing that a harsher judgment might still be in store, made himself scarce at Fort Wallace. But he was soon back in service. When General Philip H. Sheridan took over as commander of the Plains army in the spring of 1868, he ordered Lieutenant Frederick Beecher at Fort Wallace to hire a few able scouts to keep tabs on the Plains tribes and act as mediators between the whites and the Indians. On May 12, Beecher put Cephas W. "Dick" Parr and Frank Espey on his payroll at $100 a month. Four days later, he signed up the errant Will Comstock at $125, and tradition has it that Comstock returned to duty only after getting Sheridan's personal guarantee that he would face no further prosecution for the murder of H. P. Wyatt.

Spring and summer were relatively quiet on the Kansas and Nebraska plains. Then on August 10 a band of more than 200 Cheyennes, Arapahos and Sioux struck at unsuspecting white settlements in the Saline River valley; more attacks followed along the nearby Solomon and Republican rivers. The uneasy peace of Medicine Lodge—which many Indians had opposed from the start—was shattered.

Word of the outbreaks reached Lieutenant Beecher while he was out on a surveillance mission with Comstock and Abner "Sharp" Grover, another scout who had signed on for duty in June. Beecher immediately asked Comstock and Grover to find their way to the village of the Cheyenne chief Turkey Leg, who was well known to both men. There, perhaps, they could learn more about the raids and persuade Turkey Leg to help bring the rampaging braves under control. It was clearly a hazardous proposition; both scouts nevertheless agreed to go.

On August 14 they reached Fort Hays where they probably learned that Captain Frederick W. Benteen had caught up with a party of raiders at the Saline River and killed several of the Indians. Now that the Army had retaliated, their job might be more difficult, but Comstock and Grover rode on. Traveling with all the stealth they had spent years learning, guided by a tutored sense of where Turkey Leg might be camping that season, they raised the chief's lodges at the head of the Solomon River on August 16. Custom decreed that even an enemy could claim sanctuary in the lodge of an Indian who had been his friend, and the scouts crept warily into the Cheyenne village.

Although he was surprised to see the two white men who had once lived among his people, Turkey Leg made them welcome. But not for long. That evening, runners arrived bearing news of Benteen's punitive strike at the Saline, and the chief ordered Comstock and Grover to leave immediately. So far, the scouts had been lucky—if their mission had failed, at least they were still alive and had a sporting chance of making their way to safety.

About two miles from Turkey Leg's village, their luck ran out when a small party of Indians overtook them. They seemed friendly at first; then, without warning, they opened fire. Comstock, shot through the back, was killed almost instantly, while the gravely wounded Grover played dead until the Indians moved on. Luckily for him, the warriors did not scalp their victims, possibly out of respect for the scouts' courage. The next day Grover staggered 25 miles south to the nearest railroad, where he flagged down a train and made his way to Fort Wallace.

Will Comstock's body was left where he had fallen on the prairie. He was not the first civilian scout to die in service to the Army, nor would he be the last.

In early August 1874, George Armstrong Custer was in an exultant mood. A month before, he had left Fort Abraham Lincoln at the head of a long column of troopers and civilian scientists—and a 16-piece Army band tootling "The Girl I Left Behind Me." His mission had been to survey the forbidding Black Hills region of the Dakota Territory, and he was now ready to send an electrifying report to his commander, General Philip H. Sheridan: "Gold has been found in several places," wrote Custer, adding with uncharacteristic

---

THE WAGES OF A PERILOUS PROFESSION

The hazards of scouting are evidenced by the notation—"All except Comstock paid"—scrawled across this Army paymaster's ledger. The words were a grim epitaph for William Comstock (right), an experienced guide and interpreter, who was shot out of the saddle by Indians on August 16, 1868—the ledger incorrectly dates his death August 18. Comstock was being paid $125 per month—almost 10 times the rate for a private soldier. Rather than state that soldiers were not qualified to do a scout's job, the quartermaster certified on the bottom of his account that civilians were signed on only because the post could not spare any enlisted men for the assignment.

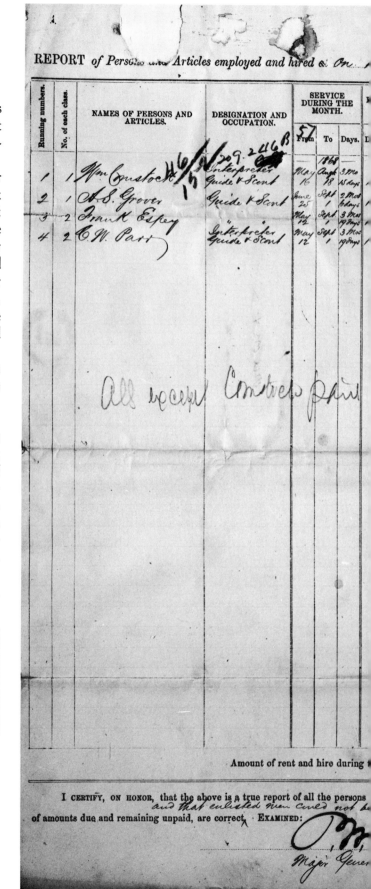

.... during the months of *May June July & Aug.*, 1868 , by *Lt Fred H Beecher 3d Inf a.a.* Quartermaster U. S. Army.

DATE OF CONTRACT, AGREEMENT, OR ENTRY INTO SERVICE.	BY WHOM OWNED.	AMOUNT OF RENT OR PAY IN THE MONTH.		REMARKS. Showing by whom the buildings were occupied, and for what purpose, and how the vessels and men were employed during the month. Transfers and discharges will be noted under this head.	TIME AND THE AMOUNT DUE AND REMAINING UNPAID.			
		Dolls.	Cents.		From—	To—	Dollars.	Cents.
May 16, 1868	209.2 26 B 57	387	50	*Wm Comstock Killed by Indians Aug. 18. 1868* *Employed on the plains in*				
June 25 "		220	00	*the Dept. of the Missouri as*				
May 12 "		363	33	*Interpreters, Guides and Scouts*				
" 12 "		363	33	*under special instructions of*				
				the Major General Comdg				
				the Department.				
May June, July & August 1868		1334	16	Total amount due and remaining unpaid				

........employed and hired by me during the months of *May, June, July & Aug.* 1868 , and that the observations under the head of "Remarks," and the statement

.....*without manifest injury to the service, to perform the duties of the civil employees herein reported*

Fred H. Beecher
Lt 3d U.S. Infty. a.a. Quartermaster.

prudence that it was still too early to tell how rich the deposits might be.

Someone would have to carry the report to Fort Laramie, 120 beeline miles to the southwest. The whole route was certain to be swarming with hostile Sioux angered by Custer's intrusion into lands that belonged to the Indians under terms of a solemn treaty with the United States government. It was surely no job for a novice plainsman, but then, no one had ever called Lonesome Charley Reynolds a novice.

Legend has it that Reynolds took on the hazardous mission only after no one else responded to a call for volunteers. In truth, he had known when he signed on as chief scout and guide at $100 a month that he might well be called upon to carry messages out of the Black Hills to civilization. And now as his time of departure neared, Reynolds cleaned his weapons, stuffed his saddlebags with hardtack and cooked bacon, and filled his ammunition belt. For his mount, he chose an animal so spirited that it had been judged unfit for regular cavalry service; such a horse, he knew, would be ideal for the long, hard ride that lay ahead. And to make that ride as safe as possible, he devised special leather sandals, cinched with drawstrings, for the horse. Pulled over the animal's ironshod hoofs, the sandals would leave tracks like those of a shoeless Indian pony.

When he picked up the canvas dispatch bag, Reynolds saw that the expedition adjutant, Lieutenant James Calhoun, had labeled it:

Black Hills Express
Charley Reynolds, Manager
connecting with
All Points East, West, North, South
Cheap Rates; Quick Transit; Safe Passage
We are protected by the
Seventh Cavalry!

The 7th Cavalry did protect Reynolds, but only for part of the way. Early on August 3, Custer and five companies of his soldiers left camp for an exploratory mission that would escort the scout to the fringes of the Black Hills. After a hard day's march, the party bivouacked near the South Fork of the Cheyenne River. Shortly after midnight, Custer walked with Reynolds to the edge of camp. There he shook hands with his scout and wished him Godspeed, and Reynolds vanished into the night. From here, Fort Laramie was 90 miles distant as the crow flies—and the journey would be longer for a man traveling by stealth through unfamiliar enemy territory.

Before sunrise, Reynolds camped along a summer-parched stream. His path would cross too many Indian trails for travel during daylight hours, and he had decided to move only in darkness, holing up by day in brush-lined stream beds that would provide only scanty water in this dry season of the year. On his hands and knees, Reynolds gathered grass to feed his famished horse, and then munched on hardtack and bacon washed down with what little water he could find to share with his mount. By the time night fell, he was off again, only to discover that his next campsite was drier than the first; this time, he was forced to dig deeply with his bowie knife to turn up a meager pool of water. According to Elizabeth Custer, who later wrote an account of what Reynolds told her about his ride, several parties of Indians passed nearby that day, one of them so close that he was able to hear their voices clearly.

On his third night out, Reynolds walked, to spare his thirsty mount. But there was no water for man or beast at the next stream-bed camp, where the scout dug down four feet and struck nothing but dirt and gravel. Now his lips were cracked and his tongue was so dry and swollen that he could not close his mouth. Reynolds took a desperate gamble. Long before sundown, he mounted up and—removing the hat that would mark him from afar as a white man—rode openly across the prairie. Twice he was spotted by warriors in the distance who, mistaking him for an Indian, allowed him to move on unmolested.

After some 10 miles, Reynolds came upon a welcome pool of sweet water. He stayed there all that night and through the next day before setting out on the final leg of his journey. On the morning of August 8 he rode into Fort Laramie and turned Custer's dispatches over to an Army telegraph operator.

The scout still had one more duty to attend to. Along with the dispatches, he had carried a small bundle of private mail that Custer had permitted his soldiers to send out. Reynolds took a stagecoach to Cheyenne, 90 miles to the south. There he boarded a Union Pacific train, delivered his mailbag to a railway postal clerk and rode to Omaha, 516 miles to the east. Then

General Custer's elaborately equipped reconnaissance expedition spreads its encampment over a large site en route to the Black Hills in 1874. To guide a party of this size, scouts had to put their skills to the most severe test.

95

he went back north by train to Bismarck. He arrived at Fort Abraham Lincoln on August 19, just 16 days after he had left. Eleven days later, Custer came riding back from the Black Hills at the head of his cavalry battalions; only then did he learn that his courier had gotten through alive.

As with Will Comstock, there had been nothing in the family background of Charles Alexander Reynolds to suggest that he would become an accomplished plainsman and Army scout. Born in Illinois in 1842, Reynolds was the son of a prominent physician and nephew of a clergyman, and his schooling had included a year of preparatory work at Abingdon College in Abingdon, Illinois. But the frontier beckoned to many a young man in his generation, and it is thought that Reynolds first answered the call in 1860 by hiring on as a teamster for a Denver-bound wagon train. Civil War service as a private in the 10th Kansas Volunteers took Reynolds over the Santa Fe Trail to New Mexico, and by the time he was mustered out in 1864, he had chosen a life on the Plains.

By 1870 he was well established in the Dakota Territory as a professional hunter, supplying fresh deer, elk and antelope to Army posts and Missouri River steamboats. So great was his skill at stalking game, and so deadly was his marksmanship, that Indians who watched him at work believed that he had mystical powers and called him "Lucky Man."

Inevitably, to meet the Army's need for trustworthy men who knew their way around the trackless northern plains, Reynolds turned to scouting. In 1872 he guided General David S. Stanley's surveying party to the Yellowstone River; the following year, on Stanley's second expedition to the Yellowstone, Reynolds met Custer for the first time, and the two men formed a lasting friendship. Thus it happened that Custer chose Reynolds as chief of scouts for his exploration of the Black Hills in 1874.

The Army had justified Custer's Black Hills mission as a legitimate military reconnaissance, although it was never fully explained why he was accompanied by two civilian gold prospectors. Once gold had been discovered, the Sioux found that their lands were overrun with white fortune hunters. The Indians had had enough of broken treaties, and they refused the government's demand that they withdraw to reservations.

By early in 1876 a military expedition was ready to move against the aroused forces of Crazy Horse and Sitting Bull.

Charley Reynolds again was hired as Custer's chief scout, and when the 7th Cavalry marched out of Fort Abraham Lincoln on May 17, Reynolds rode at the head of the column. Custer and his officers believed that the Indians would be brought to heel by the mere sight of such military power, but Reynolds thought otherwise. The scout told a friend that the summer of 1876 would witness "the greatest Indian battle ever fought on this continent."

Reynolds kept a sketchy diary of the campaign. On June 22 he recorded the discovery of several abandoned Indian camps, "the first of which was about 20 days old, the Indians seemed to be traveling leisurely along, last camp passed was probably 12 days old." It was his last entry.

Custer divided his forces in the afternoon of the 25th of June, sending Reynolds to guide Major Marcus Reno in the opening sortie against an enormous Sioux and Cheyenne camp on the Little Bighorn River. Before he reached the village, Reno encountered an overwhelming force of Indians. Reno ordered his men to make a stand in the timber on the riverbank, but he soon panicked and led the way in a retreat so unexpected that many of the soldiers did not even realize that it had been ordered. Charley Reynolds was among those left behind in the timber.

Dr. Henry R. Porter, a 7th Cavalry surgeon who was one of the few to make it back to Reno's command, described Reynolds' fate: "I was tending a dying soldier in a clump of bushes. The bullets were flying, and Reynolds noticed that they were making a target of me. He sprang up and cried: 'Doctor, the Indians are shooting at you!' I turned to look and the same instant he threw up his hands and fell, shot through the heart."

Charley Reynolds was not alone in death that day. Later in the afternoon, Custer and some 200 of his men were annihilated about two and a half miles away, in a battle that has ever since been shrouded in mystery and legend.

According to one legend, the first white man to arrive at the site after the Custer massacre was Army scout Frank Grouard, who at one time had lived in Sitting

California Joe's brief career as Custer's chief scout

In the fall of 1868, as he assembled the 7th Cavalry for a winter campaign along Oklahoma's Washita River, George Armstrong Custer selected as his chief scout a man he knew little about, but who looked as if he would fit the part. California Joe was a tall, bearded, pipe-smoking character who wore a black slouch hat and caped overcoat, carried an old-fashioned breech-loading musket and rode a mule. His appearance, said Custer, "would have attracted the notice of any casual observer."

California Joe's scouting credentials matched his looks. His real name, which Custer never knew, was Moses Milner. At 14, he ran away from home in Kentucky and became a trapper in Wyoming. At age 17, he served as an Army guide in the Mexican War, beginning a sporadic scouting career punctuated by mining, hunting, ranching and mule skinning. By the time Custer met him, the 40-year-old scout was known among frontiersmen to be one of the most able guides, canniest Indian fighters and heartiest drinkers in the West.

The night Custer appointed him chief scout, California Joe filled his canteen with rotgut whiskey and led a column of soldiers out to look for Indians. Congratulating himself on his promotion, he drank steadily while his unreined mule carried him rapidly away from his column.

Suddenly, the troops heard blood-curdling screams up ahead. As the soldiers prepared to fire on the noisy enemy, they discovered it was their own scout, dead drunk and in such a frenzy to fight Indians that he had to be bound hand and foot and tied to his mule to get him back to camp.

The incident precipitately ended California Joe's career as chief scout. Nevertheless he remained a regular scout and one of Custer's favorite companions, entertaining the soldier at every opportunity with "peculiar, but generally correct" notions of how to conduct an Indian campaign. After the winter of 1868-1869 he wandered off, but kept up with General and Mrs. Custer—and with his own much-neglected wife and four sons in Oregon—via a lively, if irregular, correspondence. His last letter to the Custers, dated March 16, 1874, announced he was "still on top of land yet," but had "not got a red cent."

In 1876, busily leading the Army into the Black Hills to chase out prospectors—and sneaking into the Hills to do some prospecting of his own—he missed Custer's disastrous last campaign. Four months later he made a drunken show of trying to avenge his commander, shouting "I'll show you how you killed Custer!" as he beat up a small group of unarmed agency Indians. Three nights afterward, Joe himself was killed, but not in any heroic stand against Indian warriors. He was shot in the back by an old enemy from the mining camps.

California Joe, photographed in 1875, was seldom seen without his pipe, gun and dog.

Four white scouts *(left)* strike the postures of victorious heroes amid the carnage of a Sioux village they massacred in 1868 in retaliation for an attack on a stagecoach. Many of the scouts considered that such brutal reprisals were the most effective response to Indian attacks—and some of them, no doubt, enjoyed the savage forays.

In a joke photograph *(right)* taken during his later life, Frank Grouard gets the drop on two friends. After three years of scouting for General George Crook, Grouard made a living helping authorities pursue outlaws who were plaguing the frontier.

Bull's camp. In reality, Grouard was far from the scene. And he was disgusted with the lurid account that a newspaperman, Joe DeBarthe, concocted years after the event. In an "autobiography" of the scout, De Barthe described Grouard, groping around in darkness to find out what had caused his horse to bolt, encountering a freshly scalped soldier's head.

But it is altogether fitting that Grouard's career was embellished with such fanciful tales, for he was surely the most mysterious figure who ever scouted for the Army. Even those who knew him disagreed about Frank Grouard—where he came from, what he was, what he really stood for.

They had reason to wonder. Here was a man who had won the trust and admiration of three such different and mutually hostile men of war as Sitting Bull and Crazy Horse of the Sioux nation and General George Crook of the U.S. Army. At different times he advised, spied for and fought for all three. With a record like that it was small wonder that some men thought him the most effective civilian scout the Army ever had, while others damned him as a renegade.

Grouard was a true exotic among plainsmen. Born in 1850 on the island of Tubuai, south of Tahiti, he was the son of a Mormon missionary and a Polynesian girl named Nahina. He reached the Western Plains when he was 8 years old, brought to Utah by a Mormon foster mother. At 16 he ran away to Montana,

where he worked for a brief period for a freighting outfit and carried mail. What he did later was a mystery that only deepened when he showed up in Nebraska at the Red Cloud Indian Agency one day in 1875, wearing an Indian breechcloth, and said that he had lived with the Sioux for six years and knew them intimately. When General Crook, preparing for his spring campaign against those same Sioux, heard about Grouard, he hired him as a scout.

In his autobiography, Grouard claimed that his first brush with hostile Indians had come in 1869, when he escaped from a band of Blackfeet after being stripped and severely beaten. But George W. Boyd, a well-known Montana scout and frontiersman who was one of Grouard's most active detractors, told an entirely different story.

Boyd branded Frank Grouard a renegade horse thief who deserved to be hanged. According to Boyd, who told his story in a long letter to the Bismarck *Tribune* in 1876, Grouard had stolen some mail horses in the fall of 1867 and fled with them to a camp of the Prairie Gros Ventres. After spending the winter with that tribe, said Boyd, Grouard stole horses from his Indian hosts and joined first the Assiniboins and then the Yanktons. By 1870, Boyd continued, Grouard was living with the Sioux as a trusted member of Sitting Bull's entourage.

By Grouard's own account, he was not a willing re-

cruit of Sitting Bull but a hapless captive. As Grouard told the story to Joe DeBarthe years later, he was riding alone one winter day wearing a bulky buffalo overcoat when he was accosted by Indians. They pulled him to the ground and tried to remove the coat. As Grouard fought back, keeping one assailant between himself and another Indian who was trying to shoot him, a mounted warrior appeared and spoke sharply to the armed Indian. "I couldn't understand what he said," Grouard recounted. "The first thing I knew, the Indian who was on horseback dismounted, went up to the one who had the gun and knocked him down with a heavy bow he carried in his hand." Grouard's captors then put him on a horse and led him on a three-day trek to a tipi village. Along the way, he learned that his savior was none other than Sitting Bull, who was so amused at the sight of Grouard in his furry coat that he spared the captive's life and named him Standing Bear.

According to Grouard, he was not allowed to hunt alone or to move freely about the Plains until he had been in the Sioux camp for a year or two. It is more probable that his previous experience with Indians made him an apt student of Sioux ways and that he was accepted as a member of the tribe within six months. In any case, he would have had ample opportunities for escape to white society—if he had felt truly at home in that society.

Possibly Grouard found Indian life more to his liking. His dark skin and black hair, inherited from his Polynesian mother, had caused some people to speculate that he was the son of a Sioux woman and a black man. Men with mixed antecedents were known scornfully as half-breeds and commanded scant respect from white frontiersmen. Among the Sioux, perhaps, he was treated as an equal.

But in 1875, for reasons that were never quite clear, Grouard put Indian life behind him. By his own account, he had considered the move for some time, and when he rode out with a war party in the spring, he slipped away to the Red Cloud Agency. Not long afterward, the Indian commissioners sent him with a large group of peaceful Indians to the camp of Crazy Horse and Sitting Bull, where he tried to persuade the two warlords to make peace. Grouard spoke more as a fellow tribesman than as an emissary from the whites, but it may be that Sitting Bull's reply led to his final

break with the Sioux. "He told me," Grouard said later, "to go out and tell the white men at Red Cloud that he declared open war and would fight them wherever he met them from that time on."

When he got back to the agency, Grouard cast his lot with the white man. But he found it hard to adjust to some civilized ways: a month passed before he cut his hair and exchanged his Indian garb for a suit of clothes.

No matter what had impelled Grouard to join the Indians or why he left them, his encyclopedic knowledge of their language, lands and habits made him an ideal candidate for employment with the Army as a scout. To be sure, there was ample cause to doubt his ultimate loyalties. More than one plainsman maintained that Grouard had been a trusted and willing warrior with the Sioux, and a government peace commission had blamed Grouard for the failure of a round of negotiations with Sitting Bull in 1872. "In order to fully understand the situation with regard to Sitting Bull," said the commissioners in their report, "it may be well to state that he has in his company a Sandwich Islander, called Frank, who appears to exercise great control in the Indian councils and who excels the Indians in their bitter hatred to the whites."

Small wonder that General Crook, although eager to make use of Grouard's knowledge of Indian ways, was careful to instruct two other scouts, Baptiste "Big Bat" Pourier and Baptiste "Little Bat" Garnier, to keep a very close eye on his new recruit. If Grouard showed the slightest sign of betrayal, said Crook, he should be shot out-of-hand.

Crook's distrust of Grouard turned out to be ill-founded, and it may well have contributed to the humiliating failure of a crucial expedition in early 1876. On March 1, Crook had moved northward out of Fort Fetterman, Wyoming, at the head of 10 companies of cavalry and two companies of infantry, expecting to engage 4,000 to 5,000 Sioux warriors at the mouth of the Little Bighorn. A week later he left his supply wagons under infantry guard and pressed on, traveling light with 15 days worth of rations on pack mules. The weather was bitterly cold; Crook's aide, Lieutenant John G. Bourke, wrote later that the bread was frozen "hard as flint and cold as charity."

Bourke was much warmer in his description of Frank Grouard, who was one of the 31 civilian scouts.

assigned to the expedition. Grouard was, the officer said, "one of the most remarkable woodsmen I have ever met; no Indian could surpass him. No question could be asked him that he could not answer at once and correctly." And on this campaign, there were plenty of questions to be answered.

Eager to engage the enemy, Crook badgered his scouts to tell him where the Sioux could be found. Most believed that they would be camped on either the Tongue or the Little Bighorn rivers, and Crook took their advice and dispatched a reconnaissance party to scour the Tongue. The only campgrounds they found had been abandoned for a month or more.

By the eighth day of fruitless searching, Crook was growing more impatient, and he summoned his scouts once again. With their rations more than half gone, he said, his men would have to fight the Indians soon or turn back for fresh supplies. Now Grouard stepped forward. Indians, he said, had the same migratory habits as animals and would be holed up along the Powder River at that time of year. If Crook would do as he told him, the scout said, he would lead the troopers to a village within three days.

"That is what we want," Crook said. The next morning, the column marched toward the Powder River. Grouard, riding far in the lead, saw that he was on the right track when he spotted a pair of Indian hunters about five miles off. The Indians hastily withdrew, but Grouard knew that they had already left behind them a trail that would lead him directly to the village he was searching for.

Informed that Indians had been sighted at last, Crook ordered a strike force commanded by Colonel J. J. Reynolds to follow Grouard as he backtracked the Indian hunters to their camp. It grew dark not long after the troops moved out, and snow flurries began to blur the trail, but Grouard stuck to it. A newspaper correspondent who accompanied the expedition described the scout in action that night: "now down on his hands and knees in the deep snow, scrutinizing the faint footprints, then losing the trail for an instant, darting to and fro until it was found, and again following it up with the keenness of a hound and a fearlessness that would have imbued almost anyone with fresh vim and courage. . . ."

Apparently, Reynolds was not equally inspired by Grouard's example. After the scout had guided the way to the village, Reynolds launched an early morning attack that caught the Indians completely by surprise. But all of a sudden, just after his troops had managed to turn back an Indian counterattack, he ordered a withdrawal, abandoning not only the victory but also a store of supplies that could have kept Crook's hungry command in the field for many more weeks of campaigning. Reynolds never totally explained the reason for his abrupt withdrawal, but there were those who believed that a rival scout had told Reynolds that Grouard had led the soldiers into a trap.

Much chagrined when he learned of the aborted assault, Crook abandoned his expedition and returned to Fort Fetterman. There, he lodged court-martial charges against Reynolds, and prepared for the upcoming summer campaign against the rampaging Plains tribes. On May 29 he was on the march once more, this time at the head of 15 companies of cavalry, five of infantry, a company of civilian scouts and 103 supply wagons. Moving north northwest, he hoped to engage Sitting Bull and Crazy Horse and help end the Sioux war that summer.

Frank Grouard, by now Crook's most trusted scout, had already gone into action. With a 10-man cavalry squad, Grouard left Fort Fetterman on the 21st of May to find a route as well as a Powder River crossing for Crook's wagons and troopers. But he had not gone far when he saw that his party was being closely observed by Indians.

That evening, Grouard ordered the soldiers to set up a bogus camp, complete with dummies and roaring cookfires. After the men had gone through the motions of bedding down for the night, the scout led them to a creek bed where they had tethered their mounts. Then, at times barely eluding bands of hostile Sioux, he guided the troopers on a roundabout ride back to Fort Fetterman. There, they joined Crook's column as it snaked out in search of the enemy.

For Crook, it was not a particularly noteworthy campaign. At a battle on Rosebud Creek, on June 17, his advance was turned back by Crazy Horse's warriors; Crook and his men then spent several weeks hunting, fishing and waiting for reinforcements. When Crook returned from a three-day hunting trip on the 5th of July, he found out that Grouard and Big Bat Pourier, out scouting as usual in his absence, had ob-

Standing on a Colorado mountain pass in 1874, a scout named Harry Yount scans the ridges for game. Yount served seven summers as provisioner for scientists compiling a geological atlas of the territory.

served a major Sioux war party not more than 20 miles away from camp. The following day, Crook dispatched Lieutenant Frederick W. Sibley and 25 hand-picked cavalrymen to accompany the two scouts on a reconnaissance mission.

Early on the morning of July 7, as the heavily armed party neared the head of the Little Bighorn, Grouard motioned the men to a halt and moved alone to the crest of a rocky ridge. A moment later, he signaled for Pourier to join him, and the two men scanned the countryside through their field glasses. Then they galloped back to the waiting troopers. "Be quick," said Grouard, "and follow me for your lives."

"What did you see, Frank?" Sibley inquired after Grouard had led the soldiers to a place of concealment behind a high bluff.

"Only Sitting Bull's war party," the scout replied. And as the two men peered cautiously back over the way they had just come, they saw an Indian on horseback riding slowly in a circle, staring at the ground. "Now we had better look out," Said Grouard. "That fellow has found our trail, sure, and they will be after us in five minutes."

Guided by Grouard, who had often hunted in the region during his sojourn with the Sioux, the troopers moved away at a brisk pace. But they were soon overtaken and driven into a tight skirmish line among trees and fallen timber. Under withering fire from the Indians—who had recognized Grouard and were taunting him and calling him by his Sioux name, Standing Bear—the detachment seemed doomed, and Sibley ordered his men to fight to the death rather than fall alive into Indian hands.

Then Grouard proposed a way out. If the soldiers would leave their horses behind, he said, there was a good chance that they might escape through the rugged mountains and make their way on foot to the safety of Crook's camp. Sibley ordered the withdrawal.

Carrying nothing but their weapons and ammunition, the troopers crept away from their position and followed Grouard into a trackless, boulder-strewn forest. After crossing a waist-high tributary of the Tongue River, they clambered up slippery rocks to a mountain ridge and began the 50-mile trek to their main camp. Stopping only briefly to rest, the soldiers pressed steadily onward, staying out of sight of passing Indian bands.

A Sioux Cemetery.

"Yellowstone Kelly"
Chief Scout.

Fort Peck - on the Missouri River.

Cantonment on Tongue River.

Cheyenne Captives.

Yellowstone Kelly, chief scout for General Nelson A. Miles, is featured in an 1877 *Harper's Weekly* montage dramatizing the Army's decisive winter campaign against the Cheyennes and Sioux.

At about 6:30 in the morning on July 9 the men came upon two troopers of Crook's 2nd Cavalry, who were out on a hunting expedition. As the hunters galloped back to camp to fetch horses and food, most of Sibley's men flopped onto the ground, too exhausted to move another step. Lieutenant Bourke, who watched the contingent ride into camp several hours later, observed that "the whole party looked more like dead men than soldiers of the army."

According to John F. Finerty, a newspaperman who accompanied and chronicled the Sibley expedition, there was no doubt that the men owed their lives to Frank Grouard, and to Lieutenant Sibley for heeding his scout's counsel. Experienced officers in Crook's camp, said Finerty, agreed that "escape from danger so imminent and so appalling, in manner so ingenious and successful, was almost without a parallel in the history of Indian warfare." Crook, giving credit where it was due, sent off a dispatch to General Sheridan himself. In it, he praised Grouard's "coolness and judgment . . . in the face of the whole force of the enemy."

But when General Nelson Miles arrived on the northern Plains in August, he was not impressed with General Crook's own behavior toward the enemy. Crook, perhaps dispirited by the Custer disaster on June 25 at the Little Bighorn, seemed to be marching almost aimlessly in pursuit of hostile Indians, who usually managed to stay far from harm's way. "The campaign thus far," wrote Miles to his wife, "would not have been creditable to a militia organization."

The ambitious and aggressive Miles intended to do himself much more credit than that. He was determined to find the elusive tribes and give them no rest. Soon, he would meet two civilian scouts who would help him succeed where other soldiers had failed— Luther S. "Yellowstone" Kelly and John "Big Leggins" Bruguier.

One day in the late summer of 1876, Yellowstone Kelly was riding along the Yellowstone River not far from Miles's camp near present-day Miles City, Montana. Tied to his saddle was the foot-long forepaw of a giant cinnamon bear that he had shot not long before. Kelly stopped to talk for a while with an Army captain, who told him that the General would surely be eager to meet someone who knew the surrounding country as

well as Kelly did. Kelly agreed and waved the bear's paw aloft. "I will send it up as my card," he said, and as he hurriedly wrote his name on the paw, the captain summoned an orderly to carry it to the general's tent. Miles was impressed with Kelly's calling card. The scout, he decided, "was a person who could be put to a very useful purpose at that juncture of affairs."

Kelly was another Easterner; he had been born in 1849 in the Finger Lakes region of upstate New York. When not yet 16 years old, but yearning for glory in the Civil War, he enlisted in the Army, and only later discovered that instead of joining up only for the duration of the War, he had signed on for a Regular Army hitch of three years. When his enlistment finally ran out in 1868, Kelly was serving at Fort Ransom in Dakota Territory.

By then, the vastness and excitement of the Plains had claimed him. He drew his mustering-out pay in St. Paul and turned westward. Green but lucky, he was befriended by able tutors who taught him the ways of the wilderness. First there were the blue-smocked, red-sashed Métis trappers of French and Indian blood, who ranged along the Red River on either side of the Canadian border. Farther south, at Fort Berthold, Kelly became friends with an old trapper named Red Mike Welsh, and he later explored the area around the Yellowstone River with Ed Lambert, a veteran French-Canadian *voyageur*.

By the time of his interview with Miles, Kelly was a consummate plainsman and hunter, and Miles was surely pleased when Kelly agreed to become his chief scout. Kelly, the general wrote later, "was destined to prove very valuable to me." The new scout's first assignment was a reconnaissance run to the North. "The attitude of these Indians, as far as I may judge, is defiant," he reported. When he returned to camp in mid-October, he was just in time to guide Miles and his infantry in a sortie against Indians who had attacked an Army supply train.

Four days out, the column came upon two Indians. The Indians carried a flag of truce, and reported that Sitting Bull wanted to confer with Miles in a council of peace. Miles agreed to meet with Sitting Bull, and at the hastily arranged conference he spoke to his Sioux adversary through Sitting Bull's interpreter, a young man called Big Leggins. Big Leggins' real name was

Johnnie Bruguier, and he would soon switch his allegiance and become one of Miles's most trusted scouts and mediators with the Plains tribes.

Johnnie Bruguier was born in 1849 to the second of two Sioux wives of Theophile Bruguier, a prosperous merchant who settled at the future site of Sioux City and sent his sons to St. Louis, where they were educated at the College of Christian Brothers. After the deaths of both Indian wives, the elder Bruguier married a white woman who never quite understood her half-Indian stepchildren. In time, they moved back to their Sioux relatives, and by his early twenties, Johnnie was working for the Army as scout and interpreter for troops stationed at the mouth of the Grand River on the west bank of the Missouri. Once he was sent as escort and interpreter with a delegation of peaceful chiefs to Washington.

But in 1875, while serving as interpreter at the Standing Rock Indian Agency in Dakota Territory, he got into serious trouble. Trying to break up a drunken

quarrel between his brother Billy and an agency employee named William McGee, he clubbed McGee so hard that the man died the next morning. Johnnie fled, seeking refuge in the camp of Sitting Bull. His white man's clothing angered the Indians at first, but Sitting Bull is said to have told his followers, "Well, if you are going to kill this man, kill him; and if you are not, give him a drink of water, something to eat and a pipe of peace to smoke." Like Frank Grouard before him, Bruguier was spared.

By the month of October 1876, Johnnie was a trusted resident of Sitting Bull's lodge. During the supply-train attack that had brought Miles into the field, it was reported that Johnnie, to impress his host, made a spectacular "brave run"—a brazen dash under enemy fire—along the flanks of the train. One day later Sitting Bull used Big Leggins as his scribe and dictated a letter, which was left on the trail for the advancing troops and wagoneers:

"I want to know what you are doing traveling this road. You scare all the buffalo away. I want to hunt in this place. I want you to turn back from here. If you don't, I'll fight you again. I want you to leave what you have got here and turn back from here. I am your friend, Sitting Bull."

Sitting Bull was anything but friendly, however, when he conferred face to face with Miles and heard his call for the Sioux to submit to white authority. Speaking through Johnnie Bruguier, the Sioux warrior told Miles, as recorded in the general's memoirs, that "the white man never lived who loved an Indian, and that no true Indian ever lived that did not hate the white man. He declared that God Almighty made him an Indian and did not make him an agency Indian either."

Something that Sitting Bull did not realize was that his own half-white interpreter was yearning to return to white civilization. Nevertheless, when the fruitless conference broke up the following day with Miles's announcement that he would open fire in 15 minutes unless the Indians surrendered, Bruguier retreated along with the Sioux.

Five days and 42 miles later on the banks of the Yellowstone River, 2,000 of the hotly pursued Sioux gave in. Sitting Bull was not among them, and neither was Johnnie Bruguier, who still feared facing a murder charge for his part in the Standing Rock incident.

Even so, he had no stomach for a bitter war against the whites and joined a chief named Iron Dog, who intended to make peace at Fort Peck. There, as evidence of good faith, Bruguier turned over an Army paycheck that had been looted from the Custer battlefield. When he learned of the check, Miles called for Bruguier, who explained why he had joined the Indians. If Miles would help him in the McGee affair, he said, he would join the general in his campaign against Sitting Bull. Convinced of the young man's sincerity, Miles promised to do what he could and gave Bruguier his first assignment.

In probably no other war anywhere would it have seemed even remotely feasible for a betrayer to treat with the betrayed, but this is what Bruguier agreed to do. Alone, and in bitter winter weather, he set out to find Sitting Bull and persuade him to surrender. He failed to wangle a capitulation, but he did manage to talk with the defiant chief and returned with accurate information on his intended movements. Miles was so impressed that he hired Bruguier as a regular scout and gave him a $300 bonus.

If his turncoat civilian employee could get away with calling on the chief who had the most reason to distrust him, Miles reasoned, he could do the same with others. Bruguier was dispatched on many similar ventures, the most notable, perhaps, coming in the wake of an action by Yellowstone Kelly.

Early in January 1877, Miles was moving up the Tongue River through foot-deep snow with a wagon train of supplies, two pieces of artillery and 436 men of the 5th and 22nd Infantry. Out ahead was Kelly with a half-dozen white and Crow Indian scouts, feeling out the country and looking for the northern Cheyennes and for Crazy Horse and his Oglala warriors. On January 7, as Kelly hunkered down behind the boll of a big cedar and scanned the country ahead, he saw walking toward him down the valley a small party of Indian women and children. When they reached his position, Kelly stepped out and told the startled wayfarers in sign language that they were his prisoners but that they would not be killed.

Miles, advised by Kelly that the captives had come from prominent lodges, drove off spirited rescue attempts that night and again the next morning and returned with the prisoners to his cantonment. A month or so later, the general summoned Bruguier and asked if he would take a chance on escorting two of the women back to their people, carrying with him an offer to talk peace. Big Leggins said he would try.

When he reached the Indian village, Bruguier doubtless wished that he had not come. Sweet Woman, one of the captives, had agreed to help him on his mission, telling him that he would be safe from harm if he could get into the tipi of Coal Bear, keeper of the Cheyennes' Sacred Hat. But Coal Bear, standing outside his tent flap, refused even to shake the scout's outstretched hand. As a crowd of suspicious tribesmen gathered around him, Bruguier quickly pushed past Coal Bear and slipped into the tipi. Once he was inside the tipi, tribal custom decreed not only that he was safe but also that the Indians were bound to listen to what he had come to say.

Many of them did not like the message that Bruguier had brought, and they feared that General Miles's invitation would turn out to be a trap. For the next two days, the chiefs and their warriors discussed what they should do, until the powerful Two Moons announced that he would go with Bruguier to confer with the general. When the scout rode back to report to Miles, he brought with him 19 Indian leaders to negotiate a surrender. It was a major step toward ending forever the wars on the northern Plains.

Johnnie Bruguier had performed critical military duties, but he still faced a serious civil charge. In 1879 he was finally arrested for killing William McGee. General Miles appeared as a character witness at the trial. His testimony was a tribute to Bruguier, but many of his words applied also to the other civilian scouts, men who had served with honor and who had sometimes given their lives in the settlement of the West. "His services have been exceedingly valuable," said Miles, "and his reports always reliable; his character has been one of a quiet, a valuable man; he attends to his own business and I never knew him to trouble anyone; through his personal information to me a junction of the forces of Crazy Horse and Sitting Bull in January 1877 was prevented."

Bruguier waited nervously as the jurors deliberated his case. When they returned in half an hour with a verdict of not guilty, spectators burst into applause.

An artist-scout who dabbled in war paint

Charles Stobie had a most unusual motive for becoming a scout: he wanted to capture the scouts' world on canvas. Unwilling to rely on his imagination and dime novels, as did some other artists who painted frontier life, Stobie packed up his sketchbooks and paints in 1865, abandoned the city comforts of Chicago and headed for Colorado. Joining a wagon train, he met California Joe, a famous scout, who began sharing his skills with the tenderfoot. By the time Stobie reached Denver, his fellow travelers conceded that he had "made good" on the trail.

For the next decade, Stobie roamed the West, working as a scout for Indian agencies and for the Army, and, on his own, living among Indians, hunting and painting. He kept company with some of the West's most celebrated scouts—Jim Baker, Kit Carson, Jim Beckwourth and Buffalo Bill Cody.

For a summer the young artist-scout lived with a band of Utes, once joining them in a bloody ambush of an Arapaho hunting party. Following the skirmish he became one of the few whites ever to join in the tribe's ritual scalp dance. "I sailed in along with the others," he wrote later, "dancing and singing until I was hoarse and stiff."

For the most part, the scouts he painted were self-portraits and, although he left no record that he had actually faced the harrowing dangers that some of the paintings depict, there is little doubt that in details of landscape, dress and weaponry the scenes are among the most accurate to have come out of the 19th Century West.

Artist Stobie scouts a mountain valley with an Indian in this self-portrait. In 1891 a critic praised Stobie's accuracy: "His Sioux are not adorned with Apache bead-work, nor are his Utes decked out with Fenimore Cooper's trappings."

Hampered by an arrow piercing his calf, a scout fights for his life in an 1895 painting by Charles Stobie. Though this is a self-portrait, there is no record of Stobie himself ever having been wounded by Indians.

4 | Indians in uniform

Sporting regulation Army bluecoats in the chill Dakota air, the Indians at right—and many others like them—played a curious and crucial role in the campaign of the Western Plains. As scouts, they helped the Army fight other Indians. Their advice on how to move against hostile tribes—and their skill in tracking the adversary—was in large measure responsible for the final conquest of Indian lands by whites.

By capitalizing on animosities between tribes, the Army found it easy to recruit Plains warriors as scouts. Indians from small, relatively pacified nations—Pawnees, Crows and Arikaras—welcomed the chance to safely seek revenge against powerful enemies like the Sioux and Cheyenne.

The scouts were selected with great care. "The tribe from which they came," wrote one Army commander, "would be chosen according to the country in which we were to operate and the tribe against which we were to operate. Now and again there would be some willing to combine against their own tribe."

Indian scouts offered the Army its best chance of negotiating with the enemy, for they knew their warring brethren's fears. At the Battle of Wounded Knee, one scout persuaded his commander to cease fire so he could reason with a group of hostiles. "It took half an hour talking," said the officer, but the Indians—some of them relatives of the scout—surrendered peaceably.

Lieutenant Charles W. Taylor (*center, foreground*) drills his Oglala Sioux scouts on Pine Ridge reservation, South Dakota. Standing Soldier, a scout who persuaded the Hunkpapa Sioux to peacefully surrender in 1890, was a member of this troop.

Turning old antagonisms to the Army's advantage

In October 1876 a wagon train carrying winter clothing to U.S. Army troops at Camp Robinson, Nebraska, stopped for the night at the Niobrara River. "Hostile bands were reported to have been seen along the route," wrote a newspaper correspondent on his way to join Crook's expedition, "and with some apprehension of attack upon the train, strict watch was kept from the start for signs of approaching Indians." Around midnight, the journalist wrote, strange noises drifted into camp on the wind. "The sounds at first somewhat resembled the crying of coyotes, but soon neighing of horses was distinctly heard; and—mingling with and rising above it—the peculiar shouts and occasional shrill cries of Indians." The urgent whisper passed from tent to tent: "Get up quick! The camp's all surrounded by Injuns!" The men grabbed their guns, doused the campfires and rushed for cover behind the wagons, which were a few yards away.

Halfway between the tents and the shelter of the wagons, the newspaperman and the wagon master were caught in the open by two Indians riding directly into the camp. "They rode on without apparent hostile intent," the journalist recalled, "but we could hear the tramp of horses in the distance, with loud shouts and urgings of Indians." As they came closer the wagon master abruptly asked the one in the lead, "Do you want fight?" "No-o-o," was the drawling response. "No want fight—Good Injun!"

"Are you Sioux or Pawnees?" asked the wagon master. "Pawnee!" the Indian replied, as if affronted. Those behind the barricaded wagons were not con-

vinced. "Pawnee, be damned!" retorted one man. "In a minute the whole band will be here." The men of the wagon train stayed behind cover, rifles poised.

But before anyone could panic and pull a trigger, an Army officer rode out of the darkness. He was Major Frank North, he quickly explained, and the Pawnees were part of his company of scouts, heading for Fort Laramie with ponies taken in raids on two camps of hostile Indians. "The scare subsided almost as quickly as it began," the newspaper correspondent wrote, "and our fires were relighted. Our visitors remained awhile to warm themselves and accept any loose trifles we might be disposed to part with. Those of us with an extra commissary in a convenient bottle re-examined it, and retired for another sleep."

This nighttime near miss, which could have ended in tragedy rather than in a celebration of relief with a "convenient bottle," demonstrated one peril of the Army policy of using Indian scouts to help prosecute the Indian wars. Had the wagon party started shooting, men on both sides might have died before the case of mistaken identity was cleared up. The tribesmen enlisted as scouts were often in double jeopardy. Likely to be scalped by the warriors they helped the white man to track down, they were also likely to be mistaken for the enemy by white soldiers or frightened settlers. But the success of the policy was to prove that its benefits outweighed any risks. For a quarter of a century, hundreds of Indians working as scouts fought alongside the U.S. Army in the West, and their service was a major factor in the final subjugation of powerful and defiant bands of Plains Indians.

Large-scale use of Indians as scouts began in 1864, when General Samuel R. Curtis recruited 76 Pawnees to help put down Cheyenne and Sioux turbulence on the Great Plains in what is now Kansas and Nebraska. The experiment was successful, and two years

---

Proudly dressed in a discordant mixture of both Army attire and tribal regalia, the Pawnee scout White Horse clutches the armament of his two allegiances—an Indian tomahawk and a white man's revolver.

later, in 1866, the U.S. Congress passed an act authorizing the President to "enlist and employ in the Territories and Indian country a force of Indians, not to exceed one thousand, to act as scouts."

The program made good economic sense. It cost two million dollars a year to maintain a single Army regiment on the Plains, and yet the Army was not particularly effective in its fight against Indians. The soldiers made advantageous use of civilian scouts to direct the troops to hostile forces, but good white scouts were scarce and expensive, sometimes getting 10 times as much pay as a private soldier. By comparison, Indian scouts were a bargain. Not only did they know the country and the ways of the Indian better than white men did, but they also could be mustered in for short hitches when needed—usually only six months at a time—and they were pleased to receive a private's pay of $13 a month.

And their skills were unique. General Crook, a strong advocate of the use of native scouts, declared that "to polish a diamond there is nothing like its own dust." Indians scoff at white soldiers, he said, "whom they easily surpass in the peculiar style of warfare which they force upon us, but put upon their trail an enemy of their own blood, an enemy as tireless, as foxy, and as stealthy and familiar with the country as they themselves, and it breaks them all up."

The advantage to the white Army of using native scouts was obvious. Less readily apparent was why these warriors would hire on with the very people who were inexorably taking over their land and destroying their way of life. From one point of view, this service could be viewed as a form of treachery, Indians betraying fellow Indians for the sake of another race. But, in fact, there was bitter warfare among the Plains tribes—rivalries and feuds that outweighed the more recent conflicts with the whites. When General Curtis sought allies against the Sioux, the Pawnees were a logical first choice. For generations the Pawnees had been mauled and preyed upon by Sioux and Cheyennes.

Other likely prospects were the Arikaras, known as Rees for short, river people of the upper Missouri in Dakota Territory. Though they had made life hell for fur traders earlier in the century, they, too, had endured so much abuse from the Sioux that they welcomed an invitation to shoot back. So the Pawnees and Arikaras

were among the first and, over the long pull, perhaps the most reliable Indian scouts the Army hired.

Farther west, the Sioux and Cheyennes had still more enemies among the Shoshoni and the Crows, who also provided bands of scouts willing to work for the bluecoats for the sake of revenge. The Crows had many grievances against the Sioux in particular. "The face of the Sioux is red, but his heart is black," remarked Old Crow, chief of the Crow nation, when he brought his warriors to General Crook. "These are our lands, but the Sioux stole them from us. They hunt upon our mountains. They fish in our streams. They have stolen our horses. They have murdered our squaws, our children. But the heart of the pale face has ever been red to the Crow. The scalp of no white man hangs in our lodges, but they are thick as grass in the wigwams of the Sioux. The great white chief will lead us against no other tribe of red men. Our war is with the Sioux and only them. Where the white warrior goes there shall we be also."

Desire for vengeance against hereditary enemies, a chance to win the fame and honor accorded by Indian tradition to the warrior, freedom from the confines and poverty of the reservation: the Pawnees, Rees and Crows had many motives for joining the bluecoats in pursuit of the Sioux and Cheyennes. Toward the end of the Indian wars even some Sioux and Cheyenne warriors scouted for the white Army, leading soldiers to the last hiding places of their own people. Some of these men took the job out of self-interest—for money to feed a hungry family, for adventure, for freedom of movement. But, because they were operating against their kinsmen, the Sioux and Cheyenne scouts did their work with restraint and compassion, trying to prevent unnecessary bloodshed, to preserve the exhausted remnants of their tribes.

Whatever their drives or doubts, the native scouts over the years compiled a military record that the commander of any army might envy. General Crook testified that without these Indian scouts, "white men would be outwitted, exhausted, circumvented, possibly ambushed and destroyed." It has often been contended that if the impetuous George Armstrong Custer had listened to his Ree and Crow scouts he might have lived to fight another day and a better battle than the one in which he and much of his command were massa-

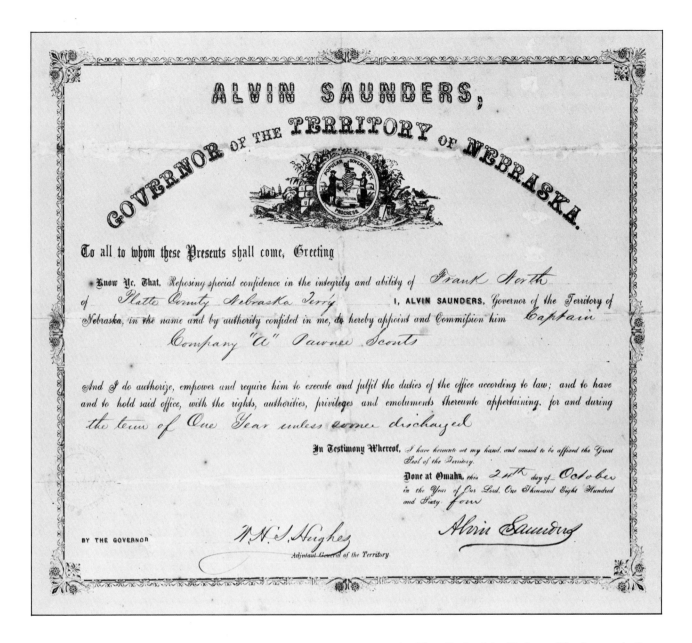

ALVIN SAUNDERS,
GOVERNOR OF THE TERRITORY OF NEBRASKA.

To all to whom these Presents shall come, Greeting

Know Ye, That, Reposing special confidence in the integrity and ability of *Frank North* of *Platte County Nebraska Terry* I, ALVIN SAUNDERS, Governor of the Territory of Nebraska, in the name and by authority confided in me, do hereby appoint and Commission him *Captain* *Company "A" Pawnee Scouts*

And I do authorize, empower and require him to execute and fulfil the duties of the office according to law; and to have and to hold said office, with the rights, authorities, privileges and emoluments thereunto appertaining, for and during *the term of One Year unless sooner discharged*

In Testimony Whereof, I have hereunto set my hand, and caused to be affixed the Great Seal of the Territory.

Done at Omaha, this *24th* day of *October* in the Year of Our Lord, One Thousand Eight Hundred and Sixty *four*

Alvin Saunders

BY THE GOVERNOR
W. H. S. Hughes
Adjutant General of the Territory

cred at the Little Bighorn in 1876. The scouts could foresee what was coming, but they stuck with him even when Custer chose to ignore their warnings. Three paid with their lives.

Despite their loyalty, courage and unquestioned usefulness, Indian scouts were often shabbily rewarded. Sometimes the neglect or outright mistreatment of these men seemed to result from lack of understanding or sheer bureaucratic fumbling. More often it was rooted in the white man's ingrained contempt for the Indian. "It is absurd to talk of keeping faith with Indians," said General Philip Henry Sheridan, and examples of white faithlessness were legion. The very first contingent of Pawnee scouts—those who had been mustered in by General Curtis in 1864—were summarily mustered out again without being paid once their job was

done. At Fort Buford in Dakota Territory, Arikara scouts had to appeal to the commander—through their white lieutenant—to stop drunken white soldiers from molesting their women. A Ree scout, Bloody Knife, died on the Little Bighorn, but it took four years before Bloody Knife's widow, She Owl, finally collected the $91.66 owed the scout at his death.

No matter what valuable service he might have rendered, the native scout's usual lot was anonymity. A white officer might praise his scouts to their faces, but when it came to writing official reports or his memoirs, he was likely to regard his Indian troopers as nameless extensions of his own good right arm. There was also the practical difficulty resulting from the Indian's custom of changing his name in the afterglow of a battle in

In a group portrait framed by tribal symbols, Pawnee scouts exhibit the dignity they shared as members of the North brothers' 1869 Army troop. Qualifying standards were high, and to be chosen, wrote a North scout, "was a great honor."

The leaders of the first and largest company of Indian scouts, Luther and Frank North, were widely known for their fearlessness. "These men were brave," wrote one contemporary, "because they thought of their work and not of themselves."

CAPTAIN LUTHER NORTH

MAJOR FRANK NORTH

which he felt he had distinguished himself by one bold deed or another. Names on the quartermaster's muster roll were inscribed with dubious accuracy at enlistment, often losing much in translation. And nobody knew, when a native recruit "touched the pen," whether his name would be the same when payday arrived.

Thus it was that the deeds of the Pawnee scouts became known to history largely as the work of the North brothers, Frank and Luther, their white officers. The brothers were born east of the Mississippi, Frank in New York in 1840 and Luther in Ohio in 1846, but in early youth they followed their surveyor father to Omaha, where they came to know the Pawnees on the Plains. In 1861, Frank North, who spoke fluent Pawnee, was hired by the appointed trader at the Pawnee reservation about 100 miles west of Omaha to be interpreter and clerk. The trader preferred to stay at home in Illinois, so 21-year-old Frank was left to conduct all business.

In 1864, when General Curtis recruited Pawnees for his expedition out of Fort Kearny against the Sioux and Cheyennes, North and another reservation employee who spoke some Pawnee headed the company. Although their maiden effort for Curtis was brief and uneventful, the general then gave North authority to enlist 100 Pawnees for the following year and arranged for him to be commissioned a captain. Largely due to Army fumbles, North nearly lost his command even before it began: the Pawnees he recruited got tired of waiting for the Army to enlist them officially and went off on their fall buffalo hunt. The would-be captain had to scramble to fill his roster, but Company A, Pawnee Scouts, was finally mustered into service in January of 1865.

Frank North was not quite 25 when he began what was to be a long association with Pawnee scouts. Later his brother Luther claimed that the scouts would serve under no other officer, a claim substantiated by at least one general who pointed out that "unwilling scouts were untrustworthy and useless; it was always the practice to let them out at once. Their fidelity depended largely upon confidence in their commander."

And much of this confidence, Luther North felt, stemmed from the fact that he and his brother spoke the scouts' language. "Of course there were other Indian scouts during that period, and later; but, so far as I know, it was necessary in all such cases to employ interpreters, and the officers changed with about each expedition—perhaps on it." The Pawnees knew the North brothers as neighbors and friends from their homeland and showed their great respect for Frank North in particular, seeking his arbitration of tribal disputes despite his youth.

At first acquaintance, the Pawnee scout force tended to amuse people unaccustomed to seeing Indian soldiers in a white man's army. When they were formally enlisted, the Pawnees were given regular cavalry uniforms, but no two of the Pawnee uniforms seemed to agree. Buffalo Bill Cody, who first saw them when he was serving as an Army scout, wrote that "some of them had heavy overcoats, others large black hats with all the brass accoutrements attached; some were minus trousers and wore only breechcloths. Part of them had cut the breech of their pantaloons away, leaving only the leggings. Still others had big brass spurs, but wore no boots nor moccasins."

An attempt was made to teach them the manual of arms, but since their language contained no equivalents for such terms as "Present Arms," the English commands were incomprehensible, even if the Indians could have been persuaded that stiff-arming a rifle in front of one's face made any sense. After a while, Frank North refused to continue to try to teach his scouts this drill, but they were still required to perform picket duty. Pawnee sentries did learn to cry "Halt!" but nobody could teach them what to do next. Unable to communicate with the sentry, the person halted could neither advance nor retreat until Frank North could come to the rescue. After the post commander at Fort Kearny was himself caught in this predicament, the Pawnees were permanently relieved of routine guard duty.

But skeptics soon learned that Pawnee scouts were good for something more substantial than spit and polish. Once, when out on a scouting patrol with Luther North and his men, Buffalo Bill Cody pointed to a Pawnee ranging ahead over a grassy tableland and asked if the scout thought he was following a trail left by passing Indians. North said he believed so but confessed that he himself could see no tracks. The two whites rode up to the scout and North told him, "The Long Hair says he doubts if there is a trail." The Indian pointed ahead to a gap in a ridge of hills and said, "Tell

the Long Hair that when we get there he will see." Three miles later in the sandy gap—where anything that passed would have to leave its spoor—they came on a plainly visible trail left by many Indian ponies. At that point Cody graciously acknowledged a superior talent. "Well, I take off my hat to him," he said. "He is the best I ever saw."

The Pawnees' blooding came in the summer of 1865 with General P. Edward Connor's Powder River campaign. In May of that year the Sioux had begun a series of brutal attacks on stagecoach stations and ranches in what is now Nebraska. Connor sent three bodies of troops to scour the country north of the Platte River for the rampaging Indians and to rendezvous on or about September 1 in Montana Territory on the lower Rosebud Creek above its mouth on the Yellowstone. The first element, 1,400 men under Colonel Nelson Cole, moved out from Omaha on the 1st of July. The second prong left Fort Laramie in Dakota Territory on August 5: 600 men under Lieutenant Colonel Samuel Walker. Connor, in overall command, left Fort Laramie in early August with 650 cavalrymen and Frank North's 75 Pawnee scouts.

For decades the Pawnee chiefs had been beseeching the government to protect their reservation from Sioux and Cheyenne raiders. Now the Pawnee scouts were overjoyed at the chance to march against their enemies—especially since they were also getting paid. A civilian traveling with the expedition remembered that the Pawnees were "phenomenal trailers, whom I have known to follow the trail of a band of Sioux for hours after night, overtake them and return to camp with scalps as evidence of their success. No hostile Indian ever approached near enough to even see our camp and succeeded in getting away with his scalp."

In mid-August, while Connor was setting up a base camp on a fork of the Powder in what is now northeastern Wyoming, the Pawnees raised the trail of a party of hostiles and Connor ordered North's whole company to pursue it. The soldiers then learned something about the Indian's attitude toward the white man's cumbersome battle rig. Within moments the Pawnees stripped the saddles from their horses and the cavalry uniforms from their own bodies. Then, rid of the dirty cloth that could be driven into a wound by an arrow or bullet, the Pawnees were ready to put themselves in harm's way.

Baptiste Bayhyalle, a half-Pawnee scout who fought
Cheyennes and Sioux, stands like a schoolmaster behind
fellow scouts, who wear government-issued peace medals.

The war party's tracks revealed the passage of about 40 horses traveling at a good clip. One was dragging a travois, which could mean a wounded man in the group. The scouts were still on the trail when night fell. Half the company, whose mounts were exhausted, were sent back to base camp. Two of the best trackers dismounted to trace the spoor through the darkness on foot while the other Pawnees followed on horseback.

At dawn they spied the smoke of the war party's breakfast fire rising from a copse of timber. The Pawnees pressed on. Then, almost simultaneously, pursuers and pursued sighted one another. North had his men riding in pairs, militarily proper but not Indian-like. Evidently the Cheyenne war party thought it faced white troopers and prepared to fight on the flank of a hill. But there was no mistaking the screeching *ki-de-de-de* of the Pawnee war cry as the scouts charged, slapping their chests. On hearing their attackers and realizing they were not whites but Pawnees, the hostile Indians scattered. In the running battle that followed, the Pawnees killed and scalped 22 men and one wom-

an, losing no men and only four horses in the process. Most Indian tribes rarely took adult male prisoners; once all the able-bodied foe had been dispatched, the Pawnees located and killed the wounded Cheyenne warrior, who had rolled off of his travois and taken refuge in a ravine.

This was the first engagement of Connor's campaign, and a total Pawnee victory. Back in camp, the Pawnees accepted Connor's congratulations and their ensuing scalp dance kept the camp awake nearly all night. The next day two more postbattle customs were carried out. First, Connor told Frank North to divide up the captured horses and property among the Indian scouts. Then, the battle having been such a rousing success, the Pawnees had a name-changing ceremony. The scouts asked Frank North, whose Pawnee name had been *Ski ri taka,* or White Wolf, to choose himself a new name. North said he would prefer they do the honors. So the scouts renamed him *Pani La Shar,* Pawnee Chief, a name given only once before to a non-Indian (it was granted to the explorer John

been but more apprehensive than ever about his fate, Connor sent out a small, fast scouting party—two Pawnees and two soldiers—to continue the search. Two days later, Connor's anxiety prompted him to send another rescue mission: North and a detachment of Pawnees with a squad of cavalry and a pack train of supplies. The first group found Cole and his men, most of them alive but all of them hungry, on September 13 near the Powder River, and told the colonel help was near. Six days later the Pawnee scouts led the second, larger, relief party into Cole's command. North's men immediately stripped the pack saddles from the mules and began distributing rations to the famished soldiers.

The Pawnees in fact had found not one missing command, but two. Cole and Walker had been together for nearly a month, having met on the northwestern fringes of the Black Hills, and Cole had taken command of what now amounted to an army of almost 2,000. For two weeks, as the high-country weather grew increasingly bitter, they had been fighting a series of battles with the elusive hostile bands. On September 9, after hundreds of his horses and mules had frozen to death in a giant blizzard, Cole destroyed his now useless wagons and other material and pushed southward along the Powder in an attempt to avoid Indians and find water and forage. But without the skills to survive in the wintry wilderness, Cole's men were virtually helpless. Some 1,200 of the cavalrymen, their horses dead behind them, were trudging along with feet bundled in gunny sacks and bits of saddle blankets. They were on less than one-quarter rations.

"Fatigue and starvation had done its work on both men and animals," Cole wrote later. "They were unfit to pursue with vigor the savage foe that circled around their starving way." More than a dozen troopers had died from wounds or sickness and the survivors were emaciated. By finding Cole's command when they did, the Pawnee scouts prevented Connor's expedition from ending in wholesale tragedy.

The Pawnees were in and out of the Army 13 years. The unit reached its peak strength in 1867. In March 1867, Frank North was made major of a 200-man battalion of Pawnees, with Luther North as captain of one of its four companies. That summer their primary duty was to guard the surveyors and tracklayers for the

Charles Frémont, for whom the Pawnees had great respect). As was the custom, North then made a gift to them—of the horse he had selected for himself from among those captured in the fight.

By September 1, Connor had had no word from the two prongs of his expedition led by Colonels Cole and Walker. Connor's own progress toward the rendezvous point had been delayed by battles with Sioux and Arapahos, his men were running low on supplies, and he knew the other two units by then would have expended their rations. The general dispatched North, 20 Pawnees and a squad of cavalry to look for the missing elements, holding up his own return to base camp to await news from the scouting party.

Traveling through rain that turned into a raging sleet storm, the scouts came upon alarming signs of disaster: Colonel Cole's deserted campground littered with more than 400 dead cavalry horses and mules. They also found the remains of fires in which saddles and other equipment had been burned. North turned back to report. Now, knowing at least where Cole had once

Union Pacific Railroad along the 300 miles from Plum Creek, Nebraska, to the Laramie plains. "I have never seen more obedient or better behaved troops," said General C. C. Augur later. "They have done most excellent service. They are peculiarly qualified for service on the Plains; unequalled as riders, know the country thoroughly, are hardly ever sick, never desert and are careful of their horses."

Before the Pawnees' arrival, railroad workers were constantly in danger from lightning raids by roving Cheyennes who seemed little deterred by the presence of white troops. But when 150 Cheyennes under Turkey Leg derailed a train a few miles west of Plum Creek and returned to plunder it, the Pawnees were waiting for them. In a 10-mile running fight that lasted all afternoon, the Cheyennes lost 17 men and 35 horses and mules; the Pawnees, although outnumbered 4 to 1, had only two horses killed and two scouts slightly wounded. "It was the only time I ever knew the Cheyennes to lose a fight unless they were greatly outnumbered," Luther North wrote later.

For the most part, the scouts' acts of valor gained scant recognition. The official military description of a battle was usually terse: "Chadron Creek, near Camp Robinson, Neb.—Troops engaged, B, D, E, F, I and M 4th Cavalry; H and L 5th Cavalry; Indian scouts." Luther North in later years contended that neither his brother nor the Pawnee scouts received as much recognition as they deserved. A rare exception occurred after a clash with Cheyennes in what became known as the Battle of Summit Springs, in 1869. But even this attempt to give credit where due—to a Pawnee scout named Traveling Bear—was not totally successful.

Traveling Bear was an extremely powerful, 200-pound warrior. The Norths acknowledged him to be their finest tracker, with an extraordinarily acute sense of location. Once Traveling Bear was among a company of scouts under Luther North when they got lost in a blizzard somewhere near Frenchman Creek in Nebraska. As men and animals stumbled blindly through the gale-driven snow, Traveling Bear appeared alongside North and said he believed that they were close to shelter. He turned to the left, with North and the scouts groping behind him. Within a few minutes they had found a wooded ravine where, with makeshift lodges, wood for campfires and grass for the animals,

FULL-DRESS JACKET

DRESS HELMET

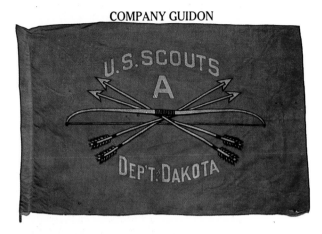

COMPANY GUIDON

A smart look to replace tribal garb

"I think it best that they should have enough distinction to wear a facing of their own," wrote Lieutenant Edward W. Casey in an 1890 letter proposing standard uniforms for Indian scouts. His idea was adopted, and within a year Indian scouts throughout the West were issued specially designed shirts, jackets, overcoats and hats as well as individual company guidons.

With few exceptions the design of the new uniforms was entirely the creation of Lieutenant Casey, who relished symbolism. Crossed arrows, the insignia of the Indian scouts, adorned helmets, campaign hats and guidons. The colors red and white were used to represent the union between Indians and white men.

Casey chose a wide-brimmed campaign hat over the traditional Army cap because "the broad cheekbones and masses of hair of the Indian make a cap a very unbecoming headgear." The guidon (*above*) was designed to carry the letter designation of the company and the name of the military department to which the scouts were attached, but variations were common. Casey's own guidon substituted the inscription "Cheyennes" for the name of the department.

FATIGUE JACKET

FATIGUE HAT WITH INSIGNIA PIN

A Cheyenne troop marked by soldierly discipline

One of the most efficient Indian scout troops—and surely the most disciplined—was the group of Cheyennes led by Lieutenant Edward W. Casey. The small unit, mustered in at a camp near Fort Keogh, Montana *(below),* in 1889, grew to a prized company of 50 expert soldiers. They were distinguished by their conformity of military drills, dress and deco-

rum. "They looked a soldier and felt a soldier and were in fact the finest I had ever seen," wrote artist Frederic Remington on a visit there.

Staunchly faithful to their new allegiance, Casey's scouts were widely praised for their service to the Army in the 1890 campaign against followers of the Ghost Dance religion. "Certainly no loyalty could be more

thoroughly tried than was theirs under those circumstances," wrote Major General O. O. Howard.

In 1891 young Lieutenant Casey, attempting to negotiate peace with the recalcitrant Sioux, was killed by Plenty Horses, a Brule warrior. "The scouts, who were greatly attached to him," wrote Howard, "were much affected by his death."

Flanked by the first members of his Cheyenne scout troop, Lieutenant Edward Casey sits on a log in the company's campground.

they holed up through the storm in reasonable comfort.

On July 11, 1869, during the Battle of Summit Springs, Traveling Bear flushed four Cheyennes who ran into a draw where several others had taken cover. Leaving his winded horse, the big warrior pursued his quarry on foot and alone. A few minutes later he reappeared, carrying four scalps and four revolvers. For this he was cited in a dispatch to Washington; in due course, back came a bronze medal decorating him for action beyond the call of duty. Unfortunately—but not surprisingly—someone had confused one scout with another and the medal was inscribed with a different man's name. With good-humored grace, Traveling Bear accepted it anyway.

In a rambling exchange with a historian long after his scouting days were over, Luther North cited countless

examples of the courage, loyalty and endurance of the scouts he helped command for nearly a decade. Once, after a journey of 80 or 90 miles, North recalled, having eaten nothing all day, "I was so tired that as soon as settled in camp, I wrapped my saddle blanket about my head to keep the mosquitoes from eating up what was left of me, and was soon sound asleep." A couple of hours later, a young scout called Nick Koots—an approximation of the Pawnee word for bird—woke North with the words. "Father, come." (All the scouts called their captains Father and addressed Major Frank North as Grandfather.)

"I got up and followed him to the bank of the river," North later remembered, "where he had a tiny fire. He gave me two hardtack, a slice of bacon and a quart of coffee. I don't recall ever having tasted anything as

In this 1890 letter to the agent at the Pine Ridge reservation, Lieutenant Casey tried to recruit a few Sioux for his Cheyenne scout troop. He wanted some artisans and men "capable of learning the trumpet."

Fort Keogh Montana
May 19 1890

US Indian Agent
Pine Ridge. S Dakota
Sir
I have received from the Hon Commissioner of Indian Affairs the names of certain young Indians living on your reservation and who are considered eligible for enlistment in the Company of Scouts now being organized at this Post, under authority granted me by the Sec of War. The same pay and allowances are allowed these Indians as is allowed the white soldiers, with the addition of 40cts per day for their horse, making their pay about $25⁰⁰ per month. The term of enlistment is for one year. The Troop is to be composed entirely of Cheyenne, but I would take the following young men on account of their occupations. It being my desire to enlist artisans and men capable of learning the trumpet.

The following names have been sent me.

Clayton Brave — Sioux — Band.
Mack Kutepi " Saddler
Frank Jannis " Carpenter.

They could be enlisted at the nearest post, and transportation furnished to this place. Will you be kind enough to let these young men (or other desirable ones) know they have the opportunity to enlist should they so desire. The strength of my Troop is limited to one hundred. I have now about fifty with enlistments each day.

Very Respectfully
Your Obedient Servant
E W Casey
1st 22 Infty
Comdg. Troop US Scouts

---

good, and gobbled it down as fast as possible, asking no questions. When finished, I happened to think that Nick Koots was standing by me, and asked him, 'Where are your crackers and coffee?' He answered, 'I will wait until the wagon train comes.' There was no possibility of the wagon train pulling in before noon the next day, and he had given me the only food he had."

Nick Koots—who could run 50 miles a day, then make camp for North and curry his horse—was also with North and nine other scouts one day when they were surprised by a war party of about 150 Cheyennes. It was below zero, North recalled, "but our horses were in good condition, as we had a big wagon train of grain back with the command. The Cheyenne horses were so thin and weak that I felt we could easily outrun them, and we started toward camp on a gallop."

It soon became evident that they could not outdistance the Cheyennes, so North told his men, who were armed with Spencer carbines, to head for a nearby dry creek where they would make a stand. "When we were about a half mile from the creek my horse slipped on some ice and fell," North recalled. "I landed on my head and was knocked unconscious. Those 10 boys stopped, dismounted and surrounded me with their horses and while nine of them fought the Cheyennes, the other one rubbed snow in my face and finally brought me out of it, but not until four of their horses were killed and three more wounded."

Keeping the Cheyennes at bay until sundown, when they departed, the Pawnees lost no men in the skirmish. (In fact, in all the years the Norths worked with the Pawnees, only one scout was ever killed in battle.)

Surrounded by the other members of an 1874 Army Expedition, Custer's Indian scout Bloody Knife stands in front of the open flap of a tent, while Custer himself reclines on the ground before him.

A Crow scout named Curley, wearing a tribal necklace, claimed to be the only survivor of those who fought under Custer at the Little Bighorn. But other scouts said Custer sent him to safety before the battle.

"My boys were so well mounted," a grateful North remembered, "that they could easily have ridden away if they had been willing to leave me to my fate; but with odds of some 15 to 1 against them, they saved my life—which took cast-iron nerve. Is it any wonder that I have always stood up for the Pawnee scouts?"

The North brothers lived to testify to the loyalty and bravery of the Pawnee scouts, but the Arikaras who scouted for George Armstrong Custer were long the subject of controversy for their role in the disaster on the Little Bighorn. Some critics contended that they abandoned Custer in his hour of need. Their assignment, however, had been to capture horses from the enemy, and they had done so. Ten of the scouts, exceeding their orders, did fight in Major Marcus Reno's skirmish line when Reno encountered the Sioux several miles from the spot where Custer made his stand, and three of the scouts were killed. The Arikaras admired Custer, whom they called "Long Hair" and "Son of the Morning Star," and he in turn admired them and sometimes counseled with them as equals. But in the end, Custer's faith in his scouts faltered, with disastrous consequences. He refused to believe their repeated

warnings about the numbers of Sioux waiting ahead.

Forty-five Indian scouts were on the roster at Fort Abraham Lincoln when Custer's 7th Cavalry set out as part of a force led by General Alfred Terry on May 17, 1876. Of these, 13 were left behind to perform courier service for the expedition, and during the next few weeks three of those with the party would be dispatched on similar assignments. The remaining 29 Indian scouts were with Custer when he ventured up the Little Bighorn. Most were Arikaras, but there were also four Sioux, early defectors from the cause of Sitting Bull, and three mixed-blood scouts.

Later, Custer acquired from another Army detachment six Crow scouts who were totally familiar with the country. They pledged themselves to Custer because, as he wrote his wife on June 21, "they had heard that I never abandoned a trail; that when my food gave out I ate mule. That was the kind of a man they wanted to fight under; they were willing to eat mule, too."

One scout, Bloody Knife, held special status as Custer's favorite, confidante and friend. Bloody Knife was in the war against the Sioux for compelling private reasons. Half Arikara, half Sioux, he had been born in the lodges of the Hunkpapa Sioux and had endured a

In near-perfect formation, impeccably uniformed Cheyenne scouts under Lieutenant Edward Casey await inspection at their camp west of Fort Keogh in Montana.

childhood of humiliating torment, bullied by his young contemporaries as an inferior half-caste. He burned for revenge, particularly against one boyhood tormentor, Gall, now a Sioux war chief.

Once, when Bloody Knife was about 25, he had missed a chance to wreak permanent vengeance on his lifelong enemy. Gall had set up camp just south of Fort Berthold, where Bloody Knife had begun to make a reputation for himself among the white soldiers as a guide, courier and hunter. Bloody Knife led the soldiers in an assault on "the bad Sioux who has been killing these white men found dead and scalped in lonely places along the river." A fierce fight ensued, and in the confused struggle Gall was bayoneted several times.

When Bloody Knife raised his gun to finish the job, the white lieutenant, believing Gall was already dead, struck the gun aside and the weapon discharged into the ground beside Gall's head. The soldiers left the Sioux's body where it lay. But Gall's people bound up his wounds and carried him away. Although he had been stabbed twice in the body and once in the neck, Gall recovered—and he survived to take an active part

in the battle on the Little Bighorn 11 years later.

By 1873, Bloody Knife had served 10 almost continuous six-month hitches as an enlisted Indian scout. That year he performed so well for Custer, on General David S. Stanley's Yellowstone expedition, that Custer persuaded Bloody Knife to transfer into his command. Even on this first venture together Bloody Knife found that Long Hair was not always inclined to follow his scout's advice. When Custer refused to cross the Yellowstone to make a surprise attack on a sizable Sioux village—with the result that the Sioux discovered the soldiers on the trail and in turn made a surprise attack on them—a furious Bloody Knife accused Custer and his troops of being men with "little bird hearts." Nonetheless, it was on this expedition that the scout and the soldier, both willful men, formed the friendship that would end in their deaths when Custer once again disregarded his scout's advice.

Thirty-six years after the Custer massacre, the personal recollections of nine of Long Hair's Ree scouts were gathered together as *The Arikara Narrative* by the North Dakota Historical Society. These bits of

memoir—full of remarkably accurate detail—vividly portray what it was like to be an Indian fighting Indians in a white man's army. The account also presents the singular personality of Custer as he revealed it only to his scouts. A scout named Red Star, who was 18 and a first-time enlistee, remembered that Custer frequently joined the scouts in camp along the trail, talking with them in sign language, which he used reasonably well, or through the interpreter Fred Gerard. Custer was partial to both 17-year-old Young Hawk and his friend Goose because of their youthful good spirits. Young Hawk was a sharpshooter who kept the scouts well supplied with game and could prepare Custer's favorite cut of meat just the way Long Hair liked it. Goose, too, was a hunter and during the expedition earned $128 selling meat to the soldiers.

Soldier, Goose's uncle, was a 44-year-old veteran beginning his 13th tour of duty. Soldier recalled a meeting that he and another scout, Bob-tailed Bull, had with Custer in which Long Hair told them that during the campaign they were to "live and fight together, children of one father and one mother." If any were

killed, Long Hair promised that their families would be provided for. "Their relations will be saddened by their death but there will be some comfort in the pay that the United States government will provide." Bob-tailed Bull answered, "I am glad you say this for I see there is some gain even though I lose my life." Custer then made Bob-tailed Bull a sergeant and named Soldier second-in-command of the scouts.

Custer may have been careful about voicing his ambitions to white men, but not to his scouts. If he had a victory this time, he told them, "even against only five tents of Dakotas"—the Sioux called themselves "Dakotas," meaning "allies"—it would be enough to make him the Great Father in Washington, and if they beat the Sioux, he would take Bloody Knife, and perhaps some of the others, to Washington with him.

On June 22, after a report from Major Reno—whom the Rees called Man-with-the-Dark-Face—that the scouts had found a Sioux trail on Rosebud Creek, Custer prepared to lead his command in pursuit. But first he sent Fred Gerard to advise the Rees that they would be in a fight soon and he wished them to sing their death songs. "Custer had a heart like an Indian," Red Star recalled. "If we ever left out one thing in our ceremonies he always suggested it to us. We got on our horses and rode around, singing the songs. Then we fell in behind Custer and marched on."

The whole valley of the Rosebud was "scratched up by trailing lodge poles," wrote Lieutenant George D. Wallace afterward, and all the signs indicated large numbers of Sioux. On June 24 the scouts led the command to an abandoned Sioux camp where, inside the remains of a large sun-dance lodge, they found a white man's scalp and evidence that the Sioux had made medicine there. "The sand had been arranged and smoothed," Red Star recalled, "and pictures had been drawn." The four Sioux scouts with Custer said this showed the enemy knew of the Army's presence.

As they found more old campgrounds—large ones, Red Star said, "one-half to one-third of a mile across"—the scouts read signs that were increasingly ominous. Two buffalo skulls, those of a bull and a cow, lay facing each other on opposite sides of a pile of stones. A stick planted next to the bull slanted toward the cow. To the Rees this meant that when the soldiers came, the Sioux would fight like bulls and the whites would run like cows. In a sweat lodge Young Hawk saw three red stones in a row, a sign that the Great Spirit had promised victory to the Sioux.

That night Custer and some of the other officers visited the scouts' camp and Gerard translated Long Hair's words as they stood around the fire: "My only intention in bringing these people to battle," Custer said, extending his arms to the scouts, "is to have them go and take many horses away from the Sioux." Nothing would cripple the Dakotas more than to have their horses captured, leaving them without fresh mounts either for renewed attack or for escape. Sheridan had said: "A Sioux on foot is a Sioux warrior no longer."

By daybreak on June 25, a scouting party that had been out all night sighted the smoke of the Dakota village on the Little Bighorn River, and Red Star and another scout were sent back to inform Custer. As Red Star approached the camp, he began to zigzag his horse, a signal that he had found the enemy.

Around 8 a.m., just before the troops were ready to march, Custer had a powwow with his scouts. "The General wore a serious expression and was apparently abstracted," wrote one of his lieutenants, referring to Custer by his Civil War brevetted title rather than his current rank of lieutenant colonel. "The scouts were doing the talking and seemed nervous and disturbed. Finally Bloody Knife made a remark that recalled the General from his reverie, and he asked in his usual quick, brusque manner, 'What's that he says!' The interpreter replied: 'He says we'll find enough Sioux to keep us fighting two or three days.' The General smiled and remarked, 'I guess we'll get through with them in one day.' "

The rest of that one day was vivid to the Ree scouts, even 36 years later. When Custer divided his command, he assigned all the Rees to Reno, who was to move down the Little Bighorn toward the Indian encampment while Custer circled around to attack from the east. Fully expecting to die at 17, Young Hawk prepared himself to be scalped by the Sioux. He loosened his hair and rebraided it with eagle feathers, far forward on his head. Before Reno encountered the enemy, 18 of the scouts rode off to capture herds of Sioux horses seen nearby. Young Hawk was among those who stayed with Reno's command as it crossed the Little Bighorn to confront the Sioux.

When Reno formed his men into a skirmish line, 10 scouts took places on the left flank, although they had not been ordered to fight. Young Hawk saw, far to the left of the line and nearest a ridge where the Dakotas were massing, the sergeant Bob-tailed Bull. Later, in the confusion of battle, a scout named Red Bear saw Bob-tailed Bull's horse—a big gentle pinto, so tame that the scout had never had to tie him up in camp—come crashing through some bushes near the river. "The reins and rope were flying, and the tail and mane floating in the wind. The horse was much frightened and ran snorting past." Red Bear saw the saddle, a wooden frame covered with rawhide, and it was "all bloody in front." Months later, the pinto found his way back to the Ree village at Fort Berthold nearly 300 miles away. The people called him Famous War Horse after that and made a war song in his honor.

The fight was just beginning when Young Hawk saw Bloody Knife alive for the last time. "He came right toward me," Young Hawk recalled, "and I noticed his dress. He had on the black handkerchief with blue stars on it given him by Custer. He wore a bear's

claw with a clam shell on it." Bloody Knife told Young Hawk, "What Custer has ordered about the Sioux horses is being done, the horses are being taken away." Then, Young Hawk remembered, Bloody Knife returned to the line and took his stand next to Little Brave, Bob-tailed Bull's brother. Little Brave, Bob-tailed Bull and Bloody Knife were the three scouts who gave their lives at the Little Bighorn.

When the Sioux and Cheyenne forces proved overwhelming, Reno panicked and began a precipitate retreat. Young Hawk got back across the river, his horse struggling hard in deep water. He took cover in a thick grove of trees with several other scouts, including Goose and Forked Horn, an old veteran. The Sioux kept firing at them and soon Goose called out that he was wounded. "When I heard this," Young Hawk remembered, "my heart did not tremble with fear, but I made up my mind I would die this day." He propped Goose against a tree; then he stripped off his shirt and prepared to fight. Another scout, Strikes Enemy, was hit and Young Hawk helped him to the same tree where he had left Goose. "The sight of the wounded

men gave me queer feelings," Young Hawk recalled. "I did not want to see them mutilated, so I decided to get killed myself at the edge of the timber.

"I then crawled out and stood up and saw all in front of me Sioux warriors kneeling ready to shoot. I fired at them and received a volley, but was not hit." Still determined to die, Young Hawk stood up again and once more was left miraculously unscathed. This performance drew a scolding from Forked Horn, who said, "Don't you do so again. This is not the way to fight at all, to show yourself as a mark." Momentarily this advice calmed Young Hawk, but when a Sioux on a gray horse came near him, he again threw caution aside and jumped up. He had to fire twice before he killed the enemy warrior. Then he killed the horse and gave the Arikara yell for a dead enemy. Soon after, Young Hawk killed another Sioux and jumped up to give the death shout again.

Around noon, Young Hawk remembered, he saw the Dakotas riding away downstream and he thought they must be going to counter Long Hair's attack on their camp. "After the shooting slackened," he said, "I

A notable Cheyenne chief who led his forces to victory at the Little Bighorn, then became an Army scout one year later, Two Moons sits at Fort Keogh holding an eagle wing, a symbol of his tribal rank.

soldier, carrying a scalp he had found mounted on a stick, asked Young Hawk if this was a Dakota scalp. Young Hawk took one look and recognized the gray streaked hair of Bloody Knife.

After Custer's defeat the Army stepped up its efforts to subjugate the Plains Indians, and as the white juggernaut ground down one hostile camp after another, a subtle but profound change crept into the Army's Indian scout force. No longer was it simply Pawnee, Arikara, Shoshoni or Crow coveting Sioux or Cheyenne scalps; now there were scouts, whose own bands had been defeated, fighting against their tribal brothers. Some needed the money to keep their families alive. For others, scouting for the Army was a way to continue functioning as self-respecting warriors instead of accepting the subdued existence of reservation Indians. By the time Colonel Ranald Mackenzie attacked the Cheyenne village of Chief Dull Knife on the Powder River a few months after the Custer massacre, 10 Cheyennes had joined the 350 Indian scouts and allies he had with him.

Dull Knife's Cheyennes had scouts of their own and knew the bluecoats were coming. They also knew Mackenzie had Cheyenne scouts with him. Two generations later the Cheyenne historian John Stands in Timber drew on the memories of his grandmother and other elders to recall what Dull Knife's people thought of this treachery.

When the bluecoats drove them out of their lodges, Stands in Timber wrote, the Cheyennes gathered on the rimrock above and, shivering in the cold, watched all their food and shelter for the winter "go up in a great blaze of fire. That was a time they used the Sacred Arrows. The women too came out on top, just like the men, and they opened the arrows and laid them facing the soldiers. Then they all lined up while the Arrow Priest sang a song, and when he gave a signal they cried out and stamped the ground with their feet. They did that four times. That was why all the Cheyennes on the other side against them died off."

But then something strange occurred, an act of mercy by one of the traitors upon whom they had placed the tribe's curse. As the soldiers were leaving, one of the Army's Cheyenne scouts, named Crow, shouted across to the refugees that the scouts had hidden a

stood up and looked around. On the ridge above me I saw a United States flag." In this lull, Forked Horn said to Young Hawk, "My grandson, you have shown yourself the bravest. The flag up there shows where the pack-train is which we were to meet and now we must try to reach it." With some difficulty they managed to put the two wounded scouts on horseback. Then, so that the soldiers would not mistake them for Sioux, Young Hawk tied his white handkerchief to a stick and they started down the stream.

But as they began climbing the slope toward the remnant's of Reno's command, they sighted Dakotas coming back over the ridge. The other scouts turned back down the hill, but Young Hawk rode for his life along the ridge toward the soldiers. The whites fired over his head at the pursuing Dakotas while the Dakotas fired at him. Young Hawk's horse was shot out from under him just before he reached camp, but he scrambled up, clutching his white flag, and made it to safety on foot.

Two days later Young Hawk was in the deserted Sioux camp looking for abandoned meat supplies. A

cache of ammunition for them. "And they did find a lot
of shells there afterwards, and they took them along,"
Stands in Timber recorded.

The first large-scale surrender of Cheyennes occurred in 1877, when General Nelson Miles and his
white civilian scout named Johnnie "Big Leggins" Bruguier talked Chief Two Moons into giving up. Almost
immediately several of Two Moons's warriors signed
up as Army scouts. This metamorphosis took place
when Two Moons wanted to leave Fort Keogh on the
Tongue River to bring in the rest of the tribe. Miles
insisted that some hostages remain behind. "Two
Moons called for volunteers," wrote Stands in Timber,
"but White Bull was the only one who would stay.
That afternoon Big Leggins took White Bull out and
dressed him in a soldier's uniform. When he came back
the others were surprised. They thought if he was in
uniform he might be safe after all, and two or three
others volunteered then to stay with him. They all got
uniforms, too."

Later, when the rest of Two Moons's people came
in, their guns and horses were confiscated. But soon the
warriors were fighting again, this time for the Army.
The irony of it was plain to one scout who later told an
interviewer, "My friend, I was a prisoner of war for four
years, and all the time was fighting for the man who had
captured me." That had been General Miles.

Though defeated and resigned to the white man's
road, these new Army scouts were anything but abject.
Two Moons did not hesitate to complain when the
white man's way of warfare seemed ridiculous. Miles
wanted to put white officers in charge of the scouts,
Stands in Timber wrote, but "Two Moons did not like
it. He told Miles that Indians did not need officers.
Every man fought for himself and counted his own
coups, and the chiefs stayed behind the lines. 'I am glad
to hear your rules of fighting,' Miles said. 'But I think
now you will need an officer and I want you to stay
near him in battle.'

"So they started out, crossing the river on a boat and
marching west for several days," Stands in Timber
wrote. "Then Miles sent them out ahead with their
lunches and canteens of water, and Two Moons did
not like that either. 'The white man eats and drinks all

the time,' he said. 'The Indian drinks when he finds water and eats when he kills game.' But they rode along with their officer and soon scattered out, looking for the Nez Percés."

This was in September 1877. The Nez Percés, trying desperately to escape being sent to a reservation, were fighting a valiant rear-guard action across Montana Territory when Miles set out to intercept them before they could cross the Canadian border. In his memoirs General Miles said that when he closed in on the Nez Percés at Bear Paw Mountain north of the Yellowstone, the Cheyenne scouts stripped, painted, donned their feather regalia and appeared "perfectly wild with delight" at the prospect of battle.

But in the midst of the fight the newly recruited Indian scouts seemed to lose their bloodthirstiness. A Cheyenne scout named High Wolf, who had heard Miles say that he would rather take the Nez Percés prisoner than kill them, signed to two enemy warriors to bring their leaders to talk of surrender. The Nez Percé chiefs appeared and there on the battlefield took

part in an impromptu peace conference with a group of the Cheyenne scouts. The Nez Percés agreed to discuss surrender terms with General Miles. When High Wolf rode to headquarters to report this, Miles lost his temper and berated the Indian for talking to the enemy. Cheyenne tribal elders later recalled that the general's rebuke had made High Wolf so furious that he grabbed Miles's collar and said, "You told us to try to get these people to come in and not be harmed. Why don't you talk to them?"

Miles did talk to the Nez Percés and they surrendered. Although the general did not mention the Cheyenne scouts' diplomatic efforts in his memoirs, he did record their effective role in the battle: "They maintained their position with remarkable fortitude and discharged all the duties required of them during the five days' siege. At its close I directed the officer in charge of the Nez Percé herd to give each of them five ponies as a reward for their gallant service."

By the end of the 1870s, the long, agonizing struggle seemed to be winding down. Sitting Bull held out

traditional Ghost Dance, the mystical ceremony that rallied Plains warriors with promises of freedom from the white man's domination.

for a time, but at last he too surrendered in 1881, and the Plains were relatively calm for several years. Hunger, disease, death and broken promises, however, led reservation-bound tribesmen to grow increasingly unhappy and angry. "Sullenness and gloom began to gather, especially among the heathen and wilder Indians," testified an Episcopal missionary among the Sioux. "A marked discontent amounting almost to despair prevailed in many quarters."

By 1890 many of the Sioux on the reservations in the Dakotas were ready for some kind of salvation or messiah—and he came along, in the form of a Paiute mystic named Wovoka who preached something called the Ghost Dance religion. Although Wovoka advocated nonviolence, his dreams told him that the Indian dead would arise and sweep the white man from the earth. The day of reckoning would come in the spring of 1891, but meanwhile disciples could visit the new paradise by dancing the Ghost Dance. The excitement and hysteria created during these dances, and the incessant beating of the dance drums, convinced

panicked white settlers that the Indians were about to launch a last general bloodbath against them.

The Army was called out and along with it the Indian scouts. In the ensuing conflict, the scout units most intimately involved were 30 Oglala Sioux under the command of Lieutenant Charles Taylor from the Pine Ridge Agency in South Dakota and 40 Cheyennes under Lieutenant Edward Casey from Fort Keogh in Montana. Since 1889 Casey had forged his Cheyennes into a crack outfit, drilled and disciplined. Yet, in the final stages of the so-called Sioux uprising these scouts would prove to be valuable not so much for their military discipline as for their native powers of persuasion. Casey's scouts talked almost every day with warriors from the last camp of the Ghost Dancers, defiant young men led by the Oglala Sioux, Kicking Bear. Kicking Bear bristled at the very word surrender, but as the Cheyenne scouts continued to point out the futility of more fighting, there eventually were so many defections from the hostile camp that on January 16, 1891, Kicking Bear himself finally entered the Pine

Once first sergeant of the Indian scouts serving under Lieutenant Charles Taylor, Standing Soldier is shown here wearing the silver badge of his new position—as a policeman on the Pine Ridge reservation.

Ridge Agency and laid his gun at General Miles's feet.

But perhaps the greatest achievement of an Indian scout during this period was accomplished even before Kicking Bear yielded. It was the work of one of Lieutenant Taylor's Oglala Sioux scouts, Standing Soldier, who won success by exercising compassion and sound judgment rather than force. Standing Soldier was a man of sense and substance, first sergeant of Taylor's scouts and later a judge for many years on the reservation Indian court. On Christmas Day, 1890, Taylor sent Standing Soldier and 15 of his scouts to help search for a band of Miniconjou Sioux led by Big Foot. General Miles was afraid that Big Foot was on his way to join the Ghost Dance holdouts under Kicking Bear. Two days later Standing Soldier found a group of 73 Indians, but they were Hunkpapa, not Miniconjou. They were Sitting Bull's people, they said, and had fled Standing Rock Agency nearly two weeks before when Sitting Bull had been killed while being arrested.

Standing Soldier told the frightened Hunkpapas that he wished to conduct them to safety. They said

they were hungry. Standing Soldier sent his scouts to kill some cattle he had seen running loose, and his men divided what tobacco they had with the fugitives. The Hunkpapas, reassured, agreed to go with the scouts.

The next day they came across Big Foot's trail. Standing Soldier sent scouts ahead to find Big Foot and ask the Miniconjou to wait, saying they would all go to the agency together. These messengers never reached Big Foot, at least not in time. The next day, December 29, Standing Soldier and his retinue of refugees reached Wounded Knee and heard gunfire from over some nearby hills. Standing Soldier suspected a battle was taking place, but the scout—worried that the fugitives would panic and attack him and his men—convinced the Hunkpapas that the shots were just a silly bluecoat tradition, soldiers saluting their officers with guns.

That afternoon a scout arrived with word of what had happened. In an encounter that would be remembered as the Battle of Wounded Knee, Big Foot's band had been wiped out; 146 Sioux and 25 soldiers had been killed in the fighting. The scout also brought orders for Standing Soldier to disarm the Hunkpapas and break up their guns. Standing Soldier, who considered the order too ridiculous even to contemplate, sent the scout back to Pine Ridge with word he was bringing the Hunkpapas in and the commander could disarm them himself if he wanted to. Meanwhile, Standing Soldier suggested, his charges needed food and tobacco, being weary and hungry as well as nervous. Someone back at headquarters saw the wisdom in this and sent out 30 scouts with supplies for the tired party.

At last, half a mile short of Pine Ridge Agency, Standing Soldier brought his ragged column to a halt. He raised his right hand. "God, Our Father," he said, addressing his remarks to the white man's deity, "help us that we may make peace and friendship tonight." Then, addressing his charges directly, he urged them to be at peace with the whites, adding that this hope was the reason the Oglala scouts had taken so much trouble to bring them, Hunkpapas, to safety. Finally he said the Hunkpapa warriors must show their good intentions by turning their rifles over to their women to carry into the agency. And so, with the scouts marching on either side and at the rear of the column, Standing Soldier brought the Hunkpapas safely and sensibly into camp.

From war-making scouts to peace-keeping policemen

As the tribes of the Plains gradually gave up fighting and moved to reservations, the government's need for Indian scouts to search out hostiles was in part replaced by a new requirement for Indian police forces.

Adjustment to reservation life was difficult for former warriors. Disorderly conduct, horse theft, bootlegging and arms smuggling were among the many law-enforcement problems that faced agency supervisors. Since the presence of armed white soldiers only increased the tensions, Indians were needed to police other Indians. No better recruits could be found than the tried and true Indian scouts who had served with the U.S. Army.

At some agencies, retired scouts were employed and at others whole troops of still-active scouts simply doubled as policemen. The transition was an easy one, for the duties of protecting property, bringing in renegades, guarding rations and—in some sad instances—informing on friends and relatives were already familiar chores to scouts.

Resolute fidelity to the white man's cause was demanded even when that cause tragically conflicted with sacred ties. "I have killed my own chief, my own brother," cried one policeman after a shoot-out. "He tried to kill a white man so we had to kill him."

Congress authorized the use of Indian police as an experiment in 1878, but in less than two years the forces were judged a "necessity" by the Commissioner of Indian Affairs. By 1890 almost every reservation had its own Indian constabulary.

The service rendered by the police was invaluable to the whites. "It would be impracticable and probably impossible to conduct this agency without this organization," wrote one agent of his force. Said another: "They are not perfect but we could not get along without them at all."

Indian police at the Standing Rock reservation headquarters in North Dakota form up behind Sergeant Red Tomahawk *(center)*.

Maj John Dunlop

Pictures that "tie memory to the stake of truth"

Squint-Eye

While the Army's Indian scouts normally used their superb powers of observation in tracking and fighting, some of them also employed the same keen-eyed attention to detail for artistic purposes, translating what they saw into colorful pictorial histories of their experiences. The subject matter—life in the forts, white soldiers, recent battles—was contemporary, but the tradition in which the scouts painted was centuries old.

Having no written languages, Indians since prehistoric times had created pictures to memorialize their hunts, wars, rituals, calamities and successes. Such painting was important work. As the Sioux tribal elders put it, "the picture is the rope that ties memory solidly to the stake of truth." Paintings had to be objective—they were open to challenge by anyone depicted in them—but they were commonly emblematic rather than realistic. Even though warriors normally fought only in breechcloths, tribal historians customarily pictured them in full dress regalia, their war bonnets, shields and other distinctive personal gear serving to identify them.

The coming of the white man caused profound changes in Indian art. By the time the scouts produced these pictures, Indian artists were using pens, pencils, crayons and brushes instead of traditional bone implements and sharpened sticks. And the scouts painted on paper and cloth instead of rocks, lodge walls and buffalo hides. But their work helped to keep alive the tradition of recording history in pictures, and provided for posterity a fascinating scout's-eye view of events of the era.

Squint-Eye, a scout sergeant, painted himself and Major John Dunlop hunting a bobcat in 1887. The artist depicted himself in uniform to ensure identification, but he probably did not wear it while hunting.

Chief Crazy Horse is bayoneted by a soldier at Fort Robinson, Nebraska, in 1877. This watercolor by Sioux scout

Saiji. Ogue Spa.
— Tankala. ecigapi

(okwcka tipi)

a mazawakon
ekta gesipi
ktepi keyapi.

Amos Bad Heart Bull suggests the unresisting chief was murdered, but other Indians said he struggled with his captors.

Kicking Bear.,

Oklala

Grant Sh

Oklala

In this Amos Bad Heart Bull painting, an Oglala Sioux scout named Grant Short Bull mediates between Kicking Bear and General Miles

Bull. major General, Nelson. a. miles

during the Ghost Dance troubles of 1890. The conciliatory gesture of Short Bull is symbolic of the function of the scouts as peacemakers.

Crow scout White Swan commemorated the Battle of the Little Bighorn on this canvas. The incidents depicted are scattered haphazardly,

Custer, with saber in hand (above), orders his bugler to sound assembly before the battle begins. Below Custer is a later event: an officer rescues White Swan, who has been shot through the hip.

Sitting high atop a stylized mountain before the battle, White Swan (above) uses a telescope to scout the camp of the hostile Sioux. The tipis of the encampment appear in the painting's upper left corner.

without regard to chronological sequence. The stories behind several of the vignettes have been lost. Some that are known are described below.

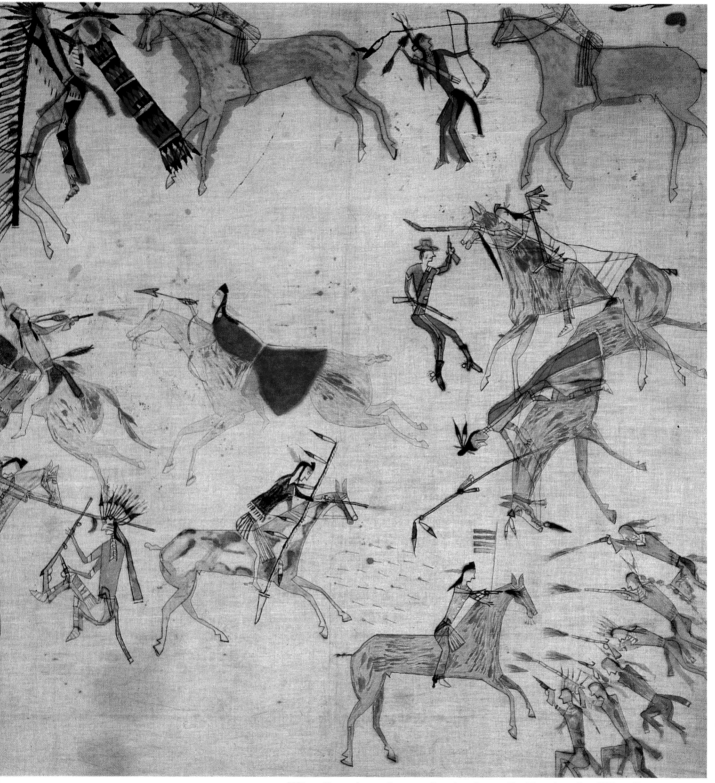

White Swan (in red cape, above), who has gone with Major Marcus Reno's detachment to attack from the south, pursues Sitting Bull's nephew, One Bull, who is riding double with a wounded friend.

On Reno's order, White Swan attempts to head off the panicky flight of a cowardly private (in uniform, above). The soldier resists, giving the scout a blow to the head that rendered him deaf for life.

5 | When Apache hunted Apache

"Nothing will demoralize the hostiles so much as to know their own people are fighting in the opposite ranks," predicted General George Crook when he was given permission to hire Apache scouts to track down and bring in fellow Apaches. "Putting a rogue to catch a rogue" is the way a Prescott, Arizona, newspaper defined Crook's strategy.

Many, including some of the Army's top brass, were highly dubious: why expect Apaches to use weapons against their own kind when they could as easily turn them on those who issued them? Apaches, the scourge of the Southwest border country that is now Arizona and New Mexico, were famous for their treachery.

Yet somehow Crook brought it off. Weaned from their outlaw status and given the proud title of scouts, Apaches proved as deadly to their kith and kin as they had been to whites. Sometimes their loyalty to the Army bordered on fanaticism. A scout named Dutchy is said to have gone out after his own father, who had killed a white man, and returned with the old man's head in a sack.

During the 1872-1874 campaigns in central Arizona, Army units without Indian scouts captured or killed fewer than 20 elusive hostiles, while the Apache scouts killed 272 of their own people and captured another 313. Such bizarre statistics speak volumes about the importance of the scouts in the taming of the Southwest.

The stresses on the loyalties of Apache scouts are dramatized in this painting of scouts obliged to arrest a fellow Apache on suspicion of murder. In the actual incident the arrested man proved to be innocent; the real culprit was never caught.

149

The unlikely scouts who subdued their own people

Snow fell heavily in the high country around Turret Peak, southeast of Prescott in Arizona Territory during the night of December 2, 1873. Fourteen Apache scouts and a Mexican tracker under Chief of Scouts Al Sieber, plus a handful of U.S. Cavalry troopers, plodded through snow that already lay two feet deep on the level. No doubt they would have preferred to stop for the night, but Lieutenant Walter Schuyler, the officer in charge, was after renegade Apaches who had fled their reservation, and would not hear of a halt. Instead Schuyler ordered his men off their horses and up a "very steep Mt. on the south of E. Fork," a prominent stream in the area. "Very difficult ascent," noted Schuyler in his log.

At the summit, the lieutenant dispatched some of his scouts to reconnoiter. They found nothing in the moonlit snowscape and Schuyler cautiously moved his small force three miles farther along the mountain. The Apache scouts went out again, this time spotting a campfire in the gloom one half mile ahead.

At this news, Schuyler halted his column for the night, but the men got no rest. To keep from freezing, they marched in circles—fires would have given them away to their quarry—and warmed their rifles inside their clothing so that fingers would not freeze to triggers when the action started. At daybreak, scouts and soldiers crept toward the sleeping Indians' brush huts, known as wickiups, "got within 20 yards," according to Schuyler's report, "and woke them up firing into the houses." Fifteen men and women died inside the huts or nearby; two men and a woman escaped into the blizzard. Schuyler's men emerged from the engagement

unscathed, although one Apache scout suffered the anguish of finding his mother among the slain Indians. So that the scout might mourn his mother, Schuyler laid over two more days on the frozen peak. Then his men, cold and wet, slithered down the mountain and rode off in search of more Indians.

This engagement and the terrain where it occurred typify most of the battles fought by the United States Army between 1872 and 1886 to force Apache Indians onto reservations and keep them there. The conflict raged sporadically across some of the most desolate and inaccessible parts of North America in what is now Arizona, New Mexico and the northern extremes of Sonora and Chihuahua in Mexico. This region—labeled Apachería on the maps of Mexico's Spanish rulers—is so arid and precipitously tilted on its own sharp edges that, a local newspaper commented, "it looks as though during the Creation it had been God's workshop, and the scraps had never been swept." Even in winter, temperatures often reached 90° at noon, although heavy snows might clog the high plateaus and mountain passes. During the summer, temperatures of 120° were not uncommon.

In most instances, the war was prosecuted by small, mobile units like Lieutenant Schuyler's, guided by scouts who, like their quarry, were Apaches. Often they all but exhausted themselves sneaking into position for surprise attacks on small bands of hostiles. In these indiscriminate battles, Indian women and children frequently were killed or wounded. And there was always the chance that scouts or renegades might kill their friends or relatives on the opposite side of a battle.

Pitting Apache against Apache was not a completely new idea. As early as 1786, the Spanish rulers of Mexico had used Chiricahua and Mimbres Apaches—bands that would later become the nemeses of white settlers in Arizona and New Mexico—as scouts

In this seemingly fraternal group of Apaches, only the ankle chains distinguish the two outlaws, soon to be hanged, from the Army scouts holding them prisoner.

against other Apaches. Subsequently, individual members of Apache bands that had not been goaded into war with whites saw intermittent employment as scouts by the U.S. Army. But it remained for General George Crook, often called the most successful Indian fighter the Army ever produced—he would later enhance his reputation on the Great Plains, working with both white and Indian scouts—to recruit whole companies of Apache scouts and to forge them into tracking and fighting units that would eventually subdue the Apache renegades who baffled the white army.

Sending Apache against Apache would seem an invitation to treachery. Indeed, one Apache scout was shot while deserting in the heat of battle; he had seen his father and brother on the other side of the fight. But there were countervailing examples of loyalty. One Apache scout killed another who, the first had learned, was plotting to murder a white Indian agent; the scouts

were brothers. And except for one incident in 1881 — when a few scouts rebelled at the arrest of a popular Apache medicine man—the Indians never turned against the white soldiers with whom they served for nearly eight decades.

When Crook took command in Arizona in 1871, a triangular struggle was in progress with the U.S. Army at one corner, civilian settlers at another and Apache Indians at the third. The Apaches were a loosely knit nation. Their several tribes—Chiricahua, Mimbres, Tonto, Warm Springs, Ariraipa, White Mountain and others—maintained only tenuous connections, occasionally uniting briefly against an outside enemy. They had no friends; their very name derives from a Zuñi word, *apachu,* meaning enemy. Forged in the image of their own harsh land, the Apaches had become human predators, who lived on what they stole from neighboring tribes—Pimas, Zuñis, Maricopas, Navajos—and Mexicans. For generations, the Apaches had plundered from Mexicans, stealing their animals, sacking their towns, killing men and enslaving women and children. Whole regions of north Mexico were desolated and depopulated by Apache depredations. When Americans began settling in Arizona and New Mexico, they too became targets for Apache plundering.

The Army had responded with a policy of extermination, which failed to stop Apache raids and made hostiles even more unruly. So the generals adopted a new program of setting up reservations where peaceful Indians could be fed, protected and policed.

By the summer of 1871, the reservation program was showing signs of success: more than 3,500 Apaches—about half the total—had voluntarily settled on reservations to avoid starvation. But there remained on the loose a large number of hostile Apaches.

Among the settlers there was almost universal disapproval of the reservation plan. Most whites felt that the only certain way to stop Apache raids was to kill all Apaches. Moreover, businessmen in Tucson made their living by supplying the Army and they resisted any peace program that would lead to a reduction in military strength and expenditures in Arizona.

General Crook arrived in Tucson, Arizona Territory, without fanfare late in June 1871. He summoned the officers of his command to report in detail the condition

of each unit. From these officers Crook chose two aides, one of whom was Lieutenant John G. Bourke, an acute observer who in 1891 published a perceptive account of his years with Crook. Wrote Bourke of his commander's zeal in his new assignment, "General Crook was not the man to delay. We were on our way to Fort Bowie, in the eastern section of Arizona, at six o'clock in the morning of July 11, 1871." Crook headed five companies of cavalry and a detachment of scouts; his mission was to explore the countryside, toughen his troops and catch some Apaches if he could.

The scouts for this march—a trek of 675 miles that ended at Fort Apache, a post south of the White Mountains near the border between Arizona and New Mexico—were a motley crew of whoever was on hand. There were a few Opata, Navajo, Yaqui and Pueblo Indians as well as one or two "tame" Apaches. There were half-breeds, Americans and 50 Mexicans hired on the recommendation of the territorial Governor, Anson Safford. It was Safford's opinion that "Mexicans were the solution of the 'Apache Problem,' that they knew the country, the habits and mode of Indian warfare, that they could go inside an Apache and turn him wrong side out."

But not on this march. Crook saw only a handful of Indians, and they eluded him. Then one of his officers bungled the single chance to intercept an Apache raiding party, which had given itself away by a dust cloud in the distance. Crook wanted troops under Captain Alexander Moore to ambush the hostiles at a spring toward which the scouts thought the raiders were headed. But Moore foolishly—Crook thought cowardly—let the Apaches see his column, and this display frightened the Indians away.

General Crook's intuition was right: an ambush was the correct tactic to employ. Apaches, unless they were cornered, would never attack or stand and fight if they perceived themselves to be at even the slightest disadvantage. It was not that they were fainthearts. As Bourke explained, "The Apache has no false ideas about courage. He would prefer to skulk like a coyote for hours, and then kill his enemy, or capture his herd, rather than, by injudicious exposure, receive a wound. But he is no coward; on the contrary he is entitled to rank among the bravest. The precautions taken for his safety prove that he is an exceptionally skillful soldier."

Well aware of Apache infamy, Crook found it "difficult to realize that there could be any of the Apache tribe who were friendly to anybody," as he wrote many years later. Nevertheless, he began recruiting Apache scouts almost as soon as he arrived at Fort Apache. Crook was convinced that only with the aid of friendly Apaches would he be able to bring recalcitrant Indians onto reservations and end bloodshed between whites and Apaches. In his 1871 annual report, Crook wrote that recruiting the scouts was "really the entering wedge in solution of this Apache question."

Crook recalled in his memoirs only the fact that he had lengthy discussions with the Indians, members of

both the Coyotero and White Mountain Apache tribes. But Bourke, his aide, reported the talks in a considerable amount of detail.

Crook told the Indians that a rapidly increasing white population would put an end to their existence as hunters. They would be much more content as farmers on reservations where the Army could protect them against predatory whites. For this plan to succeed, however, all Indians had to come onto reservations. Crook explained that he hoped to avoid war, but that after granting a reasonable grace period, "he intended to start out in person and see to it that the last man returned to the Reservations or died in the mountains."

During these conferences, Crook argued that friendly Apaches ought to help round up resisters, if that course became necessary. He said that "he should expect the good men to aid him in running down the bad ones. That was the way the white people did; if there were bad men in a certain neighborhood, all the law-abiding citizens turned out to assist the officers of the law in arresting and punishing those who would not behave themselves. He hoped that the Apaches would see that it was their duty to do the same." Influenced by Crook's persuasiveness—and also to some extent by the prospect of eating regular meals and getting pay as members of the U.S. Army—a small group of Coyo-

The sad saga of a scout who turned outlaw

One of the most tragic stories of the Indian wars is that of a scout called the Apache Kid. His talents and loyalty during the campaigns against Geronimo earned him the trust of the Army and the rank of first sergeant. But the Kid died a fugitive, sought by the troops he had served so well.

Born in the 1860s, he was befriended by the famed chief of scouts Al Sieber, who may have given him the nickname "Kid"—newspapers later made it "the Apache Kid." During a brief absence from the San Carlos Indian Agency, in the spring of 1887, Sieber left the Kid in charge of the scout unit. Investigating an Apache drinking spree, the Kid found that his father had been killed by a drunken Indian. The culprit already had been slain, but the Kid was not satisfied. With some scouts, he killed another Indian who may have had a hand in the murder.

When Sieber learned of the incident, the errant scouts were ordered to the guardhouse. Suddenly, an onlooking Indian opened fire. Sieber was severely wounded, and the Kid fled with his companions. The fugitives surrendered several weeks later. They were convicted and sent to prison; the Kid drew a seven-year term.

On their way to the jail, the prisoners overpowered their guards and escaped. Most were soon killed or captured, but the Kid eluded all pursuers, even the scouts with whom he used to track other outlaws. For years he remained a renegade with a $5,000 price on his head, and his random killings terrorized the Arizona countryside. Finally, in 1894, an Apache woman reported that she had recently left the Apache Kid dying, probably from tuberculosis, in the craggy Sierra Madre. The reward was withdrawn, but the once-loyal scout's body was never found.

The Apache Kid (*above, center*)—then a loyal servant of the Army—and two fellow scouts stand by their wickiups. Before long, the Kid was a hunted renegade.

Al Sieber (*left*), shot in the left foot, was on crutches long after the San Carlos affair. Sieber bitterly blamed the Kid for his wound and testified against him in court.

Uniformed Indian scouts (*right*) search for the trail of the Apache Kid. The Kid told an Indian boy a scout once passed by so close that the Kid could have touched him.

tero and White Mountain Apaches enlisted as scouts.

As a test, some of the Apache scouts were ordered to accompany Captain Guy Henry, three companies of cavalry and the Mexican scouts on a scouting expedition toward Fort McDowell, west of Fort Apache. The column was to attack whatever hostile Indians the scouts could find. In Crook's report of the mission, he remarked that soldiers teamed with Apache scouts exceeded Henry's "most sanguine expectations." He said the Indians were invaluable, enabling him to "kill seven warriors and take 11 women prisoners, under the most unfavorable circumstances."

While the scouts led Captain Henry to his success, Crook set off for Fort Verde on the Verde River in central Arizona, the site of another collection of friendly Indians, where he hoped to recruit more scouts. He wanted to field at least five scouting parties like Captain Henry's. They would operate simultaneously to drive onto the reservations the 500 to 700 hostiles that Crook estimated were hiding in the mountains.

But when Crook reached Fort Verde, he found his plans upset by orders from Washington to cease offensive operations. They were compromising the efforts of Vincent Colyer, of the Bureau of Indian Affairs, who was trying to talk all Apaches onto reservations. Thus began a year of chaos in the Indian affairs of Apachería.

Colyer in 1871 and General Oliver Howard, who continued Colyer's work in the summer of 1872, appeared successful in bringing the Apaches under government supervision — on paper anyway. Several reservations were set up and Howard negotiated a treaty with Apache chief Cochise that permitted his Chiricahuas, some of the most troublesome Apaches, to remain in their traditional haunts in southern Arizona.

Despite such progress, however, raids and attacks by Apaches continued and in some areas increased. On November 5, 1871, only nine days after Colyer had returned to Washington, a band of supposedly pacified Indians from the Date Creek reservation ambushed a stagecoach eight miles west of the little mining town of Wickenberg, in central Arizona near Phoenix. The driver and five passengers were killed.

Thereafter the broncos, as renegade Apaches were known, struck with increasing frequency. By midsummer of 1872 more than 50 raids and 40 murders were laid to their account. In one raid 2,000 sheep were

A stealthy Apache, almost certainly with compatriots hidden nearby, waits to ambush a covered wagon. Attacks such as these, which continued unabated even while the government negotiated with the Indians, intensified the public outcry for a military answer to the Apache problem.

driven off and their herder killed within a mile and a half of Crook's headquarters, located at Fort Whipple near Prescott, while the general delayed his offensive. Two other victims were Lieutenant Reid Stewart and Corporal Joseph Black who, riding in a buckboard, outdistanced their escort and were ambushed in a canyon near Tucson. When the escort caught up they found Stewart already dead. On a hillside above them, they saw Black tied to the flaming trunk of a dead tree while his captors tormented him with knives, lances and firebrands. His corpse bore more than a hundred wounds. The killers got away.

Crook cooperated with the peace commissioners in every way that they requested. Though he disagreed with their plan and felt all along that it would fail, he had no intention of exposing himself to some future charge that he had subverted the peace missions. Nevertheless, the Army could not stand idly by when Apache raiders killed soldiers and settlers and stole livestock. In May 1872, troopers chased Apache thieves 110 miles to retrieve a single head of cattle; two soldiers were wounded and four Indians killed. On another occasion, an 80-mile pursuit ended in the recovery of $20,000 worth of sheep, though the Indians who had stolen them escaped.

Harassed white settlers cheered the Army's successes on one hand and complained bitterly on the other, not only about the Indian raids but against Washington's peace initiatives. Colyer, the first emissary, was widely detested in Arizona. Vituperative commentary in the Western press was reprinted by Eastern newspapers. Washington, its ear attuned to public opinion, authorized Crook in November 1871, to resume military operations against Apaches. But before Crook could act, his mandate was again suspended during the winter of 1872 in anticipation of the second peace effort by General Howard.

In the meantime, Crook continued to enlist Indian scouts. Not all were Apaches; there were not enough of them. To fill out the ranks he signed up Walapais, Yavapais—a kind of cross between Apaches and Mojaves—and Paiutes, recruited far afield in Utah Territory. By now Crook had become disenchanted with Navajos as scouts; they could find Apaches all right, but became timid when battle loomed. Mexicans played no substantial role as scouts after Crook's initial

159

Exploration and adventure while the war goes on

While a geologist ponders rock specimens, Mojave scouts — who were camera shy when awake — are photographed taking a siesta.

Even while Apaches were on the warpath, the Army in the Southwest did not spend all its time fighting Indians. In 1871 Captain George Montague Wheeler began a decade-long survey of territory west of the 100th meridian by taking a party of scientists and engineers up the Colorado River from Camp Mojave in Arizona to the Grand Canyon. Wheeler's crew included 14 Mojave scouts. Traveling upstream in three open boats and one barge, the explorers deliberately bucked the great river's fiercely swift currents and rapids to test its navigability northward and

to gather other practical information.

Portaging past falls of 35 feet and more, hemmed in by canyon cliffs 1,700 feet high, the party made painfully slow progress. The Mojaves were nervous when they entered the land of their enemies, the Paiutes, and made several attempts to desert.

At Vernon Falls two boats were almost lost and for a time the party was separated and made dreary wet camps on the riverbank. One of the boats was wrecked outright at Disaster Rapids, taking with it Wheeler's notes and instruments and much of the rations. Weary and half-starved,

the explorers finally reached their goal, the supply base at Diamond Creek. Wheeler's report, not surprisingly, concluded that the river's northern reaches were not navigable.

For three of its members the expedition ended tragically: returning to California by stagecoach, they were ambushed and killed by Apaches near Wickenburg, Arizona. A young Mojave scout named Maimum, who during the journey up the Colorado River had developed a close attachment to one of the murdered men, Lieutenant F. W. Loring, helped to track down the guilty Apaches.

expedition. Crook organized his scouts into companies of 26 men attached to a column of cavalry. At the head of each scout company, Crook placed a civilian chief of scouts to control and transmit orders to the Indians.

Crook hired a dozen or so of these white intermediaries. They were men like Dan O'Leary and Gus Spear, whom the Prescott *Arizona Miner* once characterized as "better and more thorough mountaineers than whom, Kit Carson never was or will be." There was Joe Felmer, a smalltime rancher with an Apache wife, who summed up his approach to scouting against Apaches in one sentence: "When you see Apache 'sign,' be *keerful;* 'n' when you don' see nary 'sign,' be *more* keerful." But none of these men was more valuable to Crook or figured more prominently in his Apache campaigns than Al Sieber.

Sieber, the son of a German miller, was born in the Rhineland in 1844. His father died the next year and in 1849 his widowed mother brought Al and his brothers and sisters to America. After the Civil War, Sieber, with his $300 mustering-out pay, headed west to seek his fortune. He drifted awhile, worked on the railroad, prospected a little and herded horses. In the late 1860s, Al came to Arizona Territory, where he had his first encounter with hostile Indians around 1870. Sieber learned quickly; by the summer of 1872, he was known as an expert in tracking and killing Apaches.

In his prime, Sieber stood nearly six feet tall, weighed about 175 pounds and possessed enormous strength. He ruled his Indian scouts with an iron fist. "Al Sieber was head of us scouts," one Apache scout said to an interviewer many years later. "What Sieber told us to do we did."

Sieber's philosophy of dealing with Indians was simple and effective, and there is little doubt that he commanded the cooperation of his Indians as much through fear as fairness. "I do not deceive them but always tell them the truth," he said. "When I tell them I am going to kill them, I do it, and when I tell them I am their friend, they know it."

Crook, while awaiting permission to resume operations, obtained conclusive evidence that a chief named Ochocama, from the Date Creek reservation, and some of his followers were responsible for the Wickenburg stagecoach massacre five months earlier. When they found out that they were under suspicion, the Indians decided to kill Crook, thinking that they could escape afterward. Crook heard about the plot on his life from informers on the reservation and resolved to arrest the offenders.

The general, with a handful of armed men, clashed with his antagonists near the reservation in early September with inconclusive results. One of Ochocama's followers fired at Crook but missed. Several Indians were killed, but Ochocama, though wounded, escaped into the hills with most of his band.

Late in September, 86 Walapai scouts under Sieber were assigned to guide three companies of cavalry against Ochocama who, according to a friendly Indian, was camped on Burro Creek, 60 miles west of Prescott. Lieutenant Walter Schuyler, who took part in the expedition, described it in a letter to his father written a few days afterward.

The scouts, after finding the broncos' camps, "went ahead on the trail and we followed in single file as silent as could be, and very slowly as the country was very rough and we had to climb either up or down steep rocks all the time. In the dim moonlight the column presented a very weird appearance, looking like an immense snake slowly dragging itself along. If you want to see the superlative in sneaking, you ought to see one Indian hunt another. They crawled ahead of us like cats, and every little while when they saw something suspicious, we had to lie down flat until they reconnoitered the ground. Their signals were very pretty being perfect imitations of the calls of the whip-poor-will or a cricket. We crawled along in this way for 7 miles when the Indians told us we were very near the camps of which there were four."

The troops deployed silently around the Indian camps—known as rancherías in the Southwest—and charged with the dawn. Caught by surprise, about 40 Indians were killed and eight women captured. Summarized Schuyler in closing his letter: "We thus whipped one of the worst bands of Apaches in the country and performed the unparalleled feat of 'jumping' four rancherías simultaneously."

Late in 1872, Crook's patience with peace commissioners ran out. Despite their efforts, thousands of Apaches remained off the reservations, many of them

An off-duty life of relative privilege

Life on Apache reservations was somewhat easier for scouts than for their less exalted kindred. Scouts had access to Army doctors and to the medicine men (who performed special rites for them before a campaign).

They also had more money than most Indians, which made them popular with girls; at a dance at Fort Bowie, one shy young scout had to promise two Apache maidens a two-dollar credit at the commissary before they would let go of his shirt sleeves. Scouts were usually generous to their families on payday—if they managed to get back to their wickiups before being cleaned out in a betting game. Many an enthusiast lost his pay—not to mention his moccasins and saddle—playing a game known as "hoop-and-pole."

Lined up in squatting position, scouts wait to receive "the pay and allowances of cavalry soldiers" granted them by act of Congress.

In front of their conical wickiups, two San Carlos scouts stand with family members. The scouts' cartridge belts are Army issue, but their dress is pure Apache. Red headbands separated them from hostiles.

Twenty minutes after being paid, scouts huddle together for a gambling game. They often used carved sticks as dice.

killing and stealing as usual. "I think I am justified in saying," he declared in a report that year, "that I have fully carried out that portion of my instructions which required me to co-operate with the agents referred to, and believe that humanity demands that I should now proceed to carry out the remainder of my instructions, which require me to punish the incorrigibly hostile."

Backed by his Army superiors, Crook set November 15, 1872, as the deadline for all Apaches to be on reservations, and on November 16 a column of scouts and troops marched out from Fort Hualpai, 40 miles from Prescott. Crook had decided on a winter campaign in preference to operating in summer when food would be more plentiful for the Indians and the climate almost unbearable for the white pursuers. This column was the first of nine he planned to deploy; each column, led by a company of 30 to 40 scouts, was to crisscross Arizona, keeping the Indians on the move, fighting them when possible and forcing them to retreat into the Tonto Basin, their rugged but fertile valley stronghold. There the columns would converge upon and subdue any Indians who still showed fight.

Crook's instructions on this point, as noted by Bourke, were clear: "Indians should be induced to surrender in all cases where possible; where they preferred to fight, they were to get all the fighting they wanted, and in one good dose instead of in a number of petty engagements, but in either case were to be hunted

Frederic Remington

A MORAL TALE FOR GREEDY AGENTS

In 1901, Frederic Remington focused attention on corrupt Indian agents with an illustrated, semifactual tale, "Natchez's Pass." The villain was an agent who permitted Apaches to leave the reservation to murder and steal. He believed that if he did not, they would leave en masse, federal funds to his agency would be cut and he would lose his rake-off. Confronted by an honest captain, the agent denied issuing passes to marauding Indians. To the agent's mortification *(right)* the captain then plunked down on the table proof of the villain's complicity: the head of an Apache killed while attacking sheepmen, and the dead Indian's pass, signed by the agent. Shown two more heads and passes, the agent fled the reservation, never to return.

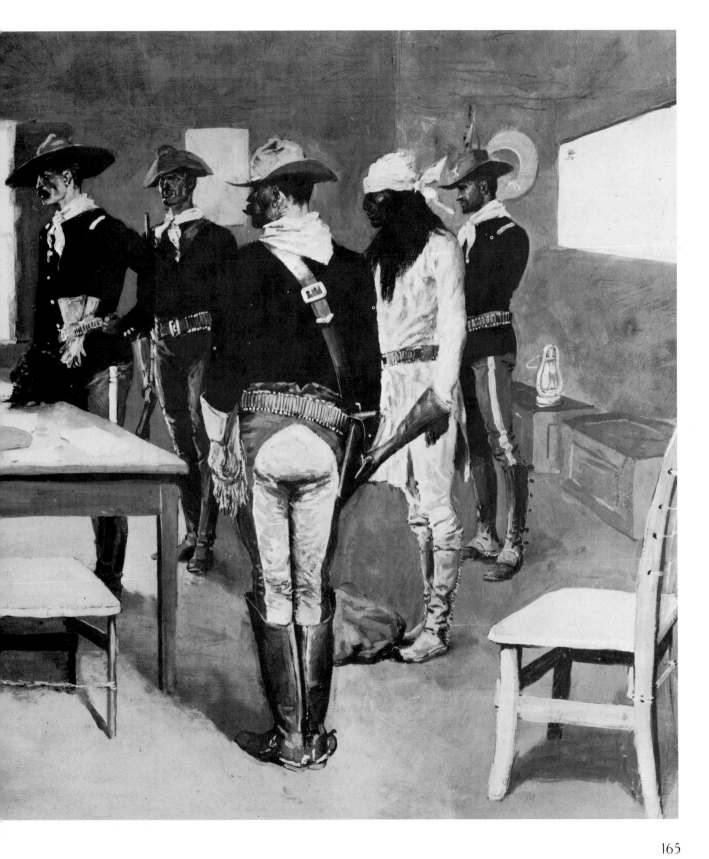

Black guardians of the Texas border country

While the Army fought Apaches in Arizona and New Mexico, it was also waging a campaign to stop murderous Indian raids along the Texas-Mexico frontier. Here, instead of depending on Apache scouts, troops relied on an extraordinary unit known then as the Seminole-Negroes.

These men, who never numbered more than 50, were descendants of runaway slaves who had attached themselves to the Florida Seminole tribe, which was forced west by the U.S. government. Many took refuge in Mexico. In 1870 the Army recruited some of them from their homes in Nacimiento, Mexico, under an enticing agreement. The U.S. government was to provide money, food and land for the men and their families in return for their services.

They were unlikely looking recruits. Most dressed in Indian style, some even sporting buffalo-horn war bonnets. In action, however, their appearance could not disguise their al-most uncanny ability to sniff out and follow trails many weeks old. They were able to survive the desolate west Texas desert on the most rudimentary diet, eating rattlesnakes in a pinch. They had a thorough knowledge of the territory and Indian ways.

In 1873, the scouts were placed under the command of Lieutenant John Lapham Bullis. The men respected Bullis because, as scout Joseph Phillips put it, "He didn't stand and say, 'Go yonder,' he would say, 'Come on boys, let's go get 'em.' "

In nine years under Bullis' command, the scouts compiled a prodigious record. In 26 engagements, 12 of them major, not a single scout was killed or seriously wounded, even though they were sometimes outnumbered by the enemy 8 to 1.

At times, the scouts' courage and loyalty to Bullis were both on the line. In April 1875, Bullis and three men ambushed a party of some 30 Comanches. In a sniping match, the tiny group of scouts killed three warriors in an hour, but then the tide turned. Swiftly the scouts mounted their horses and rode off. Glancing back, black-Seminole Sergeant John Ward saw Bullis, surrounded and unable to reach his horse. "We can't leave the lieutenant, boys!" Ward yelled, and wheeled back into the fray. While the other two men fired at the enemy, Ward scooped Bullis up onto his own horse and the four escaped uninjured. The Congressional Medal of Honor was later awarded to all three enlisted men.

The land promised to the recruits did not materialize. The War Department declared itself out of land and the Indian Commissioner gave the matter a bureaucratic shrug. A few scouts deserted, but the rest of them, loyal to Bullis, stayed on fighting Indians and, later, gangs of ruffians who terrorized the border country. For their heroism, the dust of the Texas desert was their only reward.

---

down until the last one in hostility had been killed or captured. Every effort should be made to avoid the killing of women and children. No excuse was to be accepted for leaving a trail; if horses played out, the enemy must be followed on foot, and no sacrifice should be left untried to make the campaign short, sharp, and decisive."

The war was not won by decisive battles as Crook had hoped. The typical confrontation required long days or weeks of stalking a hostile band that lost only a few members at a time as casualties or prisoners.

The Indian scouts—Apaches in particular—were crucial to even those small successes. Captain Bourke described how the scouts were deployed on the missions he accompanied: "Our Apache scouts, under MacIntosh, Felmer, and Besias, were kept from twelve to twenty-four hours in advance of the main body, but always in communication, the intention being to make use of them to determine the whereabouts of the hostiles, but to let the soldiers do the work of cleaning them out." But events rarely conformed to the plan. "It was difficult to restrain the scouts, who were too fond of war to let slip any good excuse for a fight," continued Bourke, "and consequently MacIntosh had two or three skirmishes which showed that his scouts could be depended upon both as trailers and as a fighting force. In one of these, the scouts struck the trail of the enemy, and had a sharp brush with them, killing several and capturing three."

Though recruited into the Army as scouts, Apaches remained Indians through and through. Each morning, orderly columns of soldiers ready to resume the march contrasted sharply with the ragged ranks of the scouts. Lieutenant Augustus Tassin, who was the commander of a scout company in the 1870s, described them moving out: "On breaking up a bivouac, there is no falling in, in single or double ranks or other delaying formalities. The last mule being packed, the chief of scouts gives a short, jerky order, 'Ugashe' (Get!), and the Apaches start as if shot from a gun, rapidly covering

Eight years after their last Indian battle, black-Seminole scouts stand at attention near Fort Clark, Texas, headquarters in 1889.

the ground in a rough, shambling gait, which in the long run abolishes distance in a manner wonderful to behold." Surprisingly, Apaches preferred to travel afoot. Unlike Plains Indians, they were not spectacular horsemen, often keeping their mounts only to butcher them for food. As scouts, Apaches retained their ambulatory predilection until the late 1880s when the Army persuaded them to ride.

Mounted or afoot, scouts could be utterly intractable when they were faced by something as inconsequential to white men as the appearance of an owl, which to them was a messenger of death. Reported Bourke: "I have known of one case where our bravest scouts ran away from a place where an owl had perched and begun its lugubrious ditty, and at another time the scouts made a great fuss and would not be pacified until one of the whites of our command had released a little owl which he had captured." A scout company frequently had its own medicine man to keep the Indians apprised of the significance of omens such as owls.

Although Apaches were serious about omens, they were notably less bound by religious obligations than other tribes. For instance, in the matter of purification rites that most Indians performed after victory in battle, Bourke reported that "with the Apaches these are baths in the sweat lodge, accompanied with singing and other rites." Fortunately for the Army, continued Bourke, "the Apache 'bunches' all his religious duties at these times, and defers his bathing until he gets home, but the Pima and Maricopa are more punctilious, and resort to the rites of religion the moment a single one, either of their own numbers or of the enemy, has been laid low." Such behavior no doubt contributed to the rapid decline in the use of Maricopa and Pima Indians as scouts.

The Army was more than willing to tolerate Apache idiosyncrasies, for the record clearly shows that when scouts were with the cavalry they found hostile Indians, and whenever the cavalry operated alone, the troops might as well not have bothered.

167

Mike Burns, a young Apache, captured by the Army and given an American name, accompanied one offensive expedition. Years later in his autobiography he remembered that troops "passed right by a camp of Indians on a thick flat of cedar; it was snowing and the wind was blowing right into the soldiers' faces. They never looked down on the ground to see if there were any tracks of the Indians, and went right on by."

With Apache scouts in the vanguard, however, the Army often overwhelmed the enemy, as happened once late in 1872. Nantaje, a renegade-turned-scout assigned to a column commanded by Major William Brown, suspected that hostile Indians were holed up in a wide shallow cave where he, Nantaje, had lived as a boy. The cave 500 feet below the rim of a mesa and 700 feet above the Salt River, was inaccessible except by a narrow path that led down the sheer face of the mesa. It was a bitter December night when Nantaje led Lieutenant William Ross, one of Brown's officers, and a dozen sharpshooters unseen and unheard down the hazardous trail to a spot where the path widened. Using rocks for cover, the marksmen opened fire within 40 yards of the cave, killing six Indians immediately. At the crack of the rifles, Major Brown rushed in reinforcements. All told, 76 of the enemy died on the spot; several more died later of wounds. It was an extraordinary number of casualties for a war characterized by much smaller actions.

As in most battles, there were women casualties among the hostiles, despite Crook's admonition to his troops that women should be spared whenever possible. The nature of most engagements—surprise attacks usually at dawn—made them deadly to men, women and children alike. To complicate matters, Apache women sometimes joined the fray. As William Corbusier, an Army surgeon who participated in the war, observed, "Women couldn't be distinguished from the men at a long range, and especially when they had bows and arrows to take part in the fight."

With results like those of Nantaje and Major Brown above the Salt River and virtually countless similar engagements by the other columns Crook had in the field, Apache scouts rapidly earned the esteem of the officers they served. "The longer we knew the Apache scouts," wrote Bourke, "the better we liked them. They were wilder and more suspicious than the Pimas

and Maricopas, but far more reliable, and endowed with a greater amount of courage and daring."

For all the enthusiasm the scouts generated with their tracking skills, tenacity and willingness to fight, they were not infallible. Scouts under Captain George Randall, searching a natural labyrinth of arroyos and buttes near Turret Peak for Apaches that he had been following, could not find the hostile Indians although there was an abundance of fresh sign. Fortuitously, the scouts captured a woman of the band whom they coerced into guiding them to the broncos.

Preparing to take up the pursuit, "our soldiers, before starting out, wrapped their feet and knees with gunny sacks, so as to make as little noise as possible," wrote Crook of the incident in his autobiography. "Soon after dark the command started for the camp of the hostiles under the guidance of the squaw." During the night the troops crawled silently and laboriously up Turret Peak—a 45° incline—toward the Indians. At dawn, Crook's account continues, "our people fired a volley into their camp and charged with a yell. So secure did they feel in this almost impregnable position that they lost all presence of mind, even running past their holes in the rocks. All of the men were killed; most of the women and children were taken prisoner."

This engagement and the one led by Nantaje "broke the spirit of the Apache nation," observed Bourke. By the spring of 1873, bands of hostile Apaches began to give up voluntarily. Perhaps the most significant surrender was that of an Apache-Mojave chief named Cha-lipun—Charley-Pan to the Americans—who turned in his 2,300 followers unconditionally in April. In giving up, Cha-lipun complained that his people could not sleep because they were afraid of a dawn attack, could not cook because the fires would betray them, could neither remain in the valleys nor retire to the peaks because they would be followed even there. He had never feared the Americans alone, Cha-lipun told Crook, but he feared his own people, the Apache scouts, whom Crook had turned against him.

On April 9, 1873, Crook concluded that he had in essence secured Apachería. In General Order Number 14, Crook congratulated his forces, noting that "they have outwitted and beaten the wiliest of foes with slight loss, comparatively, to themselves, and finally closed an Indian war that has been waged since the

Crouching in loincloths, their white commander in their midst, Apache scouts simulate battle action for the camera around 1880. In actual fights they were masters of stealth, cover and independent action.

days of Cortez." And in June, Crook wrote to Washington recommending 10 of his Apache scouts, including Nantaje, for the Congressional Medal of Honor, which were awarded a few years later.

Crook's proclamation of victory ignored four small bands that Crook knew he must defeat. These Indians were led by desperate holdouts named Chunz, Cochinay, Chan-deisi (called John Daisy by the troopers) and Delchay, sometimes written Delché (The Red Ant). Chunz was a murderer who had wantonly axed a 13-year-old white boy. Cochinay's various outrages made him one of the worst Apache outlaws. Chan-deisi was a former scout who turned renegade. Delchay had borne an implacable hatred toward whites since 1868 when troopers killed his brother, Rising Sun, who was already in their custody.

Crook was eager to kill these outlaws. He kept small expeditions in the field hunting them down and

offered rewards for their heads so that he could see for himself that they were actually dead. It took nearly four months—almost as long as the recent campaign had lasted—to track down and kill them all, and each success was the work of Apache scouts.

Cochinay was the first to go. A band of scouts found him within three miles of Tucson, apparently, as a contemporary account speculated, "awaiting a chance to depredate." The scouts returned with his head to the San Carlos Agency.

Chan-deisi lasted less than a month longer. On June 23, 1874, Crook sent a note to Lieutenant Schuyler at the Verde reservation noting, "Recent telegram says that John Daisy's head was brought into Camp Apache the other day, which leaves now only Chunz's head on his shoulders." Then, remembering that yet another name was still on his most-wanted list, Crook added, "Start your killers as soon as possible after the

Mickey Free: the scout nobody loved

Mickey Free was one of the most puzzling—and one of the least liked—of all the scouts used by the Army in the Apache wars. He was not an Apache; in fact, he had little Indian blood at all. His mother was Mexican and his father was said to have been part Irish (accounting for Mickey's grayish eyes and red hair). No one knew how he came by his name; he may have chosen it himself, using an Irish-sounding first name because of his father and taking the surname "Free" because, after spending his boyhood as an Apache captive, he eventually gained his freedom.

His kidnapping from a shabby Arizona ranch at age 11 or 12 led to massive trouble between whites and Apaches. In 1861 the Army sent a blunderer named George Nicholas Bascom to recover the boy from the Chiricahua chief, Cochise. A parley that began peacefully ended with killing on both sides. The incident set Cochise on the warpath: in the next 60 days his band killed 150 whites.

When Mickey Free became one of Lieutenant Britton Davis' scouts, he was blamed and hated by the Indians as "the coyote whose kidnapping had brought war to the Chiricahuas." The dislike seems to have been reciprocated. Free relished seeing the Apaches humbled and was said to have spread rumors about them to stir up trouble. He was often used as an interpreter, but the Indians accused him of deliberately twisting their words; refusing to speak through Free, Geronimo insisted on having his own interpreter for talks with General Crook in 1886.

While his white employers found him to be reliable, some of them did not like Free much more than the Indians did. Scout chief Al Sieber once said that he was "half Mexican, half Irish and whole son of a bitch."

Scout Mickey Free rarely used his rifle; the Army used him mainly as an interpreter.

When John Clum *(right foreground)* and his crack Apache constabulary brought law and order to much of southern Arizona, grateful Tucson citizens raised money to buy uniforms for the Indian police.

head of Delché & Co. The more prompt these heads are brought in, the less liable other Indians, in the future, will be to jeopardize their heads."

Credit for taking Chunz belongs mostly to the Apache scout Desalin, who had enlisted with Crook after surrendering the previous April. Leading a party of scouts from the San Carlos reservation, Desalin tracked Chunz "and a small body of desperadoes" to a hideout also near Tucson. Chunz's band held off the scouts all day, then escaped in the dark of night. They left behind a wounded warrior from whom Desalin had extracted Chunz's destination. By the time that Desa-

lin and his 30 scouts caught up with Chunz in a canyon near the San Carlos Agency, the outlaw had only six warriors left. All seven heads were taken to San Carlos and put on exhibit on the parade ground as a deterrent to other Indians.

Delchay, the last of the four, was dead by August — killed twice, according to the scouts. Three of Lieutenant Schuyler's Tonto scouts found Delchay near Turret Peak on July 29 and brought in his scalp and one ear to claim the reward Crook had posted. At about the same time the indefatigable Desalin fetched in a head complete with hair and two ears that, he claimed had

This silver peace medal was worn by mystic Noch-ay-del-klinne when he was shot in 1881. Legend said it was given by President Grant, whose likeness it bears, but there is no official record of the award.

once been part of the rest of Delchay. Crook accepted the conflicting evidence philosophically. "Being satisfied that both parties were in earnest in their beliefs, and the bringing in of an extra head was not amiss, I paid both parties."

In March of 1875, Crook left Apachería. Given a new assignment to fight the Indians on the Great Plains, he left at least a façade of peace. The renegades were momentarily subdued. But forces were already at work that would be the cause of renewed insurrection among the Apaches.

Even before Crook's departure, the Army and the Bureau of Indian Affairs had begun to compete hotly for control over the Indians. Competition between the two agencies, occasionally carried to the point of conflicting orders from civilians and soldiers, made the Indians suspicious, resentful and anxious to leave the reservations. And many of them did. In the early days of peace, these rovers caused whites little if any trouble. But the Army continued to view any Indian off his reservation, regardless of his behavior, as a hostile and hunted him accordingly.

To complicate matters, Washington had adopted a policy of concentrating Apaches on one reservation—San Carlos—where they would be easier to control. This churned up great resentment among the Indians, who did not want to leave their traditional stamping grounds. The Verde Apaches were the first to be transferred. Though they opposed the move in council, the Indians acquiesced because they lacked the numbers or the weapons to resist.

In 1876, John Clum, agent at San Carlos, sought to bring the Chiricahuas to the reservation. Clum journeyed to Chiricahua country with 54 of his Apache police force, formed at least in part from scouts who had served Crook. Clum contrived to convoy about a third of the Chiricahuas to San Carlos, but 200 eluded him by slipping into New Mexico and another 400 melted into Sonora, Mexico, under the leadership of Juh and Geronimo. Juh was an old man much respected by his followers. Geronimo, much younger, would become the last tenacious holdout and the very symbol of Apache resistance to subjugation. Juh and Geronimo along with other southern Apache leaders—Bonito, Chihuahua, Naiche, Loco, Chato, Nana and Josanie—soon came to symbolize terror in Arizona and New Mexico.

At one time or another all these men and their followers resided on reservations. And at one time or another, individually or in coalition, they all broke out. Often they had provocation enough: white incursions on the best reservation land, threatening maneuvers by the Army or boodling agents who stole supplies meant for Indians. But it was equally true that Apaches decamped out of restlessness and from disgust at being treated like children.

On the rampage, the Indians were terrors. To live and wage war an Apache needed food, guns and bullets. To get them, Apaches stole as always but with savagery that made them seem devils incarnate. They raided north out of the Mexican mountains in small, swift bands. One party reportedly led by Juh attacked two wagon trains, throwing the dead and wounded, 11 men, into the burning wagons. Nana led another band a thousand miles in six weeks. The marauders killed at least 50 Americans—nobody was ever sure exactly how many—and captured two women. They retreated to Mexico, eluding a thousand soldiers along the way.

Another band ambushed and killed three prospectors. As pursuing troops stopped to examine the still-warm bodies of the miners, the Indians attacked a ranch a few miles farther on and drove off $5,000 worth of sheep. Before taking the animals, they slaughtered seven men and one woman, then murdered two children, burning one alive and pitching the other, a helpless infant, into a patch of cactus to die of exposure.

It was during these troubled times that the Apache scouts' admirable record of loyalty and reliability received its only blemish. In 1881, near the Fort Apache reservation, there lived a medicine man and mystic called Noch-ay-del-klinne. This visionary held dances and promised better days for his people. His message was much the same as that of the Ghost Dance religion, which was to inspire insurrection

Army officers with two Apache scouts
(both at left), are dwarfed by giant saguaro
cacti in a rugged, canyon-cut part of Apachería—typical of the Apache habitat—
near Fort Thomas in southern Arizona.

A wealth of hidden sustenance in a harsh and arid land

In his 1883 "Annual Report," General George Crook explained succinctly why Apaches survived and flourished in their bleak land: "The country they inhabit is larger than New England, and the roughest on the continent, and though affording no food upon which soldiers can subsist, provides the Indian with everything necessary for sustaining his life indefinitely. The agave"—a plant, also called mescal, used for food and liquor—"grows luxuriantly in all their mountains, and upon this plant alone the Indians can live.

"They have no property nor settled habitations of any kind, but roam about like coyotes, and their temporary resting places are chosen with all the experience gained by generations of warfare. The Indian knows every foot of his territory; can endure fatigue and fasting, and can live without food or water for periods that would kill the hardiest mountaineer."

The Apaches used many desert plants for food, drink, medicine and narcotics. Even species as prickly and uninviting as those shown at right were life-sustainers to Indians on the run or to Apache scouts who were tracking them.

The fruit of the cholla cactus was a source of moisture and energy-giving glucose. The roots from the 9-foot-high ocotillo were used medicinally: boiled into a potion, they relieved fatigue; powdered, they reduced painful swellings. The fruit and flowers of the Spanish bayonet yucca were a major food source for Apaches, who also used the plant's roots, ground up, as a detergent to wash their hair and clothing. Ripe sunflower seeds, prickly-pear cactus, mesquite seeds ground into flour, even portions of milkweed, primroses and cattails: all helped to serve the needs of the ingenious Indians.

CHOLLA CACTUS

OCOTILLO

SPANISH BAYONET YUCCA

among Great Plains Indians almost a decade later. He preached that whites would go away and that two slain chiefs would rise from the dead. To Apaches confined on reservations against their will, the hope of freedom restored was heady doctrine indeed.

Some of the Army's Apache scouts went to hear Noch-ay-del-klinne preach and to take part in his dances. Scouts at Fort Apache returned from the mystic in such a surly mood that Lieutenant Thomas Cruse, their commander, disarmed them and locked their weapons in the guardhouse. The Indians claimed they were merely dancing and did not know why they should be chastised for such innocuous behavior. But General Eugene Carr, commandant of the fort, considered the mystic's activities subversive and decided to arrest him. White soldiers were to make the arrest; but Carr felt he needed Cruse's scouts, whose loyalty Cruse no longer trusted, to find the medicine man.

Carr set out at the head of 79 troops and 23 scouts to seize the source of trouble. With some foreboding, Cruse rearmed his scouts halfway to Cibicu Creek where Noch-ay-del-klinne was camped. Cruse took such comfort as he could from knowing the scouts were veterans; the company's three Apache sergeants counted 18 years of meritorious service among them.

The arrest of the mystic went smoothly, until some of his disciples from the reservation approached to speak with him where he sat guarded by soldiers. Captain Edmund Hentig, designated by Carr as officer of the day, warned the Indians away several times. Angered, the Indians ignored the officer's admonitions and surged forward, weapons at the ready. Simultaneously, the scouts loaded their rifles, and both parties of Indians fired on the white troops. Hentig fell at the first volley. In the fighting that ensued—during which the mystic was killed—all of the Apache scouts except a single sergeant called Mose fought on the side of their kinsmen. By nightfall, when the fighting ended, several Indians and soldiers had been killed or wounded. Several scouts were taken prisoner. Later, five of the scouts who escaped turned themselves in and were tried for mutiny. Three were hanged and two sent to prison.

Thus, "before the summer of 1882 had fairly begun," wrote Bourke, who had remained Crook's aide and had risen to the rank of captain during the intervening years,

"Indian affairs in Arizona had relapsed into such a deplorable condition that the President felt obliged to re-assign General Crook to the command." Immediately upon arriving in Arizona on September 3, 1882, Crook set out on his mule, with a few aides, to get the Indians' side of the story. This investigation convinced Crook that unrest among the Apaches was caused primarily by civilian plunderers and weak military officers who allowed their troops to bully the Indians.

Crook chided U.S. District Attorney J. W. Zabriskie for lack of attention to the civil side of the problem. A policy of preventing outbreaks can "only be successful," wrote Crook, "when the officers of justice fearlessly perform their duty in proceeding against the villains who fatten on the supplies intended for the use of Indians willing to lead peaceful and orderly lives."

In General Order Number 43, issued in October, Crook warned his officers against rash use of troops: "Each officer will be held to a strict accountability that his actions have been fully authorized by law of justice, and that Indians evincing a desire to enter upon a career of peace shall have no cause for complaint through hasty or injudicious acts of the military."

But letters and orders, effective as they might be in reducing future tension between Apaches and whites, had no effect on Indians already on the warpath. To subdue them Crook would again need Apache scouts, and he organized five companies of them, each with 29 Apaches, including one sergeant and two corporals. In addition to a civilian chief of scouts such as Al Sieber each company had an Army officer in charge.

To lead his scouts, Crook selected the best junior officers in his command, preferably ones in whom he could detect an empathy for Indians, men such as Captain Emmet Crawford, Lieutenant Britton Davis and Lieutenant Charles Gatewood, whose name would figure prominently in ending the struggle for Apachería. To guide these men in their duties, Crook distilled his earlier experience with Apache scouts into a concise directive: "The first principle is to show them that we trust them. We have to depend upon their fidelity, and they are quick to note any lack of confidence. They appreciate the situation and understand thoroughly what is expected of them, and know best how to do their work. They know better how to obtain the information that is needed—namely the presence of the

renegades—than we do, and should be allowed to use their own methods in getting it."

Crook believed that the wildest Apaches he could find would make the best scouts, as illustrated by his recruitment of the renegade Tso-ay. Tso-ay was one of a band of Chiricahua Apache raiders under Chato who, on March 27, 1883, caught Federal District Judge H. C. McComas and his family riding out of Silver City unescorted in a buggy. The naked bodies of the judge and his wife were recovered at the scene. Their 6-year-old son, Charlie, was captured and never seen again.

Tso-ay retreated with his comrades to their stronghold in the Sierra Madre of Mexico, but he soon began to miss his friends on the San Carlos reservation and decided he had seen enough raiding. He deserted the renegades and made his way back to San Carlos, where he was quickly arrested and taken to Crook in irons. Instead of ordering Tso-ay into the guardhouse, Crook

struck off his shackles and enlisted him as a scout.

Other Chiricahua broncos also had got away into Mexico. Crook realized that he could never corral the renegades as long as Apache raiders could retire to an untouchable sanctuary south of the border. Therefore in April 1883, he traveled into Mexico where he negotiated with the governors of Sonora and Chihuahua a two-year agreement that allowed forces of either government to cross the border in "hot pursuit" of hostiles, in this case Chiricahuas. And the trail of the McComas killers, though more than a month old, was hot enough to suit Crook.

On May 1, 1883, he marched out of San Bernardino in the southeastern corner of Arizona. Behind him followed his small staff, 193 Apache scouts serving under Captain Emmet Crawford, Lieutenant Charles Gatewood and the chief of scouts Al Sieber, and a mere 42 white enlisted soldiers. Thus for the first time,

Their enlistment term nearly over, White Mountain Apache scouts gather in 1880 for a portrait with their leader, Lieutenant Charles Gatewood *(center, in broad hat)*, known to them fondly as "Long Nose."

Crook deployed his Apache scouts as his main force.

The expedition traveled light; each man carried the clothes on his back, a blanket, his weapon and 40 rounds of ammunition. Sixty days' rations and another 160 rounds per man followed on pack mules. Once inside Mexico, the expedition turned into the mountains and after that, Bourke wrote, it was "Climb! Climb! Climb!" over precipices so steep that mules slipped from the trail and had to be rescued; men had to dodge avalanches of bounding rocks dislodged by those above them. "To look at this country is grand; to travel in it is Hell," Bourke told his diary. "And up and down these ridges, our Apache scouts, when the idea seizes them, run like deer."

Sooner than anyone could have hoped, the scouts and soldiers began to close in on the Chiricahuas. By

May 8, sign of Apaches was everywhere, and one of the scouts' medicine men predicted that Chiricahuas would be found in two days or, if not, in six days.

On May 11, Crook decided that the trail was so hot that bringing this business to climax would best be left entirely to the scouts. They agreed, complaining that the whites and the pack train were holding them back. Crook sent 150 of them ahead, led by Crawford, Gatewood and Sieber with orders to find the broncos, kill those who resisted but, pointedly, to refrain from killing women, children or any men who surrendered.

John Rope, an Apache scout who accompanied Sieber on this foray, dictated his reminiscences late in life. His description of what happened paints scouts in more realistic tones than many other accounts. "At that time I had never fought with the Chiricahua and

When Captain Emmet Crawford *(inset)* was slain in a clash with Mexican soldiers, a scout named Dutchy *(below),* enraged at his commander's death, took aim and killed the man who had shot Crawford.

A photographic exclusive from inside the enemy's camp

A talent for eliciting prime pictures from situations that breathed danger gave Arizona photographer C. S. Fly one of the biggest scoops of his life. When General George Crook went into the Sierra Madre in 1886 to negotiate with Geronimo, Fly accompanied him and came back with the only known photographs of a camp of free, undefeated hostile Indians.

Fly made his living from his Tombstone studio but his real interest was more colorful subjects: saloons, hangings, fires. He braved a rain of bullets to watch the O.K. Corral shootout in 1881, though he could get no pictures with his bulky equipment.

Fly covered the 1886 talks with comparable boldness. As Crook interrogated Geronimo, the general's aide, Captain John G. Bourke, noticed that Fly played on the old chief's mounting agitation, and "with a nerve that would have reflected undying glory on a Chicago drummer, coolly asked Geronimo and the warriors with him to change positions, and turn their heads or faces, to improve the negative." Fly's exclusive photos won him international fame.

Geronimo's renegades—including rifle-bearing children—warily eye photographer Fly's camera in their camp in the Sierra Madre.

Geronimo (*center, facing right*) negotiates with General Crook—who is among the hatted men at right—on March 27, 1886.

did not know how mean they were, so I was always in the front. We scouts in front heard someone whistle in the brush. We stopped and listened and could hear the whistle again. We all thought it was the Chiricahuas and started to run back. One man tripped and fell in a water hole. Afterward the whistle turned out to be only the wind blowing on an acorn with a hole in it, which was on a blue oak tree."

During the next three or four days, the scouts found plentiful evidence of the Chiricahua—a stray horse, signs of a dance, abandoned camps and finally a ranchería full of broncos. "We could see the camp all right," recalled Rope. "There were quite a few Chiricahuas in it. Sieber sent two scouts back to tell the other soldiers and scouts who were way behind to hurry up here and to come that same night. Some of the scouts were afraid. It was only about a mile across the valley from where we were to the Chiricahua camp. That night we could not sleep but sat and talked in whispers. Early in the morning the troops and other scouts got in there."

The scouts were to surround the camp but in the rough, broken country the maneuver proved difficult. Before the trap was complete, a scout accidentally fired his rifle. The ranchería erupted in confusion, the renegades making for cover in every direction. Nine hostiles died under the scouts' fire, including an old woman who, according to Rope, was shot against Crook's orders. The scout's account of her death suggests that Apache scouts could show their fellow Indians as little mercy as broncos showed whites.

"It was some San Carlos scouts who shot her," Rope told the anthropologist who interviewed him. "She had asked them not to kill her but just to take her captive. The San Carlos scouts had shot her anyway." When Rope and other scouts from the White Mountains asked why they had done such a thing, "the San Carlos men said they had come after these Chiricahuas and they were going to kill them."

Disconcerted by Crook's ability to attack anywhere and with tenacity, Chiricahuas began to trickle in, each bearing the same message; they were tired of fighting and if they were no longer safe in the Sierra Madre, they were safe nowhere. In all, Crook's sortie into Mexico persuaded more than 300 Chiricahuas, including many dangerous warriors—Bonito, Chihuahua,

Nana, Loco, Chato and Geronimo—to settle with the rest of the Apaches on the San Carlos reservation.

Geronimo proved to be a restless resident, as did others among the bronco leaders. They fretted over the white man's rules against beating wives who misbehaved and against guzzling tiswin, a highly alcoholic brew made from corn. For months, dissatisfaction with reservation rules mounted. On May 15, 1885, a crisis occurred at Fort Apache near the San Carlos reservation. When Lieutenant Britton Davis, in charge of the camp that morning, emerged from his tent, he found awaiting him a delegation of truculent chiefs and subchiefs. They had, they advised him, just come from an all-night tiswin spree and were fed up with Crook's regulations against this liquor, as well as against wife beating. Davis, seeing control of the situation slipping away, said he would telegraph Crook for instructions. In his wire, Davis named as chief malcontents Geronimo, Chihuahua, Mangas, Zele, Loco and Cochise's son Naiche. He added: "The guard house here is not large enough to hold them all, and the arrest of so many prominent men will probably cause trouble."

Crook never received the wire. Al Sieber, hungover himself when given the message at the San Carlos Agency, dismissed Davis' appeal as inconsequential—it was one of the few mistakes Sieber ever made about Apaches—and pigeonholed the telegram. Receiving no answer from Crook, the chiefs imagined that he was planning some fearful retribution and some broke for Mexico. It was the last mass breakout—and the worst. Before the renegades were rounded up 15 months later, the Army would bury 10 soldiers, and 100 or more settlers and peaceful Indians would die.

Crook realized that this chase would conclude in the Sierra Madre. Throughout the summer, two columns, each with two companies of Apache scouts and one company of white soldiers, probed among the Mexican mountains, crossing each other's paths, following elusive trails through craggy terrain and oppressive heat.

The pursuit became a series of anticlimaxes. Late in June, scouts picked up a trail near the Mexican hamlet of Oputo. Captain Emmet Crawford, commander of one of the columns, sent Chato, an exrenegade chief now a scout first sergeant, and 30 scouts to follow the trail. Al Sieber and Lieutenant Britton Davis, who led the scouts, stayed behind at Crawford's orders; he

feared that the whites would only encumber the scouts. Chato and his men struck a mountain ranchería in blinding rain, killed one bronco, captured 15 women and children and recaptured five stolen cavalry horses.

Six weeks later Crook received a message saying that the other column "with 78 scouts struck Geronimo's camp on the seventh of August, and killed Chief Nana, three other bucks and one squaw—one of the bucks the son of Geronimo. Geronimo was wounded and escaped." The dispatch was partly in error; Chief Nana, at least 70 years old at the time, was still very much alive when this Apache breakout finally came to an end in August 1886.

Early in January, Captain Crawford and his scouts were 100 miles into Mexico, near an enemy camp. The command moved up during a moonless night with the white soldiers, at the urging of the scouts, wearing moccasins instead of boots to avoid the giveaway scrape of hard heels against stone.

The scouts reached the camp and attacked, scattering the broncos and capturing all their animals and other belongings. It was winter and the outlaws, once more, had had enough. They sent a woman to deal with Crawford and a meeting was set for the following day. Unknown to the Americans, however, Mexican militia had been stalking the same renegade camp. In the mist of dawn the Mexicans attacked Crawford's scouts, either because they had mistaken them for the broncos or because they hated all Apaches impartially. Trying to stop the shooting, Captain Crawford was mortally wounded by a bullet in the head.

When the Mexicans withdrew, Lieutenant Marion Maus, who assumed command of Crawford's scouts, continued negotiations with the outlaws. The upshot was that Nana came in with a few others, including members of Geronimo's and Naiche's families. And they brought word from Geronimo that he, too, was ready to negotiate and would meet Crook in the Cañon de los Embudos—Canyon of the Tricksters. Crook, Geronimo specified, would have to meet him alone. "I will have to play a heavy bluff game," Crook advised his superiors, and left for the rendezvous.

But Geronimo slipped through Crook's fingers again, thanks to the efforts this time of an American bootlegger who discovered the rendezvous and sold Geronimo $30 worth of booze. Their resolve to surrender diluted by liquor, Geronimo, Naiche, 20 warriors plus their women and children fled once again.

Crook got back to San Carlos with 75 other Indians who had surrendered at the rendezvous. The results proved unsatisfactory to General Philip Sheridan, Crook's superior in Washington, D.C., and after Sheridan impugned Crook's strategy, Crook took the hint. "I believe," Crook wrote to Sheridan, "that the plan upon which I have conducted operations is the one most likely to prove successful in the end. It may be, however, that I am too much wedded to my own views in this matter, and as I have spent nearly eight years of the hardest work of my life in this Department, I respectfully request that I may now be relieved from its command." Sheridan promptly replaced Crook with Brigadier General Nelson A. Miles in April 1886.

Miles, whose relentless campaigning on the Great Plains had been most effective, did not share Crook's faith in the Apache scouts. Indeed, he suspected them of incipient treachery and discharged most of them. In their place he assembled a formidable force of 5,000 white regulars, approximately one fourth the strength of the entire U.S. Army. The target of all this military might comprised a mere 22 fighting men, including

Geronimo and Naiche, and members of their families.

Through the next four months and 12 days, Miles's regulars marched and countermarched over the canyons and deserts of south Arizona. He installed a network of 27 heliograph stations on the highest peaks of Apachería to flash by sunlight news of troop and Indian movements. Miles's heliographs drove the Apaches into Mexico and the Army floundered after them among the crags of the Sierra Madre. By August, Lieutenant Leonard Wood, second in command of the troops in Mexico, was down to "a pair of canton flannel drawers, and an old blue blouse, a pair of moccasins and a hat without a crown." They were also without Geronimo or any very firm opinion about where he was.

In the meantime, Miles heard it rumored that Geronimo was near Fronteras, about 30 miles below the border in Sonora, dickering gingerly with the Apache-hating Mexicans for liquor and supplies. His agents were two women from his ranchería.

In a providential change of policy, Miles ordered Lieutenant Charles Gatewood with a small party of Apache scouts to contact the outlaw chief. The scouts trailed Geronimo's envoys out of Fronteras. "Slowly and cautiously, with a piece of flour sacking on a stick

to the fore as a white flag, we followed the squaws the next three days," wrote Gatewood. He sent ahead two scouts, Martine and Ki-e-ta, to reconnoiter. At dark Martine returned. They had met Geronimo, who was holding Ki-e-ta, once part of Geronimo's band, as hostage for Gatewood's appearance.

On the morning of August 24, Gatewood started for Geronimo's camp, trailed by some 30 scouts. But messengers from Geronimo confronted them on the trail and warned everyone but Martine and the lieutenant to stay behind. The scout and his officer advanced alone to the bronco camp. The Chiricahuas came in a few at a time, unsaddled their ponies and waited. Finally Geronimo arrived.

"He laid his rifle down twenty feet away and came and shook hands and, the tobacco having been passed around, he took a seat alongside as close as he could get, the revolver bulge under his coat touching my right thigh," Gatewood reported. Geronimo said he was ready to hear what Miles might have to say. The only choice open to him, Gatewood informed Geronimo, was between fighting it out and going to exile in Florida. Geronimo chose Florida.

And so, in Skeleton Canyon on the Mexican border, Arizona got permanent relief from marauding Apaches, a relief delivered in the end not by 5,000 troops but by two Apache scouts and one tired white.

In Washington it had long since been decided that the only guarantee against future outbreaks of Chiricahua broncos — assuming that they were ever properly caught — would be to isolate them in Florida at Fort Marion. So, under government control at last, the Chiricahua leaders and their followers were loaded on trains and shipped away. Caught in the government's net were 60 scouts, deported along with the other exiles for no apparent reason except that they too were Apaches and that some had once been outlaws. General Crook, when he heard the news while serving up north on the Plains, was appalled and furious. He wrote: "I assert that these Chiricahua scouts did most excellent service, and were of more value in hunting down and compelling the surrender of the renegades, than all other troops engaged in operations against them, combined." Crook's acclamation of the scouts got no response and the betrayed Apaches remained under nominal arrest as prisoners of war for 26 years.

The poignant mellowing of an old warrior

Long after Geronimo was brought in by two Army scouts from his own tribe, the great Apache leader was still described as "the tiger of the human race." But captivity softened and changed the once-fearsome warrior.

In 1894, after eight years as a prisoner, Geronimo told an Army officer: "I do not consider that I am an Indian anymore. I am a white man." To most Americans, though, Geronimo re-mained "the Apache terror," and he seemed to relish his role as a living symbol of the Indian wars. He became a popular attraction at fairs and public celebrations, and slyly capitalized on his fame. Once, traveling by train to an exposition in Omaha, he peddled his coat buttons and even his hat to gawking spectators who gathered at every station along the way. Between stops, he would sew on more buttons and put on one of the new hats he had providently brought with him.

At the St. Louis World's Fair in 1904, Geronimo was part of a government exhibit on Indian culture. He laboriously printed and sold his autographs for 10 cents each, and hawked photographs for as much as two dollars. "The old gentleman is pretty high priced," said the director of the exhibit, "but then he is the only Geronimo."

Still free and still hostile, Geronimo *(center)* and his heavily armed followers assemble in the Sierra Madre during peace talks with Army representatives, in March 1886. The Apache chief surrendered less than six months later.

185

At Fort Pickens, Florida, in 1887, Geronimo *(left)* lounges on a cannon barrel with fellow prisoners Naiche *(center)* and Mangas. The "war paint" may have been for the benefit of the tourists who came to see the Apaches.

Farmer Geronimo, who turned to agriculture after being moved to Fort Sill, Oklahoma, in 1894, proudly displays one of his melons. With him are his sixth wife, two of his children and a small girl who is probably a granddaughter.

189

In his uniform as an Army scout, Geronimo *(seated, center)* lends his presence to a gathering at an 1898 exposition in Omaha. With him are visitors from the U.S. Lifesaving Service, an antecedent of the Coast Guard. They may have paid for the privilege of being photographed with him.

191

Still tall in the saddle at the age of about 75, Geronimo rides a cavalry horse at an Oklahoma Wild West show in 1905. His mount's carbine scabbard is empty, possibly because the troopers remembered the warrior's reputation.

6 | Idols in the public eye

When Buffalo Bill Cody killed a minor Cheyenne chief in a minor skirmish in 1876, he wrote to his wife, "you will no doubt hear of it through the papers." He could be confident that she would. The press had been keeping Mrs. Cody and a rapt American public up to date on Buffalo Bill—and his friend and sometime fellow scout Wild Bill Hickok—for years.

The dust scarcely had time to settle on any of their scouting exploits or Indian encounters before a journalist or dime novelist would be on the scene to record—and probably embellish—the details. Eastern readers of these thrilling dispatches found Buffalo Bill and Wild Bill endlessly fascinating. Hickok and Cody were made to order for the popular press of the period. Most of their fellow scouts were either too reticent to enjoy the publicity or too salty to be digestible except as colorful supporting characters in the Western drama. The two Bills, both genuinely capable scouts, were also handsome, reasonably civilized and willing to spend hours spinning tales for journalists. Between assignments, they even appeared on Eastern theater stages to re-create their Western heroics.

The two scouts captured the imagination of post-Civil War Americans the way Kit Carson had captured the imagination of the prewar generation. Long before Cody parlayed his publicity into a spectacular show-business career, he and Hickok epitomized the scouting trade to the American public.

The three men in the center of this 1874 photograph—*(from left to right)* Hickok, Cody and Texas Jack Omohundro—all had stage as well as scouting careers. The other men cannot be positively identified.

A heroic progress: from the prairies to the popular press

In the fall of 1864, a strapping 18-year-old scout in the 7th Kansas Volunteer Cavalry, wearing nondescript gray jeans instead of his Union Army private's uniform, rode alone in the countryside along the Little Blue River near Independence in far western Missouri. The scout, whose name was William Frederick Cody, was in no man's land, riding out ahead of his brigade to pick up whatever information he could about the disposition of Rebel troops.

Coming upon a farmhouse, he decided to stop in and neighbor around a little, confident that his casual appearance would conceal his Army role. Walking through the open door he saw, seated at a table, a man of impressive build wearing a Confederate officer's gray uniform. Young Cody felt an involuntary tightening of nerve and muscle. Though he might bluff his way through the secessionist farm communities of Missouri, it was another thing to play that role before an officer of the Rebel Army. The man turned toward him, eyed Bill Cody with interest, and spoke: "You little rascal, what are you doing in those 'secesh' clothes?"

Startled, the youth stared back and recognized James Butler "Wild Bill" Hickok, a friend of earlier days. Not to be outdone in coolness, William Cody— later known as Buffalo Bill— said: "I ask you the same question, sir." But Hickok waved him to silence. "Hush! Sit down and have some bread and milk, and we'll talk afterwards." The men shared a milksop's lunch— which, of all the tales of two hard-living characters who became the most famous Western scouts, is one of the hardest to credit. Then Hickok paid the farm wife for the fare and walked to the gate where Cody's

horse was tethered. Hickok said he also was a Union Army scout, disguised as a Southern officer to spy on a nearby Confederate division. The meeting was providential. Hickok had urgent reports to make, but was getting so much useful information that he thought he might profitably stay inside Rebel lines a while longer. He briefed Cody on Confederate movements and gave him letters to take back to Union brigade headquarters.

It was, apparently, only a few days later that Hickok decided he had exhausted his usefulness and cover as a pseudo-Rebel and determined to make his getaway. According to Cody, it was not a stealthy escape:

"While both armies were drawn up in skirmish line near Fort Scott, Kansas, two men on horseback were seen rapidly leaving the Confederate lines, and suddenly they made a dash towards us. Instantly quick volleys were discharged from the Confederates, who also began a pursuit, and some five hundred shots were fired at the flying men. When within about a quarter of a mile of us, one fell from his horse to rise no more. His companion galloped on unhurt, and seven companies of our regiment charged out and met him, and checked his pursuers. The fugitive was dressed in Confederate uniform, and as he rode into our lines I recognized him as Wild Bill, the Union scout."

Nobody today can prove or disprove the authenticity of these swashbuckling events. Army records show that Cody was a private in the 7th Kansas Cavalry during this campaign, and that Hickok, at the same time, was a Union spy. But the only authority for the meeting at the farmhouse, and for many other stories told of the two men, is the action-packed autobiography of William F. "Buffalo Bill" Cody, first written in 1879 and later embellished by other writers.

From the moment that their real-life exploits brought them to the attention of a public eager for heroes, the flesh-and-bone Hickok and Cody were magnified and

Surrounded by scenes attesting to his triumphs in hunting, scouting, guiding and Indian-killing, Buffalo Bill Cody rests by a campfire in this 1888 promotional poster.

distorted by inventive dime novelists, gullible or irresponsible journalists, and even relatives. It was Cody's own sister Helen who manufactured the whopper that Buffalo Bill once stepped up to the formidable Confederate raider Nathan Bedford Forrest and, saying he was making a delivery for a Rebel spy, breezily handed the general a set of phony maps of Union positions.

It was so pleasing a tale as not to be denied; to Cody, who liked a good story, especially about himself, it did not matter whether the yarn was true. As a matter of fact, by 1872 he was spending a good part of his time in show business, and the deeper he got into it the more conscious he became of the real gold to be found under a rainbow of publicity. If his press agents occasionally ran short of invention, he himself rarely did.

Nor was Hickok guiltless in the grand deception that portrayed him as a superman of the Plains. Possessed of a sly sense of the ridiculous, Hickok himself told a credulous Henry M. Stanley—the journalist who later earned fame for finding Dr. Livingstone in Africa—that he reckoned he had probably slain more than 100 men. But Hickok's tall tales, unlike Cody's imaginative press-agentry, were merely mischievous. Like many scouts before him, Hickok was a noted legpuller and tale spinner, in person if not in print, and it amused him to play on the tenderfoot's innocence.

Beneath the glamorous haze of hyperbole that surrounded them, both Hickok and Cody were plainsmen of genuinely high caliber. They may not have epitomized the astute early frontiersmen like Jim Bridger and Kit Carson, both of whom brought scouting to a high art. But Cody and Hickok showed themselves more than competent in the scout's roles of pathfinder, guide, tracker, courier, hunter and Indian fighter. And because they had the knack of mixing fact with fiction, the pair did more to glamorize their profession than all the rest of their workaday comrades together. No two names made Western scouts better known to the world than those of Wild Bill Hickok and Buffalo Bill Cody.

The friendship between the two men was no invention, though there was almost a nine-year difference in their ages. James Butler Hickok was born in Illinois in 1837, the fourth child in a family of four boys and two girls. When he was 19 he made his way to Kansas Territory to seek gainful occupation. By 1858, at 21,

he had settled down so respectably as to be elected constable of Monticello Township in Johnson County.

William Frederick Cody started life on an Iowa farm in 1846 and moved with his parents and five sisters to Salt Creek Valley near Leavenworth, Kansas, in 1854. When his father died in 1857, the boy took odd jobs in an attempt to become the breadwinner. After the outbreak of the Civil War in 1861, as he later confessed with shame, Cody got involved with a gang of jayhawkers—abolitionist guerrillas whose principal activity was stealing horses from secessionist farmers across the river in Missouri. When his mother found out what he was up to and pointed out that stealing from noncombatants was neither right nor honorable, he dutifully gave up the enterprise and betook himself, for no given reason, to Leavenworth.

Though there are conflicting accounts of where and when Hickok and Cody first met, it may have been in Leavenworth in 1861. In that year Hickok, by then ex-constable of Monticello, signed on with the quartermaster at Sedalia, Missouri, as an Army wagon boss at $100 a month. The job took him to Leavenworth, where, according to Cody, the two men ran into each other and Hickok took the youth on as an assistant.

Soon they went into partnership on a sporting venture that ended in grievous disappointment. Hickok acquired, Cody said, "a fast running horse from the mountains" that he thought might do well in the St. Louis races. Hickok entered his mountain runner with Cody as jockey, and bet everything the two men had, including the horse. Cody, skilled rider though he was, failed to boot the beast home in time, and the partners "came out of that race minus the horse and every dollar we had in the world—busted in the largest city we had ever been in." Wild Bill borrowed money to buy young Cody a steamboat ticket back to Leavenworth.

During this period Hickok's reputation for being tough and virtually fearless was growing. In the spring of 1862, according to an acquaintance named George Hance, Hickok's wagon train carrying Union supplies was captured by Rebel guerrillas. Hickok escaped and rounded up a band of gunslinging friends in Independence, Missouri. Next day, his small private army tracked down the Rebels and recaptured the train.

It was while in Independence that Hickok—so another story goes—got his nickname. He came to the

In a famous Civil War incident, Union spy Hickok and a companion—who throws up his hands as he is shot—dash from Confederate lines, Rebels in pursuit. The escape helped launch the Wild Bill legend.

assistance of a bartender who had wounded a thug in a brawl and whose saloon was about to be rushed by the victim's angry and booze-emboldened friends. Outside the saloon door, Hickok drew his pistols and ordered the mob to stay back. When a few foolhardy souls edged forward he fired two shots over their heads and warned them that, if they did not disperse, he would shoot the next man who moved toward him. The mob dispersed. Later that evening, Hickok was seen standing near the edge of a crowd that had gathered to form a vigilance committee. There were shouts of approval for his bold stand outside the saloon, and one woman yelled: "Good for you, Wild Bill!" No matter that Hickok's given name was James; the appellation stuck.

Hickok was an Army wagon boss until September, after which he was assigned to infiltrate enemy lines in southwestern Missouri to gather information. Records of his undercover work for the rest of the War are skimpy, but sufficient evidence survives to establish that he served as both scout and spy. One document, Special Orders No. 89 issued at Springfield, Missouri, on April 3, 1864, says in part: "J. B. Hickok will be taken up on the Rolls of Capt Owen, A.Q.M., as Scout, at these Head Quarters, from this date and will be furnished a horse, and equipments while on duty as Scout. His compensation will be five dollars per day. By order of Brigadier General Sanborn."

In autumn 1864, Wild Bill was in disguise with the Rebel army. History loses him for a few months, then finds him on February 10, 1865, when he sent a laconic report from Cassville, Missouri, to General Sanborn, Southwest District Headquarters, Spring-

Although called "Duck Bill" by a man he bested in a gunfight, Wild Bill Hickok impressed others as a handsome figure. He obliged admirers by dressing like a dandy and anointing his hair with perfumed oils.

field. "I have been at Camp Walker and Spavinaw," Hickok wrote. "There are not more than ten or twelve rebels in any squad in the southwest that I can hear of."

Wild Bill slipped into obscurity, but reemerged at the end of the War in Kansas, where William Darnell, a member of a wagon train approaching Fort Zarah, obviously recognized him as a well-known individual. "Wild Bill Hickok, on a dandy horse," reminisced Darnell, "came riding by on a run, shouting out as he rode by, 'Lee's surrendered! Lee's surrendered!'" Apparently more impressed by Hickok's appearance than by the news, Darnell continued: "He was a striking figure as I noticed him, a large broad-brimmed hat on his head, long drooping mustache, long flowing hair that fell about his shoulders, a brace of ivory-handled revolvers strapped to his waist, and an extra pair in holsters that fitted about the horn of his saddle where he could reach them instantly. These latter were long-barreled ones, capable of carrying quite a distance. It was common talk that he had got many an enemy with them just on account of their long-range qualities."

Although Hickok's official war record is veiled, Darnell's comments suggest that Wild Bill's exploits had made him famous. William Cody's war service, on the other hand—whether or not it included eating bread and milk with James Hickok in no man's land—did little to build his reputation. After the horse-racing episode with Hickok, Cody had undertaken various minor guiding jobs for military and semimilitary units, but for the most part had led what Cody himself later called "a dissolute and reckless life."

In February 1864, a few days before his 18th birthday, Cody finally got around to joining the Army. He had not, he freely admitted, been taken by a sudden, virulent attack of patriotism. "I had no idea of doing anything of the kind," he confessed, "but one day, after having been under the influence of bad whisky, I awoke to find myself a soldier in the 7th Kansas. I did not remember how or when I had enlisted, but I saw I was in for it, and that it would not do for me to endeavor to back out."

He served for more than 19 months in the 7th Kansas Cavalry, in all likelihood engaging in some scouting. But when he was mustered out on September 29, 1865, he had not yet proved himself as a scout, nor had he given any indication that he ever would.

At the end of the War, Cody was 19 and Hickok 28. Like thousands of other suddenly footloose men, they faced the necessity of finding a future. Hickok was the first to find gainful employment. In 1866 he got a job as a civilian scout with the Army at Fort Riley in Kansas. His first year in that position was relatively uneventful, but he attracted notice nonetheless. In a letter describing Hickok, an officer remarked: "By the way, I forgot to tell you about our guide—the most striking object in camp. Six feet, lithe, active, sinewy, daring rider, dead shot with pistol and rifle, long locks, fine features and mustache, buckskin leggins, red shirt, broad-brim hat, two pistols in belt, rifle in hand—he is a picture. He goes by the name of Wild Bill, and tells wonderful stories of his horsemanship, fighting and hair-breadth escapes. We do not, however, feel under any obligation to believe them all."

In the spring of 1867, Hickok was assigned to go with George Armstrong Custer and the 7th Cavalry on a campaign against Cheyennes and Sioux in western Kansas. It was a hazardous job that entailed carrying dispatches through the night and snatching rest by day, scouting ahead of the main columns and keeping the fighting force informed about the movements of the hostiles, and staying alive by outguessing, outriding and outshooting the Indians. Wild Bill must have made quite an impression on Custer, for Custer later eulogized him as "a Plainsman in every sense of the word, yet unlike any of his class. Whether on foot or on horseback, he was one of the most perfect types of physical manhood I ever saw. Of his courage there could be no question: it had been brought to the test on too many occasions to admit of a doubt.

"His skill in the use of rifle and pistol was unerring; while his deportment was exactly the opposite of what might be expected from a man of his surroundings. It was entirely free from all bluster and bravado. He seldom spoke of himself unless requested to do so. Wild Bill is anything but a quarrelsome man; yet no one but himself can enumerate the many conflicts in which he has been engaged, and which have almost invariably resulted in the death of his adversary."

Custer's account of Hickok's value as a scout is tantalizingly free of any details of the plainsman's actual achievements, as were the stories about Wild Bill that began to appear in the popular press. The first of these

was written by George W. Nichols and was published in *Harper's New Monthly Magazine* in February 1867. Openly adulatory, gloriously inventive and wonderfully exciting, the Nichols piece catapulted Hickok into national fame as a Western folk hero. Further luster was added to the Hickok name by Henry Stanley, then a young reporter covering Custer's campaign for the *Weekly Missouri Democrat.* Stanley interviewed Wild Bill at Fort Zarah in April, and in a dispatch to his paper described his subject as "one of the finest examples of that peculiar class now extant, known as Frontiersmen, ranger, hunter and Indian scout." Even local newsmen lent support to the portrait of James Butler Hickok that was beginning to emerge by reporting, or misreporting, every available anecdote about "the celebrated scout, Wild Bill."

Before the end of 1867, fiction writers had joined in, and DeWitt's Ten Cent Romances were in full swing with thrilling dime novels such as *Wild Bill, the Indian Slayer,* and *Wild Bill's First Trail.*

While Wild Bill was thus gaining fame as a scout and general all-purpose hero, William Frederick Cody had been busy courting Louisa Frederici of St. Louis, getting married, honeymooning and attempting to settle down. In Salt Creek Valley, Kansas, he set himself up in the hotel business as the genial, 20-year-old landlord of the Golden Rule House. As Cody would have it: "People generally said I made a good landlord and knew how to run a hotel—a business qualification which, it is said, is possessed by comparatively few men. But it proved too tame employment for me, and again I sighed for the freedom of the plains." The truth is that he proved so inept at the business if not the social side of hotelkeeping that he was losing money.

Within six months, Cody sold the Golden Rule House, parked his wife in Leavenworth with his sister Helen, and headed west. His separation from Louisa proved to be the first of many; for the rest of his life he was a part-time husband, sending for his wife occasionally or dropping in on her to perform his conjugal duties and to meet the children that periodically arrived.

In the autumn of 1866 he ran into his old friend Wild Bill in Junction City. Learning that Cody was jobless, Hickok came to his rescue and got him a post as a government scout. For about a year, Cody worked intermittently as a scout in Kansas, carrying dispatches and guiding expeditionary forces along unmapped trails through Indian country. It was Cody's first employment as a civilian scout, an occupation he was to transmute into a golden career in fact and fiction.

But scouting was not steady employment, and Cody occasionally had to take less glamorous jobs to earn a living. In 1867, he went to work grading track for the builders of the Kansas Pacific Railroad. It was during this period that he received his famous nickname.

There exist at least two versions of how and by whom he was first tagged with the sobriquet of "Buffalo Bill," and either could be true. Cody was forced to subject his fleet-footed horse Brigham, which he had somehow been able to train for buffalo hunting, to the indignity of a work-horse's harness. Man and horse were at work one day when a small herd of buffalo was sighted not far from the workmen's camp. Cody unhitched Brigham, took up his .50-caliber Springfield breechloader, which he called Lucretia Borgia, and started out to get meat for supper. He was barely on his way when he met a party of officers from Fort Hays, Kansas, who allowed that they, too, were out after buffalo, but would not mind if track-grader Cody tagged along on his work horse. There were 11 buffalo in the herd, and when the party came within a mile of the animals, the officers dashed off in pursuit, condescendingly assuring Cody that they would let him have most of the meat after they had had their sport.

Cody slipped off Brigham's bridle to leave both hands free and let the trained hunting horse take him at full gallop alongside the rear of the herd, arriving there before the officers. Racing along with his targets, Cody fired off shot after shot at close range from the tail end of the herd to the front, while the officers were still giving chase from behind. Cody brought down all 11 of the beasts with 12 shots. Introducing himself to Captain George Wallace Graham of the 10th Cavalry, leader of the hunting party, Bill Cody presented the officers with the tongues and tenderloins of his kill, and was hailed on the spot as Buffalo Bill.

Another version of his naming has to do with the arrival of 1,200 tracklayers near Hays City after Cody had completed his stint as a grader. Goddard Brothers, caterers to the railroad's work gangs, hired Cody to deliver 12 buffalo a day to the railroad's cook shacks at the munificent rate of $500 a month. Cody later calculated that he slew, in all, 4,280 buffalo for the railroad pantry. Understandably, the tracklaying roustabouts grew weary of an unchanging menu of humps and hindquarters, and took to greeting Cody with such comments as "Here comes this old Bill with more buffalo." One laborer, in satiated resignation, composed this tribute to the tireless and well-paid meat supplier:

Buffalo Bill, Buffalo Bill,
Never missed and never will;
Always aims and shoots to kill
And the company pays his buffalo bill.

Divergent though the paths of the two men had been, Cody and Hickok would soon become involved—sometimes separately, sometimes together—in one of the major campaigns of the Indian wars. Cody, his services as a buffalo hunter no longer required by Goddard Brothers, raffled off his horse Brigham for 10 chances at $30 apiece, and then, in May of 1868, hired on as scout at Fort Larned in western Kansas. Not long thereafter, Hickok transferred himself to Fort Hays and signed on as a scout with the 10th Cavalry.

Through the early summer of 1868 an uneasy peace reigned on the Plains. Then, in July, bands of Cheyennes began to rampage through settlements near Council Grove, and within weeks a huge encampment of Kiowas and Comanches sprang up near Fort Larned and threatened to erupt into violence. Buffalo Bill Cody was sent on a one-man 65-mile ride from the fort to General Philip H. Sheridan at Fort Hays, carrying the news that the Indians were on the warpath.

"This intelligence," Sheridan wrote later in his memoirs, "required that certain orders be carried to Fort Dodge, ninety-five miles south of Hays." This, too, was a dangerous journey. Several couriers had already been killed on the route. "Cody, learning of the strait I was in, manfully came to the rescue, and proposed to make the trip to Dodge, though he had just finished his long and perilous ride from Larned. After four or five hours' rest he mounted a fresh horse and hastened on his journey. At Dodge he took six hours' sleep, and then continued on to his own post—Fort Larned—with more despatches. After resting twelve hours at Larned, he was again in the saddle with tidings for me at Fort Hays. Thus, in all, Cody rode about 350 miles in less than sixty hours, and such an exhibition of endurance and courage was more than enough to convince me that his services would be extremely valuable in the campaign, so I retained him at Fort Hays till the battalion of the Fifth Cavalry arrived, and then made him chief of scouts for that regiment."

The 5th's first assignment, in early autumn, was a reconnaissance along the Kansas Pacific Railroad with Major William B. Royall in temporary command. Royall and Cody had an almost instant misunderstanding. After a couple of days' march, Royall sent Buffalo Bill out to bag a few of his specialty for the regimental dinner; but when Cody asked for wagons to bring in the meat, the major retorted rather haughtily that he was "not in the habit of sending out my wagons until I know there is something to be hauled in." Cody dutifully went off, shot half a dozen buffalo, and sent for the wagons. Next day, riding out again and sighting another herd, he used his horse to cut out seven animals and haze them into the middle of the regimental camp, where he killed them one by one. Royall demanded an explanation. "I thought I would make the buffaloes furnish their own transportation," Cody replied.

Concealing his restless spirit and looking like a responsible husband, Bill Cody stands by his bride, Louisa Frederici, in 1866. Ambitious only for ordered domesticity, Louisa resented his scouting career.

Toward the end of October 1868, General Eugene A. Carr, a veteran Indian fighter, arrived to take over the 5th Cavalry. The 5th had moved to Fort Lyon in Colorado Territory when, in November, Sheridan unveiled his plans for a winter campaign. As one of several columns operating against hostile Indians, Carr's 5th was to be marched southeastward to catch up with Brigadier General William Penrose, already in the field. Penrose, with four companies of the 10th Cavalry and one of the 7th, had been out for three weeks with Wild Bill Hickok as his guide. With only a small pack train for supplies, Penrose was feared to be low on rations and forage, and in need of relief. Indeed he was; he had been caught by heavy snowstorms and was snowed in at the foot of a cliff on Palo Duro Creek, on the Texas-Oklahoma border. Many of his animals were dead and his men were near starvation.

Carr left Fort Lyon in early December with a ponderous train including ambulances, pack mules and 75 six-mule wagons. With Buffalo Bill leading the way, the column pushed through deepening drifts at temperatures that sometimes dropped to 30° below. Poking ahead through a blizzard with four other scouts, Cody found one of Penrose's old camps and traced the trail along the west bank of the Cimarron River in country too rough for the wagons. Carr followed up the opposite bank of the river until he came to what looked like a dead end. He was on a high tableland in the Raton foothills, with a downward slope to the river far too steep—Carr thought—for wagons to get down in one piece. Cody thought otherwise. Persuading the general to get his cavalry down the incline, Cody turned his attention to the doubting wagon masters.

"Run down, slide down or fall down—any way to get down," he said to rally the wagon drivers. Setting an example for them, Cody had the mess wagon brought up to the brink of the slope, then he locked all four of the wheels with chains and started down. "The wheel horses—or rather the wheel-mules—were good on the hold back," he remembered later, "and we got along finely until we nearly reached the bottom, when the wagon crowded the mules so hard that they started on a run and galloped down into the valley and to the place where General Carr had located his camp. Three other wagons immediately followed in the same way, and in half an hour every wagon was in camp."

Cody had saved days of travel by forcing the wagons down the hill, and had no trouble in following Penrose's trail thereafter. Scouting along San Francisco Creek, Cody ran into three hungry troopers from Penrose's outfit who told such a harrowing tale of their comrades' condition that Carr ordered Cody ahead with two cavalry companies and a 50-mule pack train of emergency supplies. Pulling into Penrose's snowbound camp, one of the first men Cody encountered was Hickok, hunkering over a meager fire massaging his hands to keep them in gunfighting trim.

With a supply camp established and Penrose's men thawed out, Carr picked 500 of his fittest men and headed south to the Canadian River to join Colonel A. W. Evans' column coming east from New Mexico Territory. Cody and Hickok went along as scouts. Camping on the south fork of the Canadian, they located Evans' supply depot about 12 miles away.

In the Carr camp, the two Bills became the grateful recipients of exciting news, brought in by some of Evans' men: a Mexican wagon train was coming from New Mexico with a cargo of beer for Evans' camp. Cody and Hickok decided to intercept the shipment. They lay low as the train neared Carr's camp on its way to Evans' command, and by offering money persuaded the Mexicans to part with the beer. With the loot back in camp, the brigands sold it by the pint tin cup at a profit. Since the weather was bitter, the troops warmed the beer with picket pins heated red-hot in the fire. "The result," said Cody, "was one of the biggest beer jollifications I ever had the misfortune to attend."

Beer notwithstanding, it was a hard winter for the scouts. Carr needed to keep his communications open and relied heavily on Cody and Hickok to make the long, lonely trips during the bitter winter of 1868. "Mr. Cody," Carr said later, "showed his quality by quietly offering to go with some dispatches to General Sheridan across a dangerous region, where another scout was reluctant to risk himself."

Whoever the reluctant scout may have been, it was not Hickok. A contemporary account in the *Arkansaw Traveler* reported that, on one occasion, Hickok volunteered to make the 80-mile trip from Palo Duro Creek to Camp Supply for provisions after other scouts had refused. "On arriving at Camp Supply, Bill rested a short time," said the *Traveler*, "during which he was

Bill Hickok, at the far left, lines up with the quartermaster's staff at Fort Harker in Kansas, in 1867, shortly after signing up for his post-

rubbed with whiskey, both inside and out, as he termed it," and then made the return trip to Carr's camp.

Cody most likely returned to Fort Lyon with the 5th Cavalry in February 1869. Soon after, Hickok was himself approaching Fort Lyon, alone, when he encountered several Cheyennes and got into a running fight. A warrior got close enough to thrust a lance high and deep into Wild Bill's thigh. The next morning a wood detail found him about a mile from the fort, painfully dragging himself along, using the lance as a crutch. Cody saw him when he was brought in, almost dead from loss of blood and exposure, and rushed him to the Army surgeon. The wound was serious, and effectively ended Hickok's usefulness as an Army

scout. His contract ran out at the end of February, and he made no effort to renew it. At 31, Hickok was through with the military and with his scouting career.

When his leg healed, he became a civilian peace officer, first as sheriff at Hays City and later as marshal of Abilene, Kansas. Enforcing some semblance of peace in those rambunctious towns so enhanced his reputation as a killer—and paradoxically raised the trophy value of his own life—that he would never sit at a poker table except with his back to the wall.

The year of Hickok's eclipse as a scout was also the year that Bill Cody's scouting achievements launched him on his soaring ascent to fame. But in his first action

Civil War hitch as a U.S. Army scout. Wild Bill is sporting his Colt revolvers in their customary quick-draw, grips-forward position.

that spring season with the 5th Cavalry, he came close to ending his own career. As General Carr settled the 5th into camp on Beaver Creek on May 13, Cody picked up the trail of a sizable body of Indians. Scouting ahead with a lieutenant and a dozen troopers, he crawled to a hilltop and spotted the Indians camped three miles away. When a trooper carrying the message to Carr was intercepted by mounted warriors and chased back to the patrol, Cody himself rode back to camp and alerted the general.

That afternoon the 5th attacked the force of about 500 Cheyennes, killing or wounding 30 at the cost of four dead troopers. When the Indians pulled back, the 5th pursued for three days before finding them at a place called Spring Creek. The first contact was made by an advance guard of 40 men guided by Cody—a small party that soon discovered it had bitten off almost more than it could chew. Surrounded by 200 warriors, the troopers dismounted and began fighting.

"They all, to this day, speak of Cody's coolness and bravery," Carr wrote some years later. "Reaching the scene we could see the Indians in retreat. A figure with apparently a red cap rose slowly up the hill. For an instant it puzzled us, as it wore the buckskin and had long hair, but on seeing the horse, I recognized it as Cody's 'Powder Face' and saw that it was Buffalo Bill without his broad-brimmed sombrero. On closer inspection I saw his head was swathed in a bloody handkerchief, which served not only as a temporary bandage but as a chapeau—his hat having been shot off, the bullet plowing his scalp badly for about five inches. It had ridged along the bone and he was bleeding profusely—a very 'close call,' but a lucky one.''

That night, despite his wound, Cody rode 50 miles to request supplies from the nearest Army post, Fort Kearny in south-central Nebraska. For his performance during the campaign, Cody was given a bonus of $100 by the Secretary of War—a unique award for a civilian scout in recognition of what General Carr called "extraordinarily good services as a trailer and fighter in the pursuit of hostile Indians." Even before his wound was healed, Cody would further enhance his reputation.

At the end of May, 1869, a band of Cheyennes known as the Hotamitaneo, or Dog Soldiers, led by a chief called Tall Bull, went raiding along the Solomon River in central Kansas. In one attack on a white settlement they carried off two women, Mrs. Susanna Zigler Daily Alderdice, wife of a former Army contract scout, and Mrs. Maria Weichel, an immigrant only two months out of Germany. The Indians left behind the lifeless bodies of Mrs. Weichel's husband and Mrs. Alderdice's baby.

General Carr's 5th Cavalry, complete with its chief civilian scout, Bill Cody, launched its pursuit of Tall Bull's Dog Soldiers and their female captives early in June. Attached to the 5th were three companies of Pawnee scouts under Major Frank North and his brother Luther (it was during this campaign that one of the Pawnees, Traveling Bear, won a medal that was mistakenly inscribed with another man's name).

Tall Bull's trail, trending north and west, was picked up early in July by Carr's forces as they wound upstream along the Republican River. The trackers were reasonably sure that the raiders still held the captive women alive, for, as Cody noted, "wherever they had encamped we found the print of a woman's shoe." By July 10 he was certain that the end of the trail was near. That day's march took the command through two of Tall Bull's abandoned campsites, and, that evening, the army bivouacked on a third, so recent it appeared to have been left only that morning. Next day, leaving the wagons to follow, Carr rushed forward with all available men—"that is," he said, "all whose horses were fit for service." His forces included 244

troopers of the 5th Cavalry, 200 Pawnees and Cody.

Cody, moving out front with half a dozen of the best Pawnee scouts, discovered the Indians encamped in the sand hills south of the South Platte River at a place named Summit Springs. He left the Pawnee scouts to keep watch and rode back to inform General Carr that the Indian horse herds and tipis were located some six miles distant from the command in a southwesterly direction. Thereupon, according to the regimental historian, Cody "guided the 5th Cavalry to a position whence the regiment was enabled to charge the enemy and win a brilliant victory."

The action began shortly after 2 o'clock in the afternoon when Carr told his bugler to sound the charge. That functionary was momentarily so excited that he forgot the notes. But the omission, if such it was, did no harm. The wind was blowing such a gale that he could scarcely have been heard if he had been able to toot and the troopers, seeing him go through the motions, broke into a gallop. Because of the wind and the cautious flanking maneuvers of the troops, the Indians neither heard nor saw the approaching attack force until it was too late. Carr's charge tore through a village so totally surprised and panicked that there was no effective resistance. For the 52 Indians counted dead on the field, Carr lost not a man.

Tall Bull would lead no more raids on frontier settlements, for he was among those killed. Although Luther North claimed that his brother Frank had slain the Cheyenne chief, it was generally accepted by the men of the 5th that credit for the deed belonged to Cody. Buffalo Bill's own story was that during the engagement he took a fancy to a large, fleet-footed bay ridden by an Indian of commanding appearance and that he picked off the rider to get the horse. It was only later, when he was mounted on his trophy, that he learned the dead man's identity. "One of the squaws among the prisoners," he recalled, "suddenly began crying in a pitiful and hysterical manner at the sight of this horse, and upon inquiry I found that she was Tall Bull's wife"—the same woman, he added, "that had killed one of the white women and wounded the other."

Whether the wife of Tall Bull was responsible for such savagery, the rescuing party discovered Mrs. Weichel wounded, and saved her life; Mrs. Alderdice was found dead, her skull smashed in by a tomahawk.

The Kansas plains were relatively quiet after the Battle of Summit Springs. The 5th Cavalry moved to Fort McPherson in central Nebraska later that month, and Bill Cody moved with it. The move turned out to be one of the most significant events of his life. There he met the dime novelist Ned Buntline—true name, E. Z. C. Judson—who had stopped by the fort in the course of a lecture tour. After pumping Bill about the scouting trade, Buntline went home to New York and wrote a thrilling magazine serial entitled *Buffalo Bill, the King of Border Men.* Apart from its use of Buffalo Bill's name, the story had very little to do with Cody, being mainly a luridly fanciful account of the adventures of Wild Bill Hickok. Nonetheless, the meeting with Buntline and the publicity generated by the serial were key factors in the process that would lead Bill Cody to fame and fortune in show business.

For the time, however, Cody stayed with the 5th at McPherson. Completion of the first transcontinental railroad on May 10, 1869, added a new dimension to his duties. Wealthy European and American sportsmen, encouraged by the accessibility of the West and

the lull in Indian hostilities, began arriving for the thrill of the chase, and Cody was detailed to guide them on hunting expeditions. This was not a departure in scouting; Jim Bridger had guided sportsmen through the wilderness as early as the 1830s. But Cody was to capitalize on this aspect of the job as no scout ever had.

The summer of 1871 brought on a truly splendid safari led by General Sheridan himself, who, with the Plains more or less at peace, could afford some time for relaxation. Escorted by Buffalo Bill, the party comprised a round dozen of eastern and midwestern tycoons, Army brass, wealthy sportsmen and editors, of whom the most prominent was James Gordon Bennett Jr. of the *New York Herald.* The "New Yorkers on the warpath," as the press dubbed them, traveled in style with 16 supply wagons, including one for ice, assorted transport for the less enthusiastic riders, five greyhounds, French chefs to do the cooking, and linen, china, glassware and silver for serving the cuisine.

"As it was a nobby and high-toned outfit which I was to accompany," Cody said, "I determined to put on a little style myself." He succeeded admirably, as was attested by Major General Henry Eugene Davies in a pamphlet describing the hunt. "The most striking feature of the whole was the figure of our friend Buffalo Bill riding down from the Fort to our camp, mounted upon a snowy white horse," Davies wrote. "Dressed in a suit of light buckskin, trimmed along the seams with fringes of the same leather, his costume lighted by the crimson shirt worn under his open coat, a broad sombrero on his head, and carrying his rifle lightly in his hand, he realized to perfection the bold hunter and gallant sportsman of the plains."

In a virtuoso display of showmanship and hunting skill, Cody gave the sportsmen a memorable 10 days of shooting along the Republican, Saline and Solomon rivers. The happy hunters killed more than 600 buffalo and 200 elk and left a trail blazed with empty champagne bottles for 194 miles. Cody's reputation among people of influence was beginning to soar.

At the same time, General Sheridan was thoroughly enjoying his peacetime role as host of the Plains. In the autumn of 1871, the Grand Duke Alexis, third son of Czar Alexander II, set sail for the United States with a Russian battle fleet for escort, and when Sheridan heard that Alexis had expressed an interest in seeing the American prairies, he immediately began mobilizing his resources for the grandest of all buffalo hunts.

The 5th Cavalry was due to move to Arizona Territory by the end of the year, but Sheridan issued orders "not to take Cody," who was to be the producer of the upcoming spectacle. Buffalo Bill selected a suitable site, then hurried off on a 150-mile ride from Fort McPherson to Frenchman Creek, a tributary of the Republican River, to see if the Sioux Chief Spotted Tail would bring in 100 warriors to put on a show for the royal guest. Spotted Tail, not being engaged in hostilities at the moment, agreed. Meanwhile, back on Red Willow Creek 40 miles south of the fort, troops were equipping "Camp Alexis" with elaborate tents that had wooden floors, carpets and heating stoves.

The Grand Duke, surrounded by a host of U.S. Army luminaries, including Sheridan and Custer, hove into camp on January 13. That night, Spotted Tail and his warriors staged a stirring war dance while Alexis interviewed Cody on how best to kill a buffalo.

The hunt began at 9 a.m. the next day with everybody — as was protocol — intent on seeing that the roy-

The Scouts Programme!

Messrs. CODY, JUDSON, OMOHUNDRO & NIXON, PROPRIETORS
Manager, Col. E. Z. C. Judson
Gen'l Director, J. M. Nixon
Stage Manager, W. J. Halpin
Armorer, W. J. Speck
Scenic Artist, Frank D. Skiff
Properties and Effects, Geo. Beach
Costumer, Mrs. Beach
Music, Carlo Patti

The New Sensation Drama, written by NED BUNTLINE, and founded on some of the most thrilling and interesting incidents of his great New York Weekly Indian Stories, entitled The

SCOUTS OF THE PRAIRIE

And Red Deviltry As It Is!

CAST OF CHARACTERS:

BUFFALO BILL—by the Original Hero . . . . Hon. W. F. CODY
TEXAS JACK—by the Original Hero . . . . J. B. OMOHUNDRO
CALE DURG . . . . NED BUNTLINE
DOVE EYE . . . . M'LLE MORLACCHI
Mormon Ben . . . . Mr. Wentworth
Sly Mike . . . . Mr. Walters
Phelim O'Laugherty . . . . Harry Gilbert
Carl Pretzel . . . . Walter Fletcher

INDIANS.

Wolf Slayer		W. J. Halpin
Big Eagle		W. H. Ferris
Ar-fl-a-ka,		Grassy Chief
As-e-tee,	Pawnee and Indian Chiefs,	Prairie Dog
As-sin-ah-wa,		Water Chief
Te-ko, tic-pown,		Big Elk
Kit—kot-coma,		Great River
Chuk-Kak,		Seven Stars
HAZEL EYE		SENORITA ELOE CARFANO
Nat-iah		Mrs. Beach

Synopsis of Scenery and Incidents:

ACT I.—SCENE 1.—On the Plains—Cale Durg, the Trapper—Arrival of Buffalo Bill and Texas Jack—Story of the Hunt—warning from Dove Eye—Danger—We'll wipe the Red Skins out—Off on the trail—The War-Whoop.
SCENE II.—The Renegade's Camp—Mormon Ben—Phelim O'Laugherty and Sly Mike—O'Laugherty's continued Drouth—poetic tribute to Hazel Eye—Hazel Eye Surprised—Cale Durg over.
SCENE III.—The Renegade Foiled—Wolf Slayer, the Treacherous Ute—Cale Durg over to the Rescue.—Dove Eye's poetic tribute to Cale Durg—Dove Eye's Appeal to the Chief.—"Death to the Pale Faces"—Doomed to the Torture Post—burn—The blazing Faggots—Dove Eye's knife powered—Search for the Severed Bonds—Cale Durg Defiant—"We'll Fight yet all."—Timely Arrival—Buffalo Bill and Texas Jack—"Death to the Redskins"—Rescue of Cale Durg.
ACT II.—SCENE I.—Mormon Ben, Sly Mike, and Phelim O'Laugherty—O'Laugherty declares "he is not a Mormon"—Meeting with the Indians—What Mormon Ben wanted—What O'Laugherty saw well as the White—Wolf Slayer's disdain of the Indians for the War-path—Dove Eye's Man as well as the White—The Departure of the Indians for the War-path—Dove Eye's invocation of the Great Spirit.
SCENE II.—Dove Eye and Hazel Eye, the two friends—Buffalo Bill Declares his Love—It is Reciprocal—Texas Jack arrives and interrupts the Meeting.—The Indians are Coming—"Buffalo Bill and Jack retire to Ambush 'em on the Plains.—Cochise—Cale Durg—That's a kind of a man I am"—How they Scalp 'em—Jack ropes 'em in—Contempt for the Buffalo Bill.
SCENE III.—Phelim O'Laugherty and Mormon Ben—Dove Eye's Contempt for the rescue—Jod's Beverage—Love Scene between Texas Jack and Hazel Eye.
SCENE IV.—The Search for Capture of the Forest Maidens—"The Cage is here, but the bird has down"—The Trail—Cale Durg arrives upon the scene—"Fly, Fly Your Enemies are too many"—Renegades—Cale Durg Never runs—The Capture and Death of Cale Durg—The Dying Curse—The Tr per's Last Shot.
ACT III.—SCENE I.—Dove Eye and Hazel Eye—Grief for Cale Durg—Buffalo Bill Texas Jack—Bill's Oath of Vengeance—"I'll not leave a Redskin to skim the Prairie"—Re Eye dejected—The White Girl and Red Maiden's affections—"We'll be Sisters"—Reveng
SCENE II.—The German Trader—Vengeance or Death.—The Loss of the Bottle—Carl Pretzel's Agony.
the Slain Trapper—Vengeance or Death.—Eagle and Wolf Slayer—"I Come to Kill You"
SCENE III.—The Scalp Dance—Eagle and Wolf Slayer—No prospect for the a
Knife Fight—Death of Wolf Slayer.
SCENE IV.—Phelim and Mormon Ben on their last legs—The Ind
wife, or a replenished bottle.
SCENE V.—The Trapper on the lookout—Dove Eye's faith in Manito—The Ind
Durg—The American Scout Triumphant—Great Heavens the
Buffalo Bill's red hot reception—"Give it to them boys"—One Hundred Reds for o

PRAIRIE ON FIRE

Magnificent Scenic Effects; Life-like Illustrations of a Great W
Prairie, as seen when on Fire. Imposingly Grand. K. P. Railwa
in a Herd of Buffalo—Clear the Track.

To be preceded by the Short but Terribly Laughable Farce of the

A KISS IN THE DAR

Mr. Pettibone . . . . Harry
Frank Fathom . . . . Harry Wen
Mrs. Pettibone . . . . Gussie
Mary . . . . Mrs
Unkown . . . . Miss

MATINEES WEDNESDAY AND SATURDAY
50 Cents. Children 25
D. H. ELLIOTT. (Gen'l West. Agent Kan. Pac. R'y.) Tra
for this Combination.

al visitor made the first kill. To facilitate this end, Cody mounted the Grand Duke on his own buffalo horse, Buckskin Joe. But a difficulty arose: it appeared that the Duke, who had elected to use a revolver, could not hit the broad side of a barn from inside with the doors closed. When he emptied his revolver without scoring, Cody rode alongside and exchanged weapons. But again Alexis missed with six straight shots.

"Seeing that the animals were bound to make their escape," said Cody, "I rode up to him, gave him my old reliable 'Lucretia' and told him to urge his horse close to the buffaloes, and I would give him the word when to shoot. At the same time I gave old Buckskin Joe a blow with my whip; and with a few jumps the horse carried the Grand Duke to within about ten feet of a big buffalo bull."

Cody, at the Duke's elbow, gave him his cue, and Alexis pulled the trigger of the rifle. The bull went down. Alexis pulled up and waved his hat in triumph. Celebratory champagne flowed. Later in the day, having settled down a bit, the Duke killed a buffalo cow with a pistol at 30 yards, surprising everybody. More champagne followed. "I was in hopes he would kill five or six more," commented Cody, "if a basket of champagne was to be opened every time he dropped one."

Cody's hopes were fulfilled by the end of the five-day hunt, for under his tutelage the Duke succeeded in bagging a total of eight buffalo. Alexis was delighted,

211

In a fanciful 1872 newspaper illustration, Russian Grand Duke Alexis smartly guns down his first buffalo with a revolver. Alexis, a poor shot, actually was using Cody's rifle when the beast finally fell.

and later gave Bill several valuable gifts including a set of jeweled cuff links.

Shortly after the Alexis extravaganza, Cody was given a leave of absence and headed east at the invitation of James Gordon Bennett Jr. and other members of Sheridan's '71 hunt. While in New York he sought out Ned Buntline, who seized on Bill's new fame to present a play about his exploits, scribble a couple of Buffalo Bill novels, and concoct an inspired plan—to star the real Buffalo Bill onstage.

Cody however, having been royally entertained, was ready—or just about ready—to resume scouting when he was recalled to duty that spring. Legend says that Cody was still wearing evening dress and a stovepipe hat when he appeared at Fort McPherson, having had a few too many farewell drinks and having forgotten to bring along his trunk. Whether or not that tale is true, he was back in top form when, shortly after his return, a small party of Indians raided a railroad station within five miles of the fort, killed a few men and ran off a herd of horses. Captain Charles Meinhold

of the 3rd Cavalry pursued, with Cody as his scout.

On April 26, two days out on the trail, Cody went ahead with a detachment of six men under the command of a Sergeant Foley. Spotting his quarry from a mile away, Cody led his party to within 50 yards of the raiders' camp before the Indians saw them and fired. During the fight, one Indian was killed by Cody and two more by the troopers.

It was a relatively insignificant engagement by Cody's lights; but, on the strength of Meinhold's report citing him for bravery and skill, Cody was awarded the Congressional Medal of Honor on May 22, 1872.

At the end of a year that offered him little more excitement in the scouting field, Cody succumbed to Ned Buntline's blandishments and went East to go on the stage. He settled his wife and children—now numbering three—in Rochester, New York, and launched a new career as an actor playing himself. For the next few years he toured in such stirring dramas as *The Scouts of the Plains,* with time most summers to keep his hand in as a real-life scout and hunting guide. ◉

Delighted with his novel Western adventures, the Grand Duke rewarded Buffalo Bill with this unusual patchwork robe made from 57 different rare Siberian furs.

Before he left the United States, Alexis commissioned diamond-studded, buffalo-head cuff links and a tiepin for his guide. Cody later had the jewelry made into rings and a pin to give to his wife and daughters.

For rich tourists, an excursion with the famous scout

Advance-man "Pony Bob" Haslam pours drinks as Cody *(second from right)* and his guests christen Point MacKinnon with a toast.

Whenever Indian hostilities died down, Army scouts turned to a pleasant and lucrative sideline—guiding Eastern and European dudes. Gregarious Buffalo Bill Cody was easily the most popular of the moonlighting scouts. In later years, when he mounted his own hunting and sightseeing extravaganzas, he proved as successful a host as he had been a rustic attraction.

In 1892, he invited a group of European sportsmen on a hunting trip through northern Arizona. Typically, his retinue included his press agent, the advance man for his Wild West show, a dime novelist and a photographer.

The hunters encountered spectacular scenery and shot an abundance of game. And in a high point of the trip (below), they left their mark on the American West by naming a minor Grand Canyon peak after a member of the party, Colonel W. H. MacKinnon, who had just killed his first buck.

With the day's kill proudly displayed, Cody *(right, front)* and his party camp on the Kaibab Plateau above the Grand Canyon. During the trip the group shot mountain sheep, mountain lions, deer, elk, antelope and even porcupines.

Accompanied by the dime novelist Prentiss Ingraham *(left)*, Cody, dressed in an eye-catching checkered vest, ushers part of his entourage across the Colorado River. Buffalo Bill always liked to "put on a little style"—even when in the wilderness.

Cody *(center)* strikes a theatrical plainsman's attitude amid a clutter of camping paraphernalia. To ensure that his guests did not find roughing it too rough, he brought along a French chef and provided buckboards and ambulance wagons for use when the sportsmen grew tired of the saddle.

By the end of 1871, Wild Bill Hickok was out of a job. The city fathers of Abilene had decreed that their town would not henceforth be available as a shipping point for Texas cattle, and when the hell-raising transients took their trade elsewhere there was no longer any need in Abilene for a high-priced, gunslinging marshal of Hickok's caliber.

For four years, from 1872 to the beginning of 1876, Wild Bill wandered from place to place picking up odd jobs but never again finding the right niche for a man of his particular skills. For a time he joined Buffalo Bill as a scout on stage, but he lacked his old friend's show-business flair and the thespian life bored him.

In March 1876, he married Agnes Lake Thatcher, who had been smitten by him when her circus troupe visited Abilene during his days as marshal and had pursued him ever since. After a two-week honeymoon in Cincinnati, Hickok left her with relatives and went back out West, planning to send for her as soon as he had made enough money to support them both.

By this time his opportunities for employment were even more limited: sadly, for a man who had made his living and stayed alive largely through his expertise as a quick-draw specialist, his eyesight was beginning to fail him. The gold rush to the Black Hills of Dakota Territory seemed his best and perhaps his only hope. Gathering a few like-minded friends in Cheyenne and borrowing a little capital ($22.30) from an old Army buddy, he set out at the end of June for the gold diggings at Deadwood Gulch. At Fort Laramie the Hickok party was joined by 30 more wagons bound for the Black Hills with a cargo of eager prospectors and hopeful camp followers—shady ladies with such descriptive names as Dirty Emma, Sizzling Kate and Big Dollie.

It seems likely that it was during this rollicking summer excursion that Hickok and Cody met for the last time. During the first week in July, when Cody was on temporary duty with the 5th Cavalry, Hickok's train pulled up at a ranch near the 5th camp on Sage Creek in eastern Wyoming. What passed between the two men is not known, but farewells would have been in order: within a month, Wild Bill Hickok was dead.

At the time of Hickok's arrival in the Black Hills, Deadwood was a wide-open cutthroat town dominated by gamblers, thieves and tricksters who made their living by emptying the pockets of the more honest citizens. There was no lawman to bring order, and arguments were settled quickly, with guns.

On August 2, Will Bill was playing out a poker hand in Deadwood's No. 10 Saloon when a man named Jack McCall walked in. For once, Hickok had reluctantly given up his seat against the wall. McCall later claimed he had a personal grudge to settle with Hickok. Others said that he was bribed to shoot Wild Bill, possibly by an element in Deadwood that wanted to prevent the renowned gunfighter's becoming marshal of the town and bringing law to it as he had to Abilene. Whatever McCall's motive, he walked up behind Hickok and shot him in the back of the head. Hickok died instantly, the cards spilling from his fingers as he fell to the floor. Legend says that the scout held a pair of aces and a pair of eights, a combination known to poker players ever since as "The Dead Man's Hand."

The same gold that lured James Hickok to the Black Hills was indirectly responsible for bringing Bill Cody out from behind the footlights and into one of the most spectacular engagements of his career. When prospectors swarmed to the South Dakota lands reserved for the Sioux and the government elected to evict the Indians rather than the miners, the Sioux and a number of tribes friendly to them erupted with violence.

Buffalo Bill, in response to letters from the field urging him to join the summer campaign, cut short his '76 theatrical season and went off to the Indian wars. On June 9, he arrived in Cheyenne to rejoin the 5th Cavalry as guide and scout. Among those welcoming him was his old employer, General Carr. "All the old boys in the regiment," wrote an enlisted trooper named Brown, "expressed themselves to the effect that with such a leader and scout they could get away with all the Sitting Bulls and Crazy Horses in the Sioux tribe."

By July 1, Cody was with the 5th in eastern Wyoming Territory where, under the command of Brevet Major General Wesley Merritt, the regiment was patrolling a known Indian trail near the south branch of the Cheyenne River. By this time General George Crook had fought his inconclusive battle along the Rosebud, and George Custer and 200 men of the 7th Cavalry were lying dead along the Little Bighorn.

News of these events did not reach the 5th until July 7, when it was encamped alongside Sage Creek. Four days later, Merritt received orders to move north and

Effusions of sweetness from the scouting bard

Calling himself the Poet-Scout, a plainsman named Jack Crawford won wide fame in the late 1870s by writing treacly verses about the West.

Crawford was a study in contrasts. He spent many of his adult years in the company of dispatch riders and hard-drinking scouts, but he never touched liquor, having promised his dying mother that he would not. He dressed flamboyantly, wearing long hair, "wildly fringed" buckskins and silken ties—yet a friend said his manner was "simple and easy, entirely free from affectation." He was illiterate until age 17, and then went on to write four books, three plays and more than 100 short stories.

A Union soldier at 15, Crawford was wounded twice in the Civil War. While he was recovering from the first wound, a Sister of Charity taught him to read and write. As an Army scout and messenger during the Sioux War of 1876 he was esteemed by his commanders, particularly after several daring rides through hundreds of miles of hostile territory.

Crawford's abstinence from liquor was legend. He once delivered to Buffalo Bill a gift of whiskey from a friend, which prompted Cody—a celebrated drinker—to say, "I don't believe there is another scout in the West that would have brought a full bottle of whiskey 300 miles."

A Chicago journalist who offered Crawford a drink had to submit instead to a recital of his poem "Mother's Prayers" ("Keep him in the narrow pathway/Let him not be led astray"). The reporter needed several shots to counteract that saccharine dosage, but Wild Bill Hickok was moved: "You strike a tender spot, old boy, when you talk mother that way." Hickok probably would have loved Crawford's eulogy for him:

> *Under the sod in the land of*
> *gold*
> *We have laid the fearless Bill;*
> *We called him Wild, yet a*
> *little child*
> *Could bend his iron will.*
> *With generous heart*
> *he freely gave*
> *To the poorly clad, unshod—*
> *Think of it, pards*
> *—of his noble traits—*
> *While you cover him*
> *with the sod.*

Jack Crawford's Poet-Scout regalia included a starry sash and a fur-trimmed overcoat.

After killing Cheyenne Chief Yellow Hair in combat in 1876, Cody used the Indian's scalp and war bonnet *(below and right)* to promote his stage show—until revulsed religious groups persuaded him to desist. But the *First Scalp for Custer* remained a popular artistic subject. In an 1891 illustration, Cody flourishes his grisly trophies at onlooking Army troops.

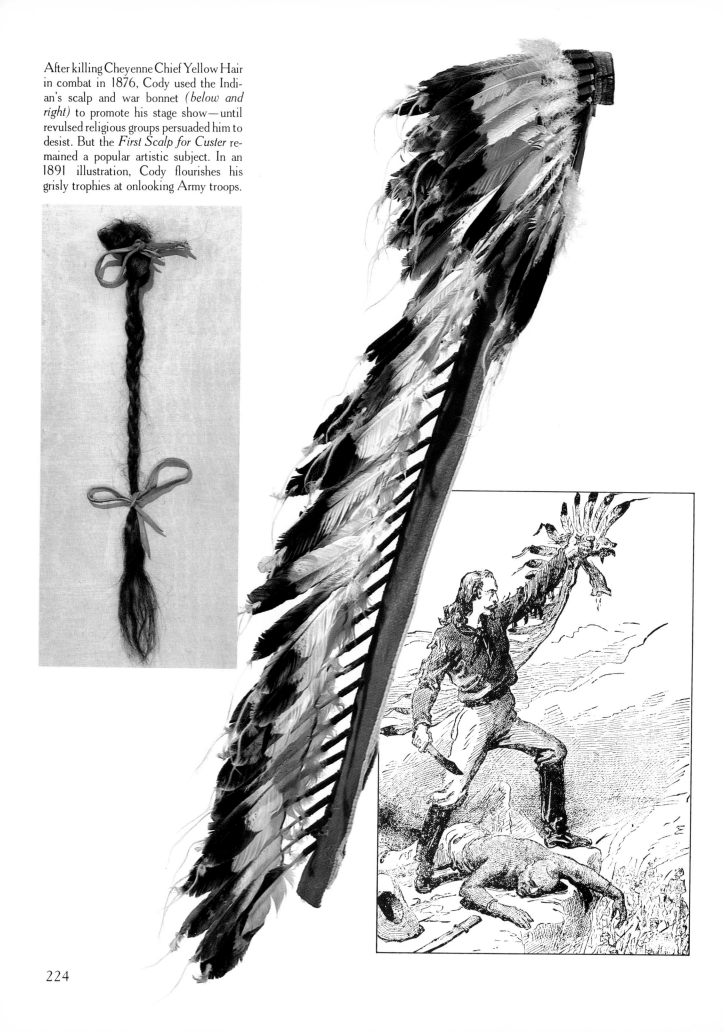

join Crook, who, dismayed by the enemy's evident strength, had held up and was awaiting reinforcements. But Merritt was sidetracked: on July 14, hearing that 1,000 Cheyennes were preparing to bolt from the Red Cloud Agency, he turned east to intercept them.

On the night of the 16th, the 5th bivouacked along Hat Creek only about 30 miles west of the Red Cloud Agency. It seemed probable that the Cheyennes—if they had indeed moved out—must be nearby. Company K, assigned to guard duty, set up pickets and outposts; and a Company A private named Chris Madsen, armed with a powerful telescope, was stationed atop a butte to signal messages by flag or torch to Merritt's headquarters. Bill Cody reconnoitered.

At first light Cody rode up to Madsen's post and told him that the Cheyennes were encamped not far away and were preparing to move. Cody then sped on to camp, alerting Merritt before the general received Madsen's message from signalmen. By 5 a.m. the Indians were in sight across a three-mile front, advancing slowly, unaware of Merritt's men but indicating much interest in something off to the west.

The target of their curiosity soon became evident: an Army wagon train was approaching. Ahead of the wagon train were two bluecoated troopers, riding toward Merritt's force—which was still hidden from the Indians in the folds of the hills. A small party of warriors broke off from the main body and rode to intercept the bluecoats. Cody, obtaining Merritt's permission, galloped off with a half-dozen troopers and two other scouts to cut off the Indian attack group. Within moments, Cody's small force was out of sight behind a hill; soon thereafter, shots were heard.

Chris Madsen, still at his post with his telescope, saw what took place. "Cody was riding a little in advance of his party and one of the Indians was preceding his group," he reported. "From the manner in which both parties acted it was certain that both were surprised. Cody and the leading Indian appeared to be the only ones who did not become excited. The instant they were face to face their guns fired. It seemed almost like one shot. Cody's bullet went through the Indian's leg and killed his pinto pony. The Indian's bullet went wild." Cody's horse stumbled, but Cody jumped clear. "Kneeling, he took deliberate aim and fired the second shot. The Indian fired at him but missed. Cody's bullet

went through the Indian's head. Cody went over to the fallen Indian and neatly removed his scalp."

The dead man turned out to be a Cheyenne subchief named Hay-o-wei, at first mistakenly translated as Yellow Hand although the correct name was Yellow Hair, bestowed upon him for the scalp of a white woman he had killed. Yellow Hair's sudden death turned out to be about all there was to the "Battle" of Hat Creek. Seeing the size and strength of Merritt's forces, the runaway Cheyennes turned around and were driven back to the agency.

Cody continued scouting until the first week of September, by which time the slow and indecisive progress of the Army's campaign against the Sioux had convinced him—and many others—that there would be no more fighting that cold and rain-drenched fall. The affair of Yellow Hair, however, was by no means ended. A suggestion of how it would be kept alive appeared in a letter Cody wrote to his wife in Rochester after the killing. "We have had a fight," he announced. "I killed Yellow Hand a Cheyenne Chief in a single-handed fight. I am going as soon as I reach Fort Laramie to send the warbonnet, shield, whip, arms and his scalp to Kerngood to put up in his window." Kerngood was a Rochester clothier. "I will write Kerngood to bring it up to the house so you can show it to the neighbors." In conclusion, Cody the showman observed that "the cheers that went up when he fell was deafening."

Applause—it was wonderful. With the sound ringing in his ears and a rousing new plot hatching between them, Buffalo Bill went back to New York and the stage. The shooting of Yellow Hand/Hair was expanded into a five-act melodrama and included in Cody's repertoire under the title *The Red Right Hand, or Buffalo Bill's First Scalp for Custer*—"noisy, rattling, gunpowder entertainment," Cody called it, "which seemed to give general satisfaction."

It gave so much satisfaction that Cody, plunging into a career as performer and theatrical entrepreneur, did no more real-life scouting. At 30, one year after James Hickok's death and with more than half of his own life ahead of him, he became instead a composite image of the Western scout, half true, half fictional, embodying the admirable characteristics of such famed plainsmen as Kit Carson, Jim Bridger, Will Comstock, Lonesome Charley Reynolds, Wild Bill Hickok—and himself.

Romantic views of a glorious life

A generation of turn-of-the-century artists, some of whom had hardly been born when Buffalo Bill was shooting down the Great Plains herds and guiding Army troops, were inspired by his exploits to paint stirring scenes glorifying scouts and scouting. Although Cody had aged, the artists found him still striking in appearance and a willing model. He was also a superb source of information about buffalo hunting and Indian fighting.

Cody showed his appreciation for their flattering interest by becoming an enthusiastic collector of Western art and a generous patron of young talent. Charles Schreyvogel, one of the most popular Western painters of the early 1900s, encountered his first Indians and buffalo in New York, on the back lot of Cody's Wild West show. Years later Cody sent the artist a full-sized Sioux tipi to lend a little frontier flavor to Schreyvogel's Hoboken, New Jersey, studio. Other artists were frequent guests at Buffalo Bill's Wyoming ranch; one young discovery was given a job as a ranch hand so he could soak up Western atmosphere while he waited for his artistic career to take off.

Cody used some of the works of his artist friends as posters for his show, and some to illustrate books about himself. But his large collection meant more to him than a promotional tool. The paintings were a bright and lingering memoir of himself and his comrades during the glory days of scouting.

Buffalo Bill and General Nelson Miles ride in the direction of a Sioux camp in this painting by Irving R. Bacon. The setting here is romanticized, but Cody was with Miles on January 16, 1891, when the last warring remnants of the Sioux nation surrendered at the Pine Ridge Agency.

227

In Charles Russell's *Buffalo Bill's Duel with Yellow Hand,* the Cheyenne chief—actually named Yellow Hair—falls as the scout fires. Though painted long after the incident, the picture was based on eyewitness accounts.

228

Galloping boldly into the 1869 Battle of Summit Springs, Cody shoots a warrior who is about to tomahawk a woman hostage. In 1907 Cody commissioned Charles Schreyvogel to paint this imaginative interpretation of the rescue.

In an idyllic scene painted by Irving Bacon, Cody the veteran scout and hunter returns to camp where his white and Indian companions await him. The painting, part of Cody's collection, is appropriately titled *The Life I Love*.

233

Irving R. Bacon

The sources for the illustrations in this book are shown below. Credits from left to right are separated by semicolons and from top to bottom by dashes.

Cover: Courtesy Newhouse Galleries. 2: Courtesy The Missouri Historical Society, St. Louis. 6, 7: Courtesy The Thomas Gilcrease Institute of American History and Art, Tulsa, Oklahoma. 8, 9: The Helen Dill Collection, courtesy of the Denver Art Museum, Denver, Colorado. 10, 11: Courtesy Northern Natural Gas Company Collections, Joslyn Art Museum, Omaha. 12, 13: *Pony Tracks in the Buffalo Trails,* by Frederic Remington; copied by Linda Lorenz. 14: Courtesy Denver Public Library, Western History Department. 17: Courtesy Collection of the Boatmen's National Bank of St. Louis. 18; 19: Copied by Charlie Brown. 21: Courtesy Library of Congress. 22, 23: Courtesy The Henry E. Huntington Library and Art Gallery, San Marino (2); courtesy Southern Oregon Historical Society; courtesy The Colorado Historical Society—Courtesy Nevada Historical Society. 25: Courtesy Library of Congress. 26: Courtesy The Meserve Collection. 27: Ken Veeder, courtesy Southwest Museum, Los Angeles. 30: Courtesy The Bancroft Library. 31: Courtesy Museum of New Mexico. 33: Courtesy Museum of New Mexico—Benschneider, courtesy Kit Carson Memorial Foundation, Taos, New Mexico. 34, 35: *Ft. Bridger. Black's Fork of Green River,* by F. R. Grist; copied by Linda Lorenz. 36: Courtesy Northern Natural Gas Company Collections, Joslyn Art Museum, Omaha. 38, 39: Ken Veeder, courtesy Carl S. Dentzel Collection. 40 through 45: Courtesy Library of Congress. 46: Henry Beville, courtesy Walters Art Gallery, Baltimore. 48: Benschneider, courtesy The Colorado Historical Society. 52 through 55: Courtesy P. J. DeSmet Papers, Washington State University Libraries, Pullman, Washington. 56, 57: Courtesy Library of Congress. 59: Map by Walter Roberts. 60: Courtesy The Missouri Historical Society, St. Louis. 62, 63: Courtesy Library of Congress (2). 65: Courtesy Duncan Galleries, Northbrook, Illinois (2). 66, 67: Courtesy The Thomas Gilcrease Institute of American History and Art, Tulsa, Oklahoma. 68, 69: From the Whipple Collection of the Oklahoma Historical Society (2). 70: Courtesy The Colorado Historical Society—Courtesy Library of Congress. 73: Frank Lerner, courtesy New York State Library. 74, 75: Courtesy National Archives and Records Service. 76: Courtesy Historical Church Archives, Church of Jesus Christ of Latter-day Saints; courtesy Library of Congress. 77: Courtesy Library of Congress. 78, 79: Courtesy Library of Congress; courtesy The Kansas State Historical Society, Topeka; courtesy Denver Public Library, Western History Department; courtesy Library of Congress. 80, 81: *Rounded-Up* by Frederic Remington. The original work of art is owned by the Sid W. Richardson Foundation and on exhibit at the Amon Carter Museum of Western Art, Fort Worth, Texas. 82: From the Turner-Workizer Papers, United States Military Academy, West Point, New York. 84, 85: *Burgess Finding a Ford,* detail from the watercolor by Frederic Remington, The Metropolitan Museum of Art, Anonymous Gift, 1962. 87: Courtesy The Kansas State Historical Society, Topeka. 88: Courtesy The New York Public Library, Astor, Lenox and Tilden Foundations. 90, 91: Courtesy The Kansas State Historical Society, Topeka; courtesy the Kansas Collection, Kenneth Spencer Research Library, University of Kansas. 93: Courtesy Amon Carter Museum of Western Art, Fort Worth, Texas. 94, 95: Courtesy South Dakota State Historical Society. 97: Courtesy Nebraska State Historical Society. 98: Courtesy The Henry E. Huntington Library and Art Gallery, San Marino. 99: Courtesy Western History Research Center, University of Wyoming. 102, 103: Courtesy National Archives and Records Service. 104: Courtesy Denver Public Library, Western History Department. 106:

Courtesy Western History Collections, University of Oklahoma. 108 through 111: Benschneider, courtesy The Colorado Historical Society. 112, 113: Courtesy Nebraska State Historical Society. 114: Courtesy National Anthropological Archives, Smithsonian Institution. 117: Courtesy Nebraska State Historical Society. 118: Courtesy Library of Congress. 119, 121: Courtesy Nebraska State Historical Society (3). 122, 123: Courtesy The New York Public Library, Astor, Lenox and Tilden Foundations. 124, 125: Henry Beville, courtesy Smithsonian Institution, Museum of History and Technology—Benschneider, U.S. Army Field Artillery and Fort Sill Museum; Henry Beville, courtesy Smithsonian Institution, Museum of History and Technology; Benschneider, U.S. Army Field Artillery and Fort Sill Museum (2). 126: Courtesy Christian Barthelmess Collection at Miles City, Montana. 127: Courtesy The Paul Dyck Research Foundation Collection, Rimrock, Arizona (2). 128: Courtesy South Dakota State Historical Society. 129: Courtesy Denver Public Library, Western History Department. 130, 131: Courtesy Southwest Museum, Los Angeles. 133: Courtesy National Anthropological Archives, Smithsonian Institution. 134: Courtesy George V. Allen Collection. 135: David Jacob, courtesy Foundation for the Preservation of American Indian Art and Culture, Inc., Chicago, Powell Family Collection. 136, 137: Courtesy Western History Collections, University of Oklahoma. 138: Courtesy National Anthropological Archives, Smithsonian Institution. 139: Courtesy Denver Public Library, Western History Department. 140, 141: Courtesy Kennedy Galleries, Inc., New York. 142 through 145: Reprinted from *A Pictographic History of the Oglala Sioux* by Amos Bad Heart Bull, by permission of University of Nebraska Press. Copyright © 1967 by the University of Nebraska Press. 146, 147: Jerry Jacka, courtesy The Paul Dyck Research Foundation Collection, Rimrock, Arizona. 148, 149: Courtesy The Thomas Gilcrease Institute of American History and Art, Tulsa, Oklahoma. 150: Courtesy Western History Collections, University of Oklahoma. 152: Courtesy The Henry E. Huntington Library and Art Gallery, San Marino. 153: Courtesy Denver Public Library, Western History Department. 154, 155: Ben Wittick photo courtesy Museum of New Mexico. 156, 157: Courtesy Fort Huachuca Historical Museum—Courtesy Arizona Historical Society, Tucson (2). 158, 159: Courtesy Library of Congress. 160: Courtesy National Archives and Records Service. 162, 163: Courtesy National Anthropological Archives, Smithsonian Institution (2); courtesy National Archives and Records Service. 164, 165: Courtesy H. Peter Findlay, New York City. 167: Private Collection of Kenneth Wiggins Porter, Eugene, Oregon. 169: Courtesy The Museum of Fine Arts, Houston, The Hogg Brothers Collection. 170: Courtesy National Archives and Records Service. 171: Courtesy Arizona Historical Society, Tucson. 172, 173: Courtesy Arizona Historical Society, Tucson (2). 174, 175: Courtesy U.S. Army Military History Institute; courtesy John Carter Brown Library, Brown University (2)—Courtesy Jenkins Publishing Company, Austin, Texas. 177: Courtesy National Anthropological Archives, Smithsonian Institution. 178: Courtesy Arizona Historical Society, Tucson. 179: Courtesy Arizona Historical Society, Tucson; courtesy National Anthropological Archives, Smithsonian Institution. 180: Courtesy Library of Congress—Courtesy Fort Huachuca Historical Museum. 182 through 185: Courtesy Arizona Historical Society, Tucson. 186, 187: Courtesy Western History Collections, University of Oklahoma. 188, 189: Courtesy Library of Congress. 190, 191: Courtesy National Archives and Records Service. 192, 193: Courtesy Western History Collections, University of Oklahoma. 194, 195: Courtesy Denver Public Library, Western History Department. 196: Benschneider, courtesy The Buffalo Bill Historical Center, Cody, Wyoming. 199: Courtesy Library of Congress. 200: From the Collection of David R. Phillips, E. E. Henry, photographer. 202: Courtesy Denver Public Library, Western History Department. 204: From the Collection of David R. Phillips, E. E. Henry, photographer. 206, 207: Courtesy The Kansas State Historical Society, Topeka. 209, 210, 211: Benschneider, courtesy The Buffalo Bill Historical Center, Cody, Wyoming. 212: Courtesy Library of Congress. 213: Benschneider, courtesy The Buffalo Bill Historical Center, Cody, Wyoming (4). 214 through 221: Courtesy Union Pacific Railroad Museum Collection. 223: Courtesy Museum of New Mexico, Ben Wittick photo. 224: Benschneider, courtesy The Buffalo Bill Historical Center, Cody, Wyoming (2)— Courtesy Iconographic Collection, State Historical Society of Wisconsin. 226, 227: Detail of *General Miles and Colonel Cody on Winter Campaign,* a painting by Irving R. Bacon and permanently on display at The Buffalo Bill Historical Center, Cody, Wyoming. 228, 229: *Buffalo Bill's Duel with Yellowhand* by Charles Russell. The original work of art is owned by the Sid W. Richardson Foundation and on exhibit at the Amon Carter Museum of Western Art, Fort Worth, Texas. 230, 231: Courtesy The Buffalo Bill Historical Center, Cody, Wyoming. 232, 233: Benschneider, courtesy The Buffalo Bill Historical Center, Cody, Wyoming.

BIBLIOGRAPHY

Alter, J. Cecil, *Jim Bridger.* Univ. of Oklahoma Press, 1962.

American Heritage, *Pictorial Atlas of United States History.* American Heritage Pub. Co., Inc., 1966.

Beeton, Barbara, "James Hervey Simpson in the Great Basin," *Montana, the Magazine of Western History,* Vol. XXVIII, No. 1, January 1978.

Bidwell, John, Hubert H. Bancroft and James Longmire, *First Three Wagon Trains.* Bindfords and Mort.

Blish, Helen H., *A Pictographic History of the Oglala Sioux.* Univ. of Nebraska Press, 1967.

Bourke, John G.:
An Apache Campaign in the Sierra Madre. Charles Scribner's Sons, 1958.
On the Border with Crook. The Rio Grande Press, 1969.

Brady, Cyrus M., *Indian Fights and Fighters.* Univ. of Nebraska Press, 1971.

Brewerton, George D., "A ride with Kit Carson," *Harper's Magazine,* Vol. VII, August 1853.

Bruce, Robert, *The Fighting Norths and Pawnee Scouts.* Copyrighted 1932, by Robert Bruce.

Burke, John, *Buffalo Bill, the Noblest Whiteskin.* G. P. Putnam's Sons, 1973.

Carroll, John M., ed., *The Two Battles of the Little Big Horn.* Liveright, 1974.

Carter, Harvey L., *Dear Old Kit.* Univ. of Oklahoma Press, 1968.

Cody, William F., *Life and Adventures of "Buffalo Bill."* Books for Libraries Press, 1917.

Crook, George, *General George Crook: His Autobiography,* Martin F. Schmitt, ed., Univ. of Oklahoma Press, 1946.

Custer, George A., *My Life on the Plains,* Milo M. Quiafe, ed., Univ. of Nebraska Press, 1966.

Dawson, Nicholas, *California in '41, Texas in '51.* Jenkins Pub. Co., 1969.

DeBarthe, Joe, *Life and Adventures of Frank Grouard.* Univ. of Oklahoma Press, 1958.

DeVoto, Bernard, *Across the Wide Missouri.* Houghton Mifflin Co., 1975.

Dodge, Grenville M., *Biographical Sketch of James Bridger.* Unz & Co., 1905.

Downey, Fairfax, *Indian-Fighting Army.* The Old Army Press, 1971.

Downey, Fairfax, and Jacques N. Jacobsen Jr., *The Red Bluecoats.* The Old Army Press, 1973.

Egan, Ferol, *Frémont, Explorer for a Restless Nation.* Doubleday, 1977.

Estergreen, M. Morgan, *Kit Carson: A Portrait in Courage.* Univ. of Oklahoma Press, 1962.

Finerty, John F., *War-Path and Bivouac.* Univ. of Oklahoma Press, 1967.

Foreman, Carolyn T., "Black Beaver," *The Chronicles of Oklahoma,* Vol. XXIV, No. 3, Autumn 1946.

Foreman, Grant, ed., *A Pathfinder in the Southwest.* Univ. of Oklahoma Press, 1968.

Frémont, John C., *Report of the Exploring Expedition to the Rocky Mountains.* University Microfilms, Inc., 1966.

Goetzmann, William H.:
Army Exploration in the American West, 1803-1863. Yale Univ. Press, 1965.
Exploration and Empire. Vintage Books, 1972.

Goodwin, Grenville, *Western Apache Raiding and Warfare.* Univ. of Arizona Press, 1971.

Gray, John S.:
Centennial Campaign. The Old Army Press, 1976.
"Frank Grouard: Kanaka Scout or Mulatto Renegade?", Chicago *Westerner's Brand Book,* Vol. XVI, October 1959.
"News from Paradise: Charley Reynolds Rides from the Black Hills to Fort Laramie," *Journal of American Military History,* Vol. III, No. 3, 1978.
"Arikara Scouts with Custer," *Montana, the Magazine of Western History,* Vol. XXXV, Spring 1968.
"Last Rites for Lonesome Charley Reynolds," *Montana, the Magazine of Western History,* Vol. XII, No. 3, Summer 1963.
"What Made Johnnie Bruguier Run?", *Montana, the Magazine of Western History,* Vol. XIV, No. 2, Spring 1946.
"Will Comstock, Scout: The Natty Bumppo of Kansas," *Montana, the Magazine of Western History,* Vol. XX, No. 3 Summer 1970.
"New Light on Will Comstock, Kansas Scout," unpublished manuscript.

Grinnell, George B.:
The Fighting Cheyennes. Univ. of Oklahoma Press, 1963.
Two Great Scouts and Their Pawnee Battalion. Univ. of Nebraska Press, 1973.

Hafen, LeRoy R.:

Broken Hand: The Life of Thomas Fitzpatrick. The Old West Pub. Co., 1973.

The Mountain Men and the Fur Trade of the Far West, Vols. I through VII. The Arthur H. Clark Co., 1965.

Powder River Campaigns and Sawyers Expedition of 1865. The Arthur H. Clark Co., 1961.

Hagan, William T., Indian Police and Judges. Yale Univ. Press, 1966.

Hine, Robert V., The American West. Little, Brown and Co., 1973.

Hodge, Frederick W., ed., Handbook of American Indians North of Mexico, Vols. I & II. Rowman and Littlefield, 1971.

Humfreville, J. Lee, Twenty Years Among Our Savage Indians. The Hartford Pub. Co., 1897.

Hyde, George E., The Pawnee Indians. Univ. of Oklahoma Press, 1974.

Innis, Ben, Bloody Knife. The Old Army Press, 1973.

Jackson, Donald and Mary L. Spence, eds., The Expeditions of John Charles Frémont, Vol. I. Univ. of Illinois Press, 1970.

Kearny, Stephen W., "Report of a Summer Campaign to the Rocky Mountains," Senate Executive Document 1, 29th Congress, 1st Session.

Kelly, Luther S., Yellowstone Kelly. Milo M. Quaife, ed., Univ. of Nebraska Press, 1973.

Lane, Jack C., ed., Chasing Geronimo. Univ. of New Mexico Press, 1970.

Lavender, David, Bent's Fort. Doubleday & Co., 1954.

Libby, Orin G., ed., The Arikara Narrative of the Campaign Against the Hostile Dakotas, June, 1876. The Rio Grande Press, 1976.

Mallery, Garrick, Sign Language Among the North American Indians. Mouton, 1972.

Marcy, Randolph B., The Prairie Traveler. Harper and Bros., 1859.

Miles, Nelson A., Personal Recollections and Observations of General Nelson A. Miles. Da Capo Press, 1969.

Möllhausen, Balduin, Diary of a Journey from the Mississippi to the Coasts of the Pacific, Vols. I, II. Johnson Reprint Corp., 1969.

Nelson, John Y., Fifty Years on the Trail. Univ. of Oklahoma Press, 1963.

Ogle, Ralph H., Federal Control of the Western Apaches, 1848-1886. Univ. of New Mexico Press, 1970.

Parkhill, Forbes, The Blazed Trail of Antoine Leroux. Westernlore Press, 1965.

Point, Nicolas, Wilderness Kingdom: Indian Life in the Rocky Mountains, 1840-1847. Holt, Rinehart and Winston, 1967.

Remsburg, John E. and George J., Charley Reynolds. H. M. Sender, 1931.

Reynolds, Charles, "Diary." Minnesota Historical Society.

Rolak, Bruno J., "The Heliograph in the Geronimo Campaign," Military History of the Southwest Seminar, Ft. Huachuca, Arizona, 1976.

Rosa, Joseph G., They Called Him Wild Bill. Univ. of Oklahoma Press, 1974.

Russell, Don, The Lives and Legends of Buffalo Bill. Univ. of Oklahoma Press, 1973.

Russell, Osborne, Journal of a Trapper. Univ. of Nebraska Press, 1965.

Sabin, Edwin L., Kit Carson Days. The Press of the Pioneers, 1935.

Saum, Lewis O., The Fur Trader and the Indian. Univ. of Washington Press, 1965.

Simpson, James H., "Report of Explorations across the Great Basin of the Territory of Utah for a Direct Wagon-Route from Camp Floyd to Genoa in Carson Valley in 1859," Washington, 1876.

Sitgreaves, Lorenzo, "Report of an Expedition down the Zuni and Colorado Rivers," Washington, 1853.

Smith, Jane F. and Robert M. Kvasnicka, Indian-White Relations: A Persistent Paradox. Howard Univ. Press, 1976.

Stands in Timber, John, Cheyenne Memories. Yale Univ. Press, 1974.

Taylor, Joseph H., Sketches of Frontier and Indian Life on the Upper Missouri and Great Plains. Private printing, 1897.

Thrapp, Dan L.:

Al Sieber, Chief of Scouts. Univ. of Oklahoma Press, 1964.

The Conquest of Apacheria. Univ. of Oklahoma Press, 1975.

"The Indian Scouts, with Special Attention to the Evolution, Use, and Effectiveness of the Apache Indian Scouts," Military History of the Spanish Southwest Seminar, Ft. Huachuca, Arizona, 1976.

Utley, Robert:

Frontier Regulars. Macmillan Pub. Co., 1973.

The Last Days of the Sioux Nation. Yale Univ. Press, 1973.

Wetmore, Helen C., Last of the Great Scouts. Univ. of Nebraska Press, 1965.

Wharfield, H. B., Apache Indian Scouts. Private printing, 1964.

TEXT CREDITS

Chapter I: Particularly useful sources for information and quotes in this chapter: J. Cecil Alter, Jim Bridger, Univ. of Oklahoma Press, 1962; George D. Brewerton, "A Ride with Kit Carson," Harper's Magazine, Vol. VII, August 1853; Harvey L. Carter, Dear Old Kit, Univ. of Oklahoma Press, 1968; Grenville M. Dodge, Biographical Sketch of James Bridger, Unz & Co., 1905; LeRoy R. Hafen, ed., The Mountain Men and the Fur Trade of the Far West, The Arthur H. Clark Co., Vol. VI, 1971; J. Lee Humfreville, Twenty Years Among Our Savage Indians, The Hartford Pub. Co., 1897; Osborne Russell, Journal of a Trapper, Univ. of Nebraska Press, 1965. Chapter II: John Bidwell, Hubert Bancroft and James Longmire, First Three Wagon Trains, Binfords & Mort; Nicholas Dawson, California in '41, Texas in '51, Jenkins Pub. Co., 1969; Grant Foreman, ed., A Pathfinder in the Southwest, Univ. of Oklahoma Press, 1968; William H. Goetzmann, Army Exploration in the American West, 1803-1863, Yale Univ. Press, 1965; LeRoy R. Hafen, Broken Hand: The Life of Thomas Fitzpatrick, The Old West Pub. Co., 1973; Stephen W. Kearny, "Report of a Summer Campaign to the Rocky Mountains," Senate Executive Document 1, 29th Congress, 1st Session; Balduin Möllhausen, Diary of a Journey from the Mississippi to the Coasts of the Pacific, Vols. I, II, Johnson Reprint Corp., 1969; Forbes Parkhill, The Blazed Trail of Antoine Leroux, Westernlore Press, 1965; James H. Simpson, "Report of Explorations across the Great Basin of the Territory of Utah for a Direct Wagon Route from Camp Floyd to

Genoa in Carson Valley in 1859," Washington, 1876; Lorenzo Sitgreaves, "Report of an Expedition down the Zuni and Colorado Rivers," Washington, 1853. Chapter III: John G. Bourke, *On the Border with Crook,* The Rio Grande Press, 1969; George A. Custer, *My Life on the Plains,* Milo M. Quaife, ed., Univ. of Nebraska Press, 1966; Joe DeBarthe, *Life and Adventures of Frank Grouard,* Univ. of Oklahoma Press, 1958; John F. Finerty, *War-Path and Bivouac,* Univ. of Oklahoma Press, 1967; John S. Gray, "Frank Grouard: Kanaka Scout or Mulatto Renegade?", *Chicago Westerner's Brand Book,* Vol. XVI, October 1959; John S. Gray, "What Made Johnnie Brughier Run?", *Montana, the Magazine of Western History,* Vol. XIV, No. 2, Spring 1964; John S. Gray, "New Light on Will Comstock," unpublished manuscript; Nelson A. Miles, *Personal Recollections of General Nelson A. Miles,* Da Capo Press, 1969; John E. and George J. Remsburg, *Charley Reynolds,* H. M. Sender, 1931. Chapter IV: Robert Bruce, *The Fighting Norths and Pawnee Scouts,* copyrighted 1932, by Robert Bruce; John M. Carroll, ed., *The Two Battles of the Little Big Horn,* Liveright, 1974; William F. Cody, *Life and Adventures of "Buffalo Bill,"* Books for Libraries Press, 1917; Fairfax Downey and Jacques Noel Jacobsen Jr., *The Red Bluecoats,* The Old Army Press, 1973; John F. Finerty, *War-Path and Bivouac,* Univ. of Oklahoma Press, 1967; George B. Grinnell, *Two Great Scouts and Their Pawnee Battalion,* Univ. of Nebraska Press, 1973; Orin G. Libby, ed., *The Arikara Narrative of the Campaign Against the Hostile Dakotas, June, 1876,* The Rio Grande Press, 1976; Jane F. Smith and Robert M. Kvasnicka, *Indian-White Relations: A Persistent Paradox,* Howard Univ. Press, 1976; John Stands in Timber, *Cheyenne Memories,* Yale Univ. Press, 1974. Chapter V: John G. Bourke, *An Apache Campaign in the Sierra Madre,* Charles Scribner's Sons, 1958; John G. Bourke, *On the Border with Crook,* The Rio Grande Press, 1969; George Crook, *General George Crook: His Autobiography,* Martin F. Schmitt, ed., Univ. of Oklahoma Press, 1946; Grenville Goodwin, *Western Apache Raiding and Warfare,* Univ. of Arizona Press, 1971; Dan L. Thrapp, *Al Sieber, Chief of Scouts,* Univ. of Oklahoma Press, 1964; Dan L. Thrapp, *The Conquest of Apacheria,* Univ. of Oklahoma Press, 1975; Dan L. Thrapp, "The Indian Scouts, with Special Attention to the Evolution, Use, and Effectiveness of the Apache Indian Scouts," *Military History of the Spanish Southwest Seminar,* Ft. Huachuca, Arizona, 1976; H. B. Wharfield, *Apache Indian Scouts,* private printing, 1964. Chapter VI: William F. Cody, *Life and Adventures of "Buffalo Bill,"* Books for Libraries Press, 1917; Joseph G. Rosa, *They Called Him Wild Bill,* Univ. of Oklahoma Press, 1974; Don Russell, *The Lives and Legends of Buffalo Bill,* Univ. of Oklahoma Press, 1973.

ACKNOWLEDGMENTS

The index for this book was prepared by Gale Partoyan. The editors give special thanks to Dr. John S. Gray, Fort Collins, Colo., and Dr. LeRoy R. Hafen, Provo, Utah, who read and commented on the text. The editors also thank: Terry P. Abraham, Adelle B. Knox, Washington State Univ. Libraries, Pullman; Martha Andrew, Smithsonian Institution, Washington, D.C.; Manon T. Atkins, Oklahoma Historical Society, Oklahoma City; Maxine Benson, Judy Golden, Joseph Morrow, Colorado Historical Society, Denver; F. Frederick Bernaski, Kennedy Galleries, N.Y.; William R. Best, Thomas Gilcrease Institute of American History and Art, Tulsa, Okla.; Ray A. Billington, Alan Jutzi, Huntington Library, San Marino, Calif.; Jack K. Boyer, Kit Carson Home and Museum, Taos, N. Mex.; Ellen Bradbury, Minneapolis Institute of Arts, Minn.; John Carter, Ann Reinert, Marilyn Stewart, Nebraska State Historical Society, Lincoln; Cynthia Chapman, Hampton Institute Archives, Hampton, Va.; Gordon Chappell, National Park Service, San Francisco; John M. Christlieb, Bellevue, Neb.; Judith Ciampoli, Missouri Historical Society, St. Louis; Carol Clark, Marjorie A. Morey, Amon Carter Museum of Western Art, Fort Worth, Tex.; Michael Cox, Arthur Olivas, Richard Rudisill, Museum of New Mexico, Santa Fe; David Crosson, Univ. of Wyoming, Laramie; Jim Davis, Idaho State Historical Society, Boise; Carl S. Dentzel, Southwest Museum, Highland Park, Calif.; Harry Drew, Klamath County Museum, Klamath Falls, Ore.; Paul Dyck, Rimrock, Ariz.; William C. Ellington Jr., Wichita Public Library, Kans.; R. M. Engert, U.S. Army Center of Military History, Washington, D.C.; Melissa H. Farnum, McLean, Va.; Forrest Fenn, Fenn Galleries, Santa Fe, N. Mex.; Paula Fleming, National Anthropological Archives, Smithsonian Institution, Washington, D.C.; Richard I. Frost, Buffalo Bill Museum, Cody, Wyo.; Sir John Galvin, Dublin, Ireland; Bonnie Gardner, South Dakota State Historical Society, Pierre; Roger Giddings, Grand Canyon Historical Park, Grand Canyon, Ariz.; Philip Gifford, American Museum of Natural History, N.Y.; Gillett Griswold, Lynda Roper, U.S. Army Field Artillery and Fort Sill Museum, Fort Sill, Okla.; Jack Haley, Western History Collections, Univ. of Oklahoma, Norman; Charles E. Hanson Jr., The Museum of the Fur Trade, Chadron, Neb.; Homer D. Hardy, World Art Services, Tulsa, Okla.; Michael Harrison, Fairoaks, Calif.; Margaret Bret Harte, Arizona Historical Society, Tucson; Peter Hassrick, Buffalo Bill Historical Center, Cody, Wyo.; Michael Heastin, Austin, Tex.; Joan Hofmann, The Beinecke Rare Book and Manuscript Library, Yale Univ., New Haven, Conn.; Alice Holmes, Arizona State Museum, Univ. of Arizona, Tucson; Warren Howell, San Francisco; Jacques Noel Jacobsen, Staten Island, N.Y.; Myra Ellen Jenkins, New Mexico State Archives, Santa Fe; Michael J. Koury, The Old Army Press, Fort Collins, Colo.; Bruce Le Roy, Washington State Historical Society, Tacoma; A. D. Mastrogiuseppe, Western History Department, Denver Public Library, Denver; Evan Maurer, The Art Institute of Chicago; Pat Michaelis, Kansas State Historical Society, Topeka; Gary Morgan, National Archives, Washington, D.C.; Dan Murphy, Jefferson National Expansion Memorial, St. Louis, Mo.; Peter Palmquist, Arcata, Calif.; Joe Park, University Library, Univ. of Arizona, Tucson; Karen Petersen, St. Paul, Minn.; Father Peter Powell, St. Augustine's Center, Chicago; S. H. Rosenthal Jr., Encino, Calif.; Paul and Florence Rossi, Tucson, Ariz.; W. L. Rusho, Salt Lake City; Harold and Peggy Samuels, Locust Valley, N.Y.; Linda P. Schulte, The Boatmen's National Bank of St. Louis, Mo.; William W. Slaughter, Church of Jesus Christ of Latter-day Saints, Salt Lake City; Dan Thrapp, Tucson, Ariz.; George Tomco, The Joslyn Art Museum, Omaha, Neb.; Barbara Tuttle, Ft. Huachuca Historical Museum, Ft. Huachuca, Ariz.; Robert A. Weinstein, Los Angeles; Valleau Wilkie Jr., Sid W. Richardson Foundation, Fort Worth, Tex.; Bonnie Wilson, Minnesota Historical Society, St. Paul; Lyle Woodcock, St. Louis, Mo.

Printed in U.S.A.